THE DAN BROWN COMPANION

THE
DAN BROWN
COMPANION

THE TRUTH BEHIND THE FICTION

With a gazetteer to the people and places featured
in the Robert Langdon novels

SIMON COX

with extra material by
Ed Davies, Susan Davies, Mark Foster and Andy Gough

MAINSTREAM
PUBLISHING
EDINBURGH AND LONDON

First published in Great Britain in 2006 by
MAINSTREAM PUBLISHING COMPANY
(EDINBURGH) LTD
7 Albany Street
Edinburgh EH1 3UG

ISBN 1 84596 197 8

All photographs by Simon Cox, Mark Oxbrow, Andrew Gough,
Mark Foster and Filip Coppens

A catalogue record for this book is available
from the British Library

Typeset in Apollo and Hamilton

Printed in Australia by Griffin Press

CONTENTS

ACKNOWLEDGEMENTS

This is one of those sections of a book that most people pass on by. It's a place that is very personal to the author but it's a very important place, too. This is about acknowledging the people and organisations that have helped along the way with the work you are about to read, without whom this wouldn't have been possible.

All books are collaborative efforts and this tome is no exception. My first debts of gratitude go to the four people who played a big part in this effort. Susan Davies and her father Ed Davies of Ancient World Research were quite brilliant in coming up with research and material when called upon. Susan in particular was a rock of calm in a sea of chaos. Mark Foster was as ever a genius of design and layout, not only with the great-looking cover art but also with his fantastic design for the gazetteer section of this book. Added research and material by

Mark rounds off a superb effort; my eternal gratitude goes out to you. Thanks also to Andy Gough for his genuinely unique and interesting take on the Rennes-le-Château mystery. It seems that the answer to the universal question is 22!

Filip Coppens for the Saunière picture and some interesting insights on Rennes; Georgina and Alan Gammon for the Spanish translation; Clive Prince and Lynn Picknett for helping out on both DVDs; Martin and Ali Woods, keep the board games coming! Kay Davies for balance; Alison, Neil and Joe Roberts for friendship and fun evenings; Mum and Dad for the never-ending encouragement; Mark Cox for bringing me back to earth! Gemma Smith and Sam, my Bicester retreat; Richard Belfield; Stephen Holmes; Marcus Mazure; Salah and Ahmed in Cairo, for being great friends always; Mohamed Nazmy; Ian Ord; the Blue Ginger boys for the supply of nourishment; Epica, Nightwish, After Forever and Kamelot for a great musical backdrop.

In the United States, Jennifer Clymer for quite simply being brilliant, capable and effervescent; M.J. Miller, because it's all about me, baby! Caroline Davies for extraordinary photography; John Anthony West; Chance Gardner and the child bride; Jason Melton 'Mr Hippoty Hoppity'; Pete Smith; Pamela McLeod for being so patient; Bob and Shirley Hicks. Mark and Tina Gloss-Finnell for the delicious food and great conversation. Joel and Lynne Schroeder, it's all about Macs, baby! Ken for rescuing the brightest girl of all; Tim and Thandy for the parties! Amanda Mottola and Jeff Johnson for keeping the faith.

On the literary front: Ailsa Bathgate for duties above and beyond the job description; Robert Kirby, Catherine Cameron and PFD, without whom . . .; Bill Campbell for the opportunity; the brilliant Fiona Brownlee and all at Mainstream; all my foreign publishers the world over, keep those sales coming!

I will, of course, have left people out. For this I apologise as ever and blame my bohemian scatter brain. You know who you are and you have my thanks and admiration.

INTRODUCTION

This is always, for me at least, the hardest part of any book to write. It's invariably the last thing that any author commits to the page and usually comprises a free flow of thoughts about the book. I often find it difficult to reflect and elucidate upon the project I have just undertaken at such close quarters and realise that most readers skip this part and get straight into the book proper. An introduction is one of those little necessities in the life of an author and, as such, I here present you with my best effort.

Why does the world need another Dan Brown reference book? Surely there are quite enough of these around – over 70 at the last count. I should know: I was part of that whole new genre when I released both *Cracking the Da Vinci Code* and *Illuminating Angels and Demons*, only to find myself plunged into a maelstrom of speculation, conjecture and theorising about what was fact and what was fiction in the two Robert Langdon novels by Dan Brown. It has been an incredible ride over the last couple of years, with a sold-out two-week run of shows at the Edinburgh Fringe 2005, where, along with Mark Oxbrow and Ian Robertson (authors of *Rosslyn and the Grail*, Mainstream 2005), I gave my version of the background themes to the novels to eager and responsive audiences. I also made numerous television and radio appearances and lectures around the world, so why another book in the same vein?

My idea for this book came about when I was actually doing some of the research for both of my previous Dan Brown-related projects. While travelling around Europe, visiting the places mentioned in the two novels, particularly in Rome and Paris, I came across a plethora of 'Dan Brown tourists', people who clutched a copy of the novel in one hand and a standard guidebook in the other. Walking down the Grand Gallery in the Louvre in Paris, as I overheard person after person making comments like 'Is that the painting Sophie lifted up?' or 'Is this where Saunière was murdered?', it became obvious to me that what was needed was a specialist guidebook for the avid Dan Brown reader. It was at this point that the idea for *The Dan Brown Companion* was born, especially the gazetteer section of the book. I wanted the Dan Brown tourist to be specifically catered for, with guides to the places featured in the novels, details of opening times and how to get there, and an explanation of the connection between the location and the novel in which it featured. This turned out to be a much harder task than I first thought but with the aid of my brilliant designer, Mark Foster, the whole concept steadily came together.

The opening section of the book is what I call the narrative. This section deals with some of the themes and sources behind the two novels in a much more in-depth and detailed way than my previous works. Within these narrative segments I have looked at and written about some of the most important (in my opinion) themes that Dan Brown seems to have used as the background to his fictional tales of murder and codified intrigue.

For the narrative section of *The Da Vinci Code*, I have chosen to discuss the story of Rennes-le-Château, the priest Bérenger Saunière and the mysterious secret society known as the Priory of Sion. It seems clear to me from *The Da Vinci Code* that Dan Brown must be familiar with the Rennes story, a tale of mysterious treasure and hidden secrets in the south of France, as he appears to allude to it in some of the names of the characters in his book. The murdered curator of the Louvre, Jacques Saunière, is a direct example. I have come to believe that the Rennes story is the backbone of the novel, though it is not actually spoken about directly, and it was with this in mind that I decided to examine this mysterious and convoluted area of research.

Convoluted is an understatement! The whole Rennes-le-Château mystery has become a can of worms for the unwary, a trap from which there is no escape if you are not careful. In my quest for some clarity, I found more confusion and conjecture than I have with any other line of research. Enter researcher Andy Gough. Andy told me about some of his interesting and unique theories and ideas about Rennes and suddenly things became clearer. I include some of his thesis within the Rennes section and hope to see more from Andy in book form in the near future.

Along with Rennes-le-Château, I also decided to investigate the so-called Priory of Sion. Again, the truth was far from clear and, if anything, just as convoluted and confusing as the story of Rennes. However, the further I researched and the more I read on the subject, the more obvious it became to me that this section was very much needed within the *Companion*.

The Priory of Sion and the Rennes stories have become inextricably linked and so these two sections became one in the final version. I hope I have made a good stab at outlining the mystery of both and of explaining at least some of the truth behind them. The stories themselves – of treasure, holy bloodlines, underground societies protecting a great secret, the mysterious comings and goings of a village priest and much else besides – are wonderful and make engrossing reading if nothing else. Beware of Rennes and the Priory, though. The deeper you delve, the more mysterious and hidden it becomes. The harder you try to understand, the more addictive it becomes.

In the narrative section dealing with *Angels and Demons*, I have chosen three of what I believe to be the fundamental themes behind the book. The Death of Popes section takes a look inside the Vatican, daring to open some of the closed doors of history to give the reader an insight into some of the more murky goings on at the Catholic HQ. It seems that there is plenty of historical precedent for Dan Brown's murdered pope, with the mysterious death of Pope John Paul I being but a small historical stone's throw from us today.

Church v. science is an obvious choice to me. The whole of *Angels and Demons* is really about the struggle between these two competing forces. I look at some of the more contentious historical issues in this area, from Galileo and Copernicus through to Leonardo da Vinci and on to the debate raging today in some US states between Creationism and Darwinism. This is an area of research with rich pickings, the only problem being what material to leave out and what to keep in.

The other obvious area to research as far as background themes for *Angels and Demons* goes is the issue of the Illuminati. This shadowy secret society seems to be blamed for more and more of the world's ills today, so I decided it was time to find out the real truth behind this mysterious order. Does it really exist at all? What were its origins? What were its aims? It was a fascinating and illuminating journey of discovery and one that I am sure I will look into again at some point.

One of my lecture sections at the Edinburgh Fringe 2005 was on the paintings of Leonardo da Vinci and whether he had left some kind of codified message within them – possibly pertaining to a Jesus/Mary

Magdalene holy bloodline. It proved to be a very popular piece of the show, undoubtedly due to its highly graphical nature, with slides showing in close-up some of the salient points of the argument. This gave me the idea to include a section in the *Companion* detailing this theory as first put forward by two friends of mine, Lynn Picknett and Clive Prince, in their excellent book *The Templar Revelation*. Hopefully this detailed and intricate section of the gazetteer will help you make your mind up about their theory. Did Leonardo leave clues to an amazing secret in his work? Go to the gazetteer to find out.

The whole cult and phenomenon of Dan Brown shows no sign of abating. As this book goes to press, Columbia Tristar Pictures are about to release the movie version of *The Da Vinci Code*, directed by Oscar winner Ron Howard and starring Tom Hanks, Sir Ian McKellen and Audrey Tautou. This major movie release promises to light once again the blue touchpaper of debate about the novels, with millions more people being exposed to their themes and theories.

With tens of millions having already purchased these novels, the clamour for more information about the factual background will only get stronger. What Dan Brown has managed to do is to make this information seem more accessible, no longer solely the domain of the theologian and the academic. I believe it is this, more than anything else, that will be the true legacy of these books. I hope that countless more people will want to delve deeper into the past, into the facts behind the fiction, not only of these novels but also behind the fiction that masquerades as history in many orthodox works today. I am proud to call myself an alternative historian – a historian of the obscure, as the BBC once called me. For I believe that it is through research and looking into some of the more esoteric and obscure chapters of our history that real truths can be divined. Dan Brown and his novels are just the catalyst. It's up to you, the individual, to actually carry this through.

So, in answer to my original question – do we need another Dan

Brown reference book? – I believe that *The Dan Brown Companion* fills a void with its lavish gazetteer section and helps to further your potential research with the narrative section. In short: yes.

Here endeth the introduction. If you have read this far, I thank you for your patience and indulgence. I sincerely hope that you find *The Dan Brown Companion* both enlightening and useful as a guide, and encourage any feedback you may have. I can be contacted at coxinvestigates@mac.com and am very happy to answer any questions that you may have about this book.

Simon Cox
March 2006

RENNES-LE-CHÂTEAU AND THE PRIORY OF SION

At my initiation I was taught to be cautious.
— Recited by the candidate during the
Masonic First Degree, or initiation, ritual

THE HIDDEN MYSTERY BEHIND *THE DA VINCI CODE*

If Cecil B. DeMille's *The Ten Commandments* is known as the 'greatest story ever told', then the mystery of Rennes-le-Château and the Priory of Sion is the most convoluted. For every fact, there are a dozen lies and twice as many half-truths. But there can be no doubt that the story has now captured the popular imagination and it appears to lurk deep inside the heart of Dan Brown's *The Da Vinci Code*.

The surname of the chief protagonist in the Rennes-le-Château story, Bérenger Saunière, will be familiar to readers of *The Da Vinci Code*. In the novel, the murdered Jacques Saunière was the Grand Master of the Priory of Sion, a highly secretive order that is one of the key threads running through the story. Bérenger Saunière, on the other hand, was a French priest who in the 1880s appears to have discovered a treasure and/or religious secret of tremendous significance in and around the Church of St Mary Magdalene in the tiny village of Rennes-le-Château in southern France. Dan Brown seems to have used the name Saunière to point us towards this mysterious village, which just happens to be steeped in the legends of the Priory of Sion.

It is also surely no coincidence that the area surrounding Rennes-le-Château, the Languedoc, north of the French Pyrenees – home to both the Cathars and the Templars – should be rich in Holy Grail lore and tales of hidden sacred bloodlines. Chief amongst these is the claim that Jesus and Mary Magdalene came to the area, bringing their daughter with them, and that the remains of this holy couple could rest beneath the hills of the region. *The Da Vinci Code* itself ends with the revelation that Mary Magdalene is in fact the long-lost Holy Grail and it is implied that her body rests on French soil – although beneath the Louvre Museum in Paris in this instance.

So, are these themes really tales of history rather than mere fiction? Does the Priory of Sion exist? What is the truth behind the legend of Rennes-le-Château and Bérenger Saunière? Is the Holy Grail really the lost bloodline of Christ and is it secreted in France?

In order to answer some of these questions, we are going to have to set out on a quest of our own, one that will have just as many shocks and surprises as *The Da Vinci Code* itself.

Let us start first with the tale of Bérenger Saunière and the mystery of Rennes-le-Château.

HISTORY OF A MYSTERY

> Discovered a tomb. At night it rained.
> – From the diary of Bérenger Saunière, 21 September
> (the autumn equinox) 1891. The diary is now on
> display in the museum at Rennes-le-Château.

François-Bérenger Saunière – known in later life just as Bérenger Saunière – was born in 1852 in Montazels, France. His family home, the Maison Natale, looked out over a lavish classical fountain that adorned the centre of the village square and adjoined Saunière's parish church. Beyond the fountain, looking due east, Saunière would have watched the sun rise over Pech Cardou, a local mountain of considerable mysterious significance. Interestingly, researchers Richard Andrews and Paul Schellenberger would much later identify Pech Cardou as the final resting place of Jesus Christ in their 1996 book *The Tomb of God*.

Beyond the church of Montazels, across the River Aude, some four kilometres in the distance, the young Saunière would have just been able to make out the silhouette of Rennes-le-Château, the village with which his name would become inextricably linked.

Saunière was the eldest of seven children. As a young man he was very athletic and was considered to be quite handsome. He attended school in Limoux and entered the seminary in Carcassonne at the age of 22. His brother Alfred also trained for the priesthood and the two were very close.

In 1879, Saunière was ordained as a priest. He accepted his first assignment in Alet-les-Bains, a prosperous village some 15 kilometres to the north of his childhood home in Montazels. Alet-les-Bains is renowned for two unusual carvings on the beam of a medieval house once said to be inhabited by Nostradamus. One appears to be a

17

dualist-inspired carving of the Chinese yin–yang symbols, the other, a curious pentagram within a circle. The ruined remains of the village abbey also featured in *The Holy Blood and the Holy Grail* by Michael Baigent, Richard Leigh and Henry Lincoln. The authors of this book found it quite peculiar that the abbey window had been carved in the shape of a pentagram – the Star of David. The pentagram has long been a symbol of alchemy and it is a quintessential emblem in the Rennes-le-Château mystery.

Saunière left Alet-les-Bains in 1882 to become the parish priest in the small village of Le Clat. Later, he taught in the seminary in Narbonne. On 1 June 1885, he was appointed the parish priest of Rennes-le-Château, an isolated hamlet with 298 villagers. The young priest wasted little time in creating a stir.

Saunière was outspoken in his support of the French monarchy and like many loyalists of the day he felt the republican government was anti-clerical. He used the pulpit as a platform from which to express his concerns and, as a result, was reassigned back to Narbonne. The young priest had been popular however, and at the request of the villagers he was reinstated at Rennes-le-Château a year later.

Having re-established himself in village life, Saunière turned his attention to restoring his dilapidated church and presbytery. For all practical purposes, each had been rendered unusable from years of neglect. His funds were limited and, after some debate, he decided to proceed with repairs to the existing structures in the face of professional advice to demolish them and rebuild.

Saunière was aided by a donation from the Countess of Chambord, whose husband was the grandson of Charles X, king of France from 1824 to 1830. It appears that Saunière met the count and countess while teaching in Narbonne. The reason for the gift, which amounted to 3,000 French francs, is unclear. It was, however, only the first of his mysterious sources of income.

Saunière was now ready to begin and it was not long after he initiated restoration of the interior of the Church of St Mary Magdalene that he supposedly made his first discovery. Concealed within a Visigoth pillar that had been overturned by workmen were four ancient parchments. Two of them were handwritten extracts from the Bible, penned in Latin. Saunière immediately halted work in order to contemplate his discovery in private.

The writing on the parchments was quite old and rather peculiar, and Saunière required expert assistance to make sense of them. After informing his superiors of the discovery, he was instructed to travel to St Sulpice in Paris to meet with the director of the seminary, Emile Hoffet. St Sulpice had long been established as a leading centre of obscure studies, and here, as in *The Da Vinci Code*, many of the key elements of our story unfold.

When decoded, the parchments allegedly revealed cryptic messages about ancient kings, treasure maps and an organisation called the Priory of Sion. The first parchment must have been especially difficult to decode, as it was apparently constructed using an elaborate technique called the Table of Vigenere. The system uses a series of knights' moves, as on a chessboard, to conceal the message, which in this case was revealed to be:

SHEPHERD, NO TEMPTATION, POUSSIN AND TENNIERS
HOLD THE KEY. PEACE 681. BY THE CROSS AND THIS
HOUSE OF GOD, I FINISH OFF THIS GUARDIAN DEMON
AT MIDDAY. BLUE APPLES.

The second parchment was comparatively less complicated and used raised letters to codify the message:

TO KING DAGOBERT II AND TO SION BELONGS
THE TREASURE AND HE IS THERE DEAD.

While in Paris, Saunière was said to have mingled with the Parisian elite, including the famous opera singer Emma Calve, who was rumoured to have become his lover. He visited the Louvre and acquired replicas of three paintings, including *Les Bergers d'Arcadie* (The Shepherds of Arcadia) by the famous seventeenth-century painter Nicolas Poussin. The painting features an ancient tomb in a mountainous landscape seemingly identical to the setting of a tomb just north of Rennes-le-Château near the village of Arques.

The inscription on the painting reads *Et in Arcadia Ego* (Even I am in Arcadia – as if spoken by Death). The presence of Poussin in the mystery is particularly intriguing as he is alleged to have possessed secrets greater than any king of his day. In 1656, the Abbé Louis Fouquet met with Poussin in Italy. Afterwards, he sent a letter to his brother, Nicolas Fouquet, the superintendent of finances to Louis XIV, describing the encounter. The letter reads:

> He and I discussed certain things, which I shall with ease be able to explain to you in detail – things which will give you, through Monsieur Poussin, advantages which even kings would have great pains to draw from him, and which, according to him, it is possible that nobody else will ever rediscover in the centuries to come. And what is more, these are things so difficult to discover that nothing now on earth can prove of better fortune nor be their equal.

Shortly after receiving this letter, and for no apparent reason, Nicolas Fouquet was imprisoned for life. Historians believe he is a likely candidate to have been the *Man in the Iron Mask*, the prisoner written about in the novel by Alexandre Dumas. Had Saunière just learned the same arcane secret of the world's most famous prisoner?

Upon his return from Paris, Saunière accelerated the renovation of his church, home and village in a lavish, esoteric design, concealing whatever his discovery was in a veil of symbolism and sacred geometry. The numbers 22 and 17 appear to be encoded in much of his work.

His renovations were rather unusual by today's standards, not to mention those of his day. The Latin inscription over the entrance of the church door reads TERRIBILIS EST LOCUS ISTE (This place is terrible). Immediately inside the church is a statue of Asmodeus – the ancient guardian of Solomon's treasure in Jewish mythology – while on the left or west wall, Saunière commissioned a strange rendering of the Sermon on the Mount. A bag erupting with gold is placed at the foot of a hill before Jesus. The flower known as Solomon's seal is featured. The whole scene feels laden with clues.

Saunière ordered the church to be decorated with depictions of the 14 Stations of the Cross and he commissioned the pieces from a Masonic statue manufacturer in Toulouse, the same place from which he had commissioned the Sermon on the Mount fresco. Again, these pieces seem unusually sombre and symbolic. One depicts an underground mine at the nearby Templar fort of Blanchfort, whilst another shows a night-time setting for a biblical story that is conventionally set during the day.

And then there are the restoration works that Saunière personally designed, such as the Tour Magdala, the beautiful stone tower dedicated to the Magdalene that Saunière constructed in his garden. Yet again, it appears to conceal more clues.

Saunière's behaviour became increasingly bizarre with each passing month. He excavated the church cemetery at night and defaced the tombstone of a noblewoman, Marie de Nègre d'Ables. Like the parchments he discovered in the Visigoth Pillar, when decoded, the tombstone apparently revealed cryptic references, this time to Poussin, Dagobert II, the Priory of Sion and pentagonal geometry.

Around this time, the priest began to take long walks in the countryside, collecting stones and placing them in a rucksack or suitcase. One of his favourite destinations was just south of the village, down in the valley, in the vicinity of a rocky outcrop and grotto dedicated to Mary Magdalene. He would return to his church via a private entrance that only he could access. Here, he inventoried the stones he collected on the day, many of which he would later use to create a replica grotto next to his newly remodelled church.

It was not long before he began to undertake longer journeys to places like Perpignan and Durban, near the south-east coast. This is where his colleagues Abbé Boudet and Abbé Giles served as priests for a brief period of time and it is believed that Saunière visited them there. It is also near Perillos, a peculiar village that we will learn more about later on.

SAUNIÈRE'S SOURCE OF WEALTH

As time passed, the villagers of Rennes-le-Château became frustrated with Saunière's increasingly insular and careless behaviour, and they issued a series of formal complaints against him. They were not the only ones who were upset with the priest. Saunière's bishop and ultimately the Vatican were perplexed by the priest's apparent wealth and extravagant lifestyle. Written records in his own hand, in which one might expect him to be conservative, reveal expenditures on renovations in excess of £1.5 million in modern equivalency. He was also known for the lavish hospitality he offered to guests and, according to Rennes-le-Château lore, Saunière is said to have entertained a plethora of esteemed visitors that included the likes of Richard Wagner, members of the Habsburg dynasty and Emma Calve.

Bérenger Saunière's inexplicable wealth is at the heart of the mystery of Rennes-le-Château. How could a poor priest possibly have obtained so much money?

The answer, according to his superiors, was that Saunière was trafficking masses to other priests and parishioners. This was supported by the fact that he was said to have received an enormous amount of mail, sometimes 150 letters a day or more. He was suspended, not for selling masses to those who desired them – which was not actually illegal at the time – but for selling more masses than he could possibly fulfil. Saunière defended himself against the allegations and was eventually supported by his bishop, but more senior authorities in the Church ruled against him.

Yet, the question remains. Would it have been possible to raise such significant amounts of money from the trafficking of masses alone?

René Descadeillas, a local journalist and respected historian, studied the matter of Saunière's wealth not long after the priest's death and wrote:

> The traffic in the Mass? He admitted it. There is no question on this matter, but this traffic, although it was significant, did not produce amounts sufficient to allow him to erect such buildings, and at the same time to live so grandly. Therefore, there was something else.

He concludes: 'The treasure of Rennes does not exist. But the secret of the Curé [Abbé] of Rennes is real. And it is there that the mystery resides.'

As is documented, the Countess of Chambord donated 3,000 francs to Saunière. We should perhaps look to see if this was a usual practice at the time or if there was something a little more suspicious taking place.

In the final decades of the nineteenth century, France was as turbulent and politically charged as at any time since the revolution. The government had annexed the Church and France was torn between the republic and the monarchy. Strange bedfellows emerged and some alliances defied logic. One such alliance is the shadowy relationship between the Countess of Chambord and Bérenger Saunière, a priest who venerated the Magdalene.

As we have seen, the Countess of Chambord was married to the grandson of Charles X, the king of France from 1824 to 1830. Saunière and his brother Alfred, a Jesuit, each enjoyed a friendship with the countess from their time in Narbonne. Furthermore, Saunière was not the only beneficiary of her generosity.

Another local priest, Louis de Coma, of the village of Le Boulou near the town of Foix, had already received a similar donation from the Countess of Chambord. Researcher and author Filip Coppens has commented on the intriguing similarities:

> Both were village priests of a church dedicated to Mary Magdalene. Both churches were located in the Cathar heartland . . . De Coma named his estate Gethsemane, Saunière his Bethanie – both areas where the Passion of Christ would occur. Faced with such parallels, the question needs to be asked whether both priests were part of a 'movement'. If they were, what kind of movement? . . .
>
> The strangest parallel is that Saunière's enigma became known to the general public in 1956, the year when the bishop of Pamiers ordered the destruction of de Coma's legacy. Coincidence, or design?

What is clear is that the Countess de Chambord and her husband found in Saunière and de Coma political allies, kindred souls in opposition to the republic. But was there another reason? Why, exactly, did these priests feverishly build shrines in memory of the Magdalene?

There is another possible candidate for the source of Saunière's wealth. Paul Smith, researcher and one of the staunchest critics of the Rennes-le-Château mystery, states:

> Abbé Saunière's Bishop was far wealthier – he inherited over a

million francs in 1891 from a rich widow and he too lived from selling masses and, like Abbé Saunière, was eventually to become suspended from his sacerdotal duties over allegations relating to financial impropriety within the Church.

Could Saunière have been the beneficiary of his bishop's inheritance? If so, why?

Saunière received other miscellaneous donations but nothing that would account for his apparent wealth. And this brings us to one last, yet intriguing, possibility. Jean-Luc Robin, the curator of Rennes-le-Château from 1994 to 2000, offers an interesting explanation.

It seems that while living in Saunière's presbytery, the Villa Bethanie, Robin discovered some bank envelopes that the priest had used, addressed to a Habsburg bank account in Budapest. The Habsburgs were the most influential family of their day and one of the wealthiest. It is said that they, not the Vatican, had the deciding vote when it came to choosing successive popes. Could the Habsburgs have been the Illuminati of their day? Had they funded Saunière? Had they instructed him where to look? Were they perhaps attempting to re-establish a position of power in Europe through staking a claim to the French throne?

Despite all of these possible sources of income, Saunière died a poor man, in debt and suspended from practising his trade. Of that we are certain. Many of his renovations were paid for over a long period of time and at the time of his death he had not worked for several years. This runs contrary to the legend that he was wealthy beyond measure. Nevertheless, it is evident that he must have received either a substantial influx of funds early on, or received a steady income from an undisclosed source, such as the Habsburgs, over time, otherwise he would not have been able to carry out his extensive building programme, the results of which still grace the hilltop of Rennes-le-Château.

It is now time to turn our attention to these buildings and, as we shall see, the nature of Saunière's renovations steer us towards an even greater mystery than the elusive source of wealth.

SAUNIÈRE'S GRAND CONSTRUCTIONS AND RENOVATIONS

One would expect a man of the cloth to be respectful of historical remnants. Not our Saunière. His behaviour seemed to indicate that he regarded archaeological remains as a means to an end. If we only knew what he knew, then we might be able to view his behaviour as justifiable; at the moment, however, his actions after his discovery appear very bizarre indeed.

Entire books have been dedicated to the individual architectural components discussed below. Let us examine them one by one in order to see what they may reveal to us of Saunière's motives.

The Old Altar (Visigoth Pillar)

When Saunière restored his church, he removed the original altar support, relocated it near the entrance of the church and inverted it to support a statue of the Virgin Mary. He carved MISSION 1891 on the bottom and PENITENCE! PENITENCE! on the top.

In 1858, when Saunière was just six, the first of a series of apparitions of the Virgin Mary occurred at Lourdes. The story appears to have made a lasting impression on the young boy, as the carving of PENITENCE! PENITENCE! seems to echo the visitations at Lourdes and the eighth apparition's utterance of 'Penance! Penance! Penance!'

The carving of the pillar is consistent with Carolingian-style design of the eighth century. The original is on display in the Bérenger Saunière Museum and a replica of it remains in situ, just outside the entrance to the church.

There is much debate surrounding the significance of MISSION 1891. For instance, 1891 was the year Saunière discovered his secret while conducting his initial renovation work and, in fact, 'Peace 681' appears in the parchments he is said to have discovered in the Visigoth Pillar.

The year 1891 is when Saunière employed his housekeeper and alleged lover Marie Denarnaud. It's also the year his name was etched on a rock alongside that of opera singer Emma Calve in a lovers' cove in Rennes-les-Bains. But remember, the pillar has been turned upside down to accommodate a statue of the Virgin Mary. When read right side up, it reads 1681. Now things get even stranger.

As we will see later on in this chapter, a Frenchman named Pierre Plantard at one time claimed that the Priory of Sion was founded in 1681, in Rennes-le-Château. Plantard claimed that he became the Grand Master of the Priory of Sion in 1981 – another combination of the numbers. But hold on, it gets even more puzzling. The tombstone of Marie de Nègre d'Ables that we will look at next appears to state that she died in 1681 but this is not true. She actually died in 1781. The date is carved in Roman numerals and has an O substituted where a C should represent 100 years, the substitution meaning that only 1681 can be read. The year 1681 is also when Isaac Newton turned to alchemy. Such is the nature of the mystery of Rennes-le-Château: it seems to attach itself to every esoteric thread in existence.

Taking the analysis of 1681 a step further, it is worth noting that, when reversed (remember, the pillar was turned upside down), the word 'Mission' appears as 'Noissiw'. The name of Isis is contained in anagram form in both words and this goddess is perhaps one of the most symbolic representations of the sacred feminine. It has also been suggested that this goddess is the archetype of our story's emerging cult heroine, Mary Magdalene.

The numbers 1891 and the way they feature in seemingly significant events in the mystery is intriguing. However, as we shall see, the simplest explanation is arguably the best: 1891 is the year Saunière dedicated the renovations in his church to the Virgin Mary, a figure who had captured his imagination since childhood. He dedicated his modifications of the pillar to Our Lady of Lourdes.

The Tombstones of Marie de Nègre d'Ables

In the churchyard of Rennes-le-Château, we find the tombstone of Marie de Nègre d'Ables. This historical figure plays a central role in the mystery. Or at least her tombstone does. It was allegedly defaced by Saunière one night, after he had deciphered the inscriptions on it. Serendipitously, however, the French author Gérard de Sède claimed that the inscriptions had been preserved in local historical journals and also claimed that there was a second inscribed tombstone, a horizontal slab. It must be stated, however, that there is no historical account of this second tombstone and Gérard de Sède was the first to reference it. He says a picture of it is recorded in the book *Engraved Stones of the Languedoc* by Eugene Stublein but the book does not appear to exist. The Aude Society for Scientific Studies also visited Rennes-le-Château at least twice and never mentioned it.

According to de Sède, the upright tombstone (1) revealed unusual word breaks, misspellings and offset letters. It also revealed a keyword, MORTEPEE. The flat tombstone (2) was equally peculiar. It highlighted the letters PS (commonly thought to represent Priory of Sion) and revealed the keyword PSPRAECUM, which was apparently necessary to decode the complex first parchment. Amongst other clues, tombstone 2 included the phrase JESUS, KING OF RHÉDAE, HIDDEN IN ARQUES as well as ET IN ARCADIA EGO, which is also featured in the previously mentioned Poussin painting.

While forming a potent part of the mystery of Rennes-le-Château, this information must be accepted only with some degree of caution, because if it were not for de Sède's reference to the second tombstone we would know nothing of it.

The Knight's Stone

This is a fascinating relic preserved in a display in the Bérenger Saunière Museum in Rennes-le-Château. Many believed that Saunière found the stone when he discovered a tomb in an ancient crypt below his church. The local historical society found it placed face down by Saunière, serving as a step outside the church, in front of the Calvary.

The Knight's Stone is horribly weathered; however, it seems to portray two scenes, each consistent with the Carolingian style. The popular interpretation is that the primary scene depicts Sigebert IV, the infant son of Dagobert II, being carried by a horseman to his mother, the Visigoth princess Gisele de Razès, in Rennes-le-Château. Others speculate that the knight is carrying the Holy Grail.

While none of this can be confirmed, the stone does appear to date the church to the time of the Carolingians or even Visigoths and thus serves to establish the sacred nature of the village in ancient times.

The Coume-Sourde Stone

Again, it is Gérard de Sède who informs us of the now lost Coume-Sourde Stone that was allegedly carved by an associate of Abbé Bigou, the priest in Rennes-le-Château from 1774 to 1790. Abbé Bigou was the confidant of Marie de Nègre d'Ables, who is said to have entrusted him with a great secret, as well as supporting documents. The stone was discovered on the mountain of Coume-Sourde, near Rennes-le-Château. De Sède's drawing reveals a date of 1292, which seems more likely to have been intended to be 1792.

Like the tombstone of Marie de Nègre d'Ables, the stone apparently portrayed a treasure map of the Knights Templars. It spells PS PRAECVM, which is translated as 'treasure of the Templars'. Noël Corbu, the later owner of the Rennes-le-Château estate, believed the stone referenced Blanchfort, the Black Rock and the Castle of Bezu, all local mystical sites. The name Bezu pops up again in *The Da Vinci Code* in the form of the French police inspector central to the story.

It is entirely possible that the Coume-Sourde Stone never existed and that it was the work of de Sède's imagination; however, if rediscovered, the stone would warrant considerable research.

The Tour Magdala

The Tour Magdala is arguably the grandest of Saunière's designs. It is not a restoration; he designed it and had it built from scratch. It was originally intended to house his immense library. He also planned to preach from the top, as if from an outdoor pulpit. Many believe that Saunière has encoded his secrets in this, his final work.

The stone tower was dedicated to the Magdalene. Author Margaret Starbird reminds us that 'the word magdala in Hebrew means "tower" (with connotations also of "stronghold" or "fortress")'. In front of the Tour Magdala is a courtyard that Saunière also designed. It is said to be symmetrically constructed to represent the pieces on a chessboard. Leaving the courtyard, two sets of 11 steps, 22 in total, lead to an observatory that connects the tower to its counterpart to the east, a gazebo built on a stone base that echoes the Tour Magdala's design and which also has 22 steps leading to its summit. The number 22 crops up again and again in Saunière's constructions. We will reveal more about why this might be significant at the end of this chapter.

Saunière's Grotto

In the vicinity of Rennes-le-Château's Church of St Mary Magdalene is a replica of a grotto constructed by the priest himself.

The original grotto built by Saunière, as well as the manner in which he assembled the materials, is highly curious but perhaps we should not be too surprised at this by now. He clearly took a lot of care with the construction, which appears to venerate the Magdalene. It is built with tufa quarried from the fields to the south of Rennes-le-Château. This is where the priest is known to have walked with a suitcase or rucksack on many occasions. In fact, he also appears to have built an extension to his church that allowed him to conceal his actions from the parishioners. He frequently went straight into these private quarters after his walks.

The grotto contained a statue of Mary Magdalene that has long since vanished. Still remaining, however, is another apparent clue. On the bench of the grotto, Saunière set in stone the legend XXSLX, in large letters that span the width and length of the seat. As there is no Roman numeral 'S', what are we to make of this apparent code? The most we can ascertain is that it incorporates three Xs, which, as we shall see, appears to be quite significant.

The grotto was originally built on an alignment with the Tour Magdala, some 75 yards in the distance, but it was vandalised by treasure seekers and has been reconstructed on a slightly different alignment.

The Interior of the Church of St Mary Magdalene

As previously noted, when approaching the Church of St Mary Magdalene, one is greeted by the Latin inscription TERRIBILIS EST LOCUS ISTE (This place is terrible), which is carved over the door. Although this would seem an inappropriate phrase to be applied to a church, when translated it actually means 'this place is amazing, great, wonderful, etc.' rather than anything sinister.

Of greater concern is the statue of the demon Asmodeus, which is the first thing one sees on entering the church. It is horrifying and sets the tone for the rest of Saunière's restorations, including the unusual Stations of the Cross and the Sermon on the Mount that Saunière had specially commissioned.

Also on display in the church are statues of saints specially commissioned and arranged by Saunière. The statue of St Antoine stands opposite that of Mary Magdalene. St Antoine's feast day is 17

January; Mary Magdalene's, 22 July: the numbers 17 and 22 crop up again.

Rennes-le-Château researcher Andrew Gough has made a series of observations using the Principle of Parsimony, which by definition states that 'One should always choose the simplest explanation of a phenomenon, the one that requires the fewest leaps of logic.' The principle is an extension of Occam's Razor, named after William of Ockham, a controversial English theologian and arguably the most influential philosopher of the fourteenth century. Occam's Razor – 'Given a choice between two explanations, choose the simplest – the explanation which requires the fewest assumptions' – is applied in many disciplines, including mathematics, philosophy and physics, and now the study of grail legends.

Gough has reviewed the intriguing configuration of saints within the Church of St Mary Magdalene. For years, researchers have mused over the possibility that the statues of the saints within the church allude to the presence of the grail and point to the Magdalene as the key.

It works like this. The French word for grail is *graal* and we find this encoded in the statues of the following saints:

- St Germaine
- St Roch
- St Antoine de Padoue
- St Antoine
- St Luc (on the pulpit)

The configuration of the statues forms a large, albeit disproportional, M and points to the Magdalene (see the diagram in the Gazetteer section on page 209).

The contention is that the grail is located in Rennes-le-Château and it appears to be related to the Magdalene. Is this what Saunière is trying to tell us here in the Church of St Mary Magdalene and is this the chief secret he took to his grave?

This intriguing question concludes our investigation into the works of Saunière. It is time we examined what happened to him towards the end of his life.

YEARS OF DEATH AND DECEIT

We left Saunière faced with accusations of selling masses and a question mark hanging over him concerning the vast sums he was spending in the village.

The priest continued to defend himself against claims of wrong-doing but to no avail. He was suspended from conducting mass in the Church of St Mary Magdalene that he loved so deeply and that he had spent so much time restoring. To avoid further punitive action, he constructed an alternative altar in the Villa Bethanie, his newly built presbytery, and proceeded to conduct his masses there.

In 1917, Saunière suffered a heart attack on 17 January and died on the 22nd, which seems a remarkable coincidence. Father Rivière, the priest summoned to Saunière's side, is said to have refused to give him his last rites after hearing his confession and the tale goes that when he left Saunière's room he was depressed, white as a sheet and never smiled again.

Fortuitously, before his death Saunière is said to have entrusted his secrets to his housekeeper, Marie Denarnaud, who had been his faithful servant since 1891. The villagers referred to her as 'the priest's Madonna' and her relationship with Saunière is rumoured to have been more than platonic.

A vast library of books has been written on the subject of Saunière's discovery. The list of possible treasure includes relics of the Knights Templars, the Cathar treasure from Montségur, Visigoth loot from Rome, secrets from the French Revolution, as well as artefacts from King Solomon's Temple in Jerusalem.

Alternatively, many researchers believe that the legacy Marie Denarnaud received from Saunière may have included heretical religious truths, such as the knowledge that Christ was a mortal man and that Mary Magdalene was his wife and the mother of his child. They believe that the secret involves the fact that the holy couple are buried in the vicinity of Rennes-le-Château, possibly with their daughter Sarah, and that their bloodline exists to this very day.

Marie Denarnaud is said to have informed Noël Corbu, a local businessman who bought Saunière's estate after his death, 'You'll see, my boy, you'll see. Before I die I'll tell you the secret, and you'll have so much money that you'll be asking people how to spend it.' But fate was cruel, as a crippling stroke ensured that Marie Denarnaud took her secrets to the grave. In 1953, 36 years after Saunière's death, the secret of Rennes-le-Château was buried along with the priest's Madonna.

So ends the conventional story of Rennes-le-Château. By the early 1980s, only a handful of researchers had explored the mystery of Bérenger Saunière, a humble French priest who is believed to have stumbled upon hidden treasure and become entwined in a web of concealed religious truths and secret societies. Writings about the mystery of Rennes-le-Château were confined to a few, predominantly French, esoteric authors. But in 1982, that all changed with the publication of *The Holy Blood and the Holy Grail*. After creating unprecedented controversy due to its suggestions that Jesus may have been married to Mary Magdalene, that together they may have had a child and that their child, the holy bloodline, was the Holy Grail, the book became a bestseller – and before you could say '*Et in Arcadia Ego*' a genre was born, centring on Rennes-le-Château.

Without doubt, the mystery is just as complex, convoluted and confusing today, and individual components warrant further scrutiny. But where do we draw the line between fact and fantasy? In the more than 100 books published on the subject since *The Holy Blood and the Holy Grail*, the mystery has been solved time and time again by ambitious and highly creative treasure seekers, grail enthusiasts and mathematicians. Their conclusions frequently stretch credulity and examples include:

- Rennes-le-Château marks the precise spot where the next life-extinguishing comet will collide with earth;
- Rennes-le-Château conceals the entrance to the hollow earth, where Rex Mundi (Satan) lives and reigns;
- Rennes-le-Château lies three degrees off the Paris Meridian (Rose Line), and the three degrees of Masonry were created to encode this fact and to draw attention to the treasure that was placed there, namely the Arc of the Covenant;
- Rennes-le-Château is a multi-dimensional/frequency gateway that utilises the Emerald Tablets of the Egyptian God Thoth to span dimensions.

Believe it or not, the story just gets weirder over time. A few years ago, a descendant of the eighth president of the United States, Martin van Buren, was reported to have purchased land adjoining the village of Rennes-le-Château. It is alleged that she was anticipating the arrival of extraterrestrials at the time of the millennium celebrations. As far as we know, she's still waiting. And so the tales continue.

A recent addition to our mystery, a model of the Calvary Mount, is nothing short of sensational. The model, supposedly made to measure for Saunière, reveals the tomb of Jesus Christ to be located not in Jerusalem but in Perillos, near Perpignan, approximately an hour's drive south-east of Rennes-le-Château. Seemingly, the research is the work of one man, André Douzet. His 2001 book, *Saunière's Model*, is the only real contemporary source for this intriguing storyline.

Douzet claims that Saunière had frequently journeyed to the area and was aware of the rumour suggesting that Christ is buried there. The model was commissioned by Saunière but never collected from its maker, as the priest died before it was completed. Douzet claims to have identified the place names on the model of the Calvary Mount in and around Perillos by using pre-French Revolution maps. The place names he has cross-referenced from the maps and the model of the Perillos landscape include 'the Hill of the Skull', 'the Garden of Olives', 'the Cistern of St Helena' and 'the Oratory of St Simon'.

The mystery surrounding this so-called Model of Saunière is regarded with considerable scepticism in the village of Rennes-le-Château. Nevertheless, a number of different facets of the story point to the potential significance of the area, for example the proximity of Louis de Coma, the priest who had revered the Magdalene in architecture only to see it later obliterated with dynamite in the same year that Pierre Plantard registered the Priory of Sion (1956). Abbés Giles and Boudet, friends of Saunière, both worked in Durban, just to the north of Perillos, so it is possible that he visited them or knew something about the area. Evidence for this, as is so often the case in the mystery, could be stronger. This is a new twist to the Rennes-le-Château story and one that requires further research.

Perillos itself has come under much scrutiny in recent years as it is the base for the Chronodrome Experiment, a project managed by scientists that is focused on the launch of the satellite KEO in 2007/08. The satellite will travel for 50 years and the Chronodrome Experiment is an attempt to leverage a vortex-like timewarp to encourage distant time travellers who may intercept the satellite to visit earth, specifically the village of Perillos.

POSTSCRIPT TO THE MYSTERY

Real-life mysteries are seldom tidy. They are not afforded the resolution often seen in contemporary fiction and Hollywood blockbusters. But that's what makes them mysteries in the first place.

In 2000, rumour spread that the mayor of Rennes-le-Château had received a letter from an American of French descent who said that his uncle's grandfather had been in charge of the builders who completed Saunière's restorations. The letter supposedly indicated that he had assisted Saunière in burying a chest or casket beneath the foundations of the Tour Magdala. The American then went on to contact Dr Robert Eisenman, of *The Dead Sea Scrolls* fame. A ground scan was conducted and a crypt was identified beneath the floor of the church.

What was most exciting was the detection of what appeared to be a chest, three feet square, buried around twelve feet beneath the floor of the Tour Magdala. An unseemly circus ensued and the French media got into quite a frenzy. And who could blame them? A theologian by the name of Dr Serena Tajé became involved and is on record as making some very bold statements, including: 'Perhaps we will discover items concerning the foundation myth of the Church.' Tajé added:

> It could be a question of a document that will challenge the history of the Catholic Church . . . Unless it is a tangible sign of the presence in this place (a presence attested to by the holy texts) of Jesus's judge, of that same Herod Antipas who stopped here, at Rennes-le-Château, on the path of exile, in the company of a certain Mary the Madgalenian.

Two years later, on 20 August 2003, Eisenman and his international team of multi-disciplined experts conducted their excavations beneath the Tour Magdala. The esteemed Professor Andrea Baratollo and other scholars, including *The Holy Blood and the Holy Grail* co-author Michael Baigent, were on hand for the much-hyped event. But the excavations proved fruitless. Nothing was discovered and it is even believed that the team simply re-excavated an earlier dig.

So, having followed the story right up to the present day we must leave Rennes-le-Château for the time being. There, with some of the greatest scholars of our day working around him, the body of Bérenger Saunière lies buried with a wry smile on his face. The evidence suggests that the mystery had something to do with the Magdalene. It is possible that Saunière simply encoded the location of his discovery in the monuments he built yet still the experts look away.

However, before we head off down that route and reveal exactly what it is that Saunière has veiled in secrets, we need to examine the shadowy organisation known as the Priory of Sion, because it is intrinsically linked to the story of Rennes-le-Château.

THE PRIORY OF SION AND PIERRE PLANTARD

The Priory of Sion features heavily in *The Da Vinci Code* as well as in the mystery of Rennes-le-Château. Is it a real order, as Dan Brown would have us believe, or is it merely the concoction of some of the more shadowy figures in the mystery? What confuses the issue somewhat is the inclusion by Dan Brown, at the beginning of *The Da Vinci Code*, of the following statement:

FACT:

The Priory of Sion – A European secret society founded in 1099 – is a real organization. In 1975 Paris's Bibliothèque Nationale discovered parchments known as Les Dossiers Secrets, identifying numerous members of the Priory of Sion, including Sir Isaac Newton, Sandro Botticelli, Victor Hugo and Leonardo da Vinci.

This is a very unusual line to take in a novel and this course of action on the part of the author is especially risky if the subject is not one that can be easily proven. As we will see, when it comes to the Priory of Sion, nothing is what it seems.

So, is Dan Brown's statement justified? Is there proof that the Priory of Sion really does exist? We need to start right at the beginning.

As we have discussed, in *The Da Vinci Code* the first introduction we have to the Priory of Sion is through the murdered Jacques Saunière, who is shot inside the Louvre right at the start of the novel. Jacques Saunière, it turns out, was the Grand Master of a mysterious group known as the Priory of Sion. It is then left to Saunière's granddaughter, Sophie Neveu, to establish what exactly the Priory of Sion is and who is involved.

Helping her in her quest is Robert Langdon, who, we are told, is familiar with the secret dossier of the Priory of Sion, the Priory Documents, held in the Bibliothèque Nationale in Paris, France.

The bulk of the Priory Documents were deposited in the national library between 1964 and 1967. They consist of a wide assortment of papers, clippings, poems, sketches and maps all relating to Rennes-le-Château, Merovingian genealogies and the Priory of Sion. While there is no question that these documents exist, doubts have been raised about their origins and authenticity. For example, one of the documents is 'Le Serpent Rouge' (The Red Snake), a poem that links Rennes-le-Château with the Rose Line and St Sulpice in Paris, both featured in *The Da Vinci Code*. Each of its alleged authors had hanged himself on or around the same day, before the document was submitted to the library.

Before we discuss the veracity of the documents in detail, however, let us first look at what the documents reveal to us of the Priory of Sion.

According to the Priory Documents, in particular a document known as 'The Secret Files of Henri Lobineau', an order by the name of L'Ordre de Sion (The Order of Sion) was founded by Godfroy de Bouillon in 1090, in Jerusalem. This is the first reference to the order that would, apparently, become the Priory of Sion approximately 100 years later.

Supposedly, a group of Calabrian monks believed that Godfroy de Bouillon was in fact a direct descendant of the Merovingian kings and, as such, could claim lineage back to Jesus and King David. It was through the actions of these Calabrian monks that Godfroy de Bouillon became the defender of the holy sepulchre in Jerusalem, after refusing the title of king. In his book *Sangraal: The Mystery of the Holy Grail*, J.J. Collins elaborates on Godfroy's holy bloodline:

> Godfroi was, by legend, a member of the Grail Family, and by lineage a Merovingian and apparently, rightful King of Jerusalem by his descent from David. It is clear that he was aware of this. When he left for the first crusade, he sold all of his property. He intended to stay in Jerusalem. Godfroi was close to de Payen and the count of Champagne and Baudoin [his brother] was integral to the founding of the Templars.

Michael Bradley, in *Holy Grail Across the Atlantic*, goes further: 'One might therefore term Godfroi de Bouillon as a sort of "king of kings", or at least a maker of kings, since he founded the Order of Sion that could crown Kings of Jerusalem.'

Interestingly, the Priory Documents tell us that at this time the Knights Templar were created specifically to act as the Order of Sion's military wing. This would suggest that the Order of Sion was more important than we could have guessed. However, it must be stated for the record that the Priory Documents is the only place where we find a mention of this fact.

Once Jerusalem had been secured by the Crusaders, Godfroy de Bouillon ordered the construction of Notre Dame du Mont de Sion and it was here that the Order of Sion was installed. The Abbey of Notre Dame du Mont de Sion was built on the remains of a ruined

Byzantine church and was located south of the Sion gate. Baigent, Leigh and Lincoln describe this abbey in *The Holy Blood and the Holy Grail*:

> To the south of Jerusalem looms the 'high hill' of Mount Sion. By 1099 an abbey had been built on the ruins of an old Byzantine basilica at the express command of Godfroi de Bouillon.
>
> According to one chronicler, writing in 1172, it was extremely well fortified, with its own walls, towers and battlements. And this structure was called the Abbey of Notre Dame du Mont de Sion.

Aside from the information included in the Priory Documents, there are other independent sources which claim that the Order of Sion did in fact exist in Jerusalem at this time in history. Researcher Dr Steven Mizrach, for example, makes reference to it on his website http://www.fiu.edu/~mizrachs/.

The story then takes us to 1152 when members of the Order of Sion left Jerusalem, accompanying King Louis VII back to France after the collapse of the Second Crusade. The order appears to have been installed at St Samson in Orleans and also at St Jean-le-Blanc just outside the town. The Priory Documents are explicit in telling us that it was at this time that the order became known as the Priory of Sion. In *The Messianic Legacy*, Baigent, Leigh and Lincoln detail the spread of the order's influence:

> By 19 July 1116, the name of the Ordre de Sion was already appearing on official charters and documents. We found another charter, dated 1152 and bearing the seal of King Louis VII of France, which conferred upon the Order its first major seat in Europe, at Orleans. We found a later charter, dated 1178

and bearing the seal of Pope Alexander III, which confirmed certain land holdings of the Order not only in the Holy Land, but in France, Spain and throughout the Italian peninsula – in Sicily, in Naples, in Calabria, in Lombardy.

As mentioned, the Priory Documents talk of the Order of Sion and the Knights Templar operating hand in hand. However, again according to the Priory Documents, this came to an end in 1188, when a major parting of the ways, known as the Cutting of the Elm, occurred at Gisors in Normandy.

The history of the Knights Templar from this point onwards is well documented. They went on to assume huge wealth and power until their destruction in 1307 by King Philip IV (the Fair) of France. The Order of Sion, on the other hand, seemingly went underground after the split of 1188.

'The Secret Files of Henri Lobineau' informs us that Grand Master Jean de Gisors founded the Priory of Sion in this very year, 1188. It appears to have grown out of an amalgamation of other orders, including the Order of Sion and another society known as Ormus. This is an interesting connection because 'orme' is the French word for elm, therefore indicating a link between the split with the Knights Templar at the aforementioned Cutting of the Elm and the formation of the new order.

As we have seen, the Priory Documents have a lot to say about the history of the Priory of Sion. Another controversial aspect of the documents is a list, again contained within 'The Secret Files of Henri Lobineau', that claims to document all of the Priory's Grand Masters from their supposed foundation in the year 1188 up until the late twentieth century. Some of the illustrious names on the list may come as a surprise:

Jean de Gisors (1188–1220)

Marie de Saint-Clair (1220–1266)

Guillaume de Gisors (1266–1307)

Edouard de Bar (1307–1336)

Jeanne de Bar (1336–1351)

Jean de Saint-Clair (1351–1366)

Blanche d'Evreaux (1366–1398)

Nicholas Flamel (1398–1418)

René d'Anjou (1418–1480)

Iolande de Bar (1480–1483)

Sandro Filipepi (1483–1510)

Leonardo da Vinci (1510–1519)

Connétable de Bourbon (1519–1527)

Ferdinand de Gonzague (1527–1575)

Louis de Nevers (1575-1595)

Robert Fludd (1595–1637)

J. Valentinus Andreae (1637–1654)

Robert Boyle (1654–1691)

Isaac Newton (1691–1727)

Charles Radclyffe (1727–1746)

Charles de Lorraine (1746–1780)

Maximillian de Lorraine (1780–1801)

Charles Nodier (1801–1844)

Victor Hugo (1844–1885)

Claude Debussy (1885–1918)

Jean Cocteau (1918–1963)

In *The Holy Blood and the Holy Grail*, Baigent, Leigh and Lincoln point out an interesting fact relating to the names included on this list:

> It would seem that Sion's Grand Mastership has recurrently shifted between two essentially distinct groups of individuals. On the one hand there are figures of monumental stature who – through esoterica, the arts or sciences – have produced some impact on Western tradition, history and culture. On the other hand, there are members of a specific and interlinked network of families – noble, and sometimes royal.

Many of the names on this list need no introduction but some are worth a special mention. Nicholas Flamel, for example, is probably the most famous alchemist ever to have lived. It is said that he achieved two of the primary goals of alchemy: first, that he managed to create the Philosopher's Stone, which can turn lead into gold, and, second, that he gained immortality. His tomb has been found to be empty and this has led some to believe that he achieved his aim of becoming immortal. Flamel became very rich in his lifetime, supposedly through his art of alchemy, and in later years he became a philanthropist. He is mentioned in the pages of Victor Hugo's *The Hunchback of Notre Dame* and, of course, Hugo is another Grand Master on the list contained in the Priory Documents.

Sir Isaac Newton, listed as Grand Master from 1691 to 1727, is often cited as the most influential scientist in history. However, it is not widely known that he also seems to have been interested in alchemy. It is therefore worth quoting one of his many sayings here:

> Just as the world was created from dark chaos through the bringing forth of the light and through the separation of the aery firmament and of the waters from the earth, so our work brings forth the beginning out of black chaos and its first matter through the separation of the elements and the illumination of matter.

The inclusion at the end of the long list of Grand Masters of the name Jean Cocteau – the poet, novelist, filmmaker and one of the founders of Surrealism – is curious to say the least. There is not much in the way of evidence to help us establish just why he might have been elevated to such a lofty position. However, Dr Steven Mizrach says of Cocteau:

> Interestingly, right around the same time, Cocteau seems to have partnered with Satie and Picasso on a 1917 production called Parade (Picasso's work was dominated by PoS-type esoteric themes), and then he and Satie went on to form a musical composing group, 'Le Six', that were based on improvisation from Debussy's work. The link between these two 'GM's was Erik Satie.

As it turns out, Jean Cocteau's membership of such an organisation is not the strangest aspect of the whole affair and there was to be a further twist to the story of the Grand Masters of the Priory of Sion.

A name that was added to the list after Jean Cocteau was that of a Frenchman called Pierre Plantard. It is here that our tale takes a turn down an alley ripe with deception and if the Priory Documents and the Priory of Sion are real, then history will have to be rewritten. The documents state that the primary objective of the Priory of Sion is the restoration of the Merovingian dynasty to the throne of France. The Merovingians were purported to be the bloodline of Christ and Mary Magdalene, and the Knight's Stone discovered by Saunière is said to portray their presence in Rennes-le-Château. During the 1960s, Pierre Plantard claimed that he was a descendant of Dagobert II, the Frankish king who died in 679 leaving no heir, and therefore Plantard put himself forward as a Merovingian claimant to the throne of France. There is, however, no evidence that these claims are true and in fact a BBC documentary made in 1996, *TimeWatch: The History of a Mystery*, established that Plantard had faked the genealogy, inserting his name into a list copied from a popular history magazine. His real ancestor was apparently a sixteenth-century peasant who grew walnuts.

More importantly, and far more disturbing, it would seem that it was not only Plantard's lineage that had been forged but the entire contents of the Priory Documents. They seem to have been fabricated by Plantard, along with the author and researcher Philippe de Chérisey, and it was these two characters who deposited the documents in the Bibliothèque Nationale in Paris.

We will come to the evidence for this claim later on but first we should examine the character of Pierre Plantard in a little more detail.

Plantard was born in Paris in 1920. In later life, he added the suffix de Saint-Clair to his name to try to add credence to the myths with which he had surrounded himself. His early life showed distinct anti-Semitic and anti-Masonic leanings, and he was a supporter of the Vichy regime in wartime France. Even before the outbreak of the Second World War, Plantard had tried to establish a right-wing group with the aim of 'purifying and renewing France' and he had sought official permission to circulate a magazine called *The Renewal of France*. He finally founded an order of knighthood in 1942, which he called the Alpha Galates, and began distribution of a periodical called *Vaincre* (Conquer). This publication contained anti-Semitic views mixed with esoteric articles on chivalry and the like. Plantard was arrested at this time and spent four months in prison for failing to register the organisation.

He was arrested a second time in 1953, this time for fraud, and was sentenced to six months in prison. Just three years later, he and three colleagues registered another group, this time called the Priory of Sion, with the French authorities. There is no doubt that one of the original aims of this organisation was to promote Plantard's claim that he had a hold over the long abandoned throne of France due to his – alleged – descent from the Merovingians.

It transpires that in the mid-1950s, Plantard had met Noël Corbu, the man who had bought Bérenger Saunière's estate after his death. It seems it was this meeting that had inspired Plantard, and the story of Saunière and his mysterious fortune may have led to the creation of Plantard's organisation, the Priory of Sion. It is even said that the story of Saunière's treasure was in fact a myth made up by Noël Corbu with the simple aim of attracting customers to his newly opened restaurant in the Villa Bethanie.

Interestingly, in the Priory Documents, the hierarchy of the Priory of Sion is outlined and as well as the list of Grand Masters there is mention of some 27 commandaries and one 'arch', or sub-group, called Beth-Ania. This name bears an uncanny resemblance to the Villa Bethanie in Rennes-le-Château. Is this yet further evidence that Plantard based the Priory of Sion around the alleged mysterious discoveries of Saunière, incorporating many of the themes he encountered in the village into the Priory Documents?

We do know that Plantard was extremely interested in the area and he bought a small plot of land nearby, on the hill beside Castle Blanchefort. In the Priory Documents, it is even claimed that Plantard visited Marie Denarnaud, Saunière's housekeeper, in 1938 – at which point Plantard would have been just 18 – however, there is no evidence to back up this suggestion.

Later, in the 1960s, Plantard would meet another individual who would have a profound effect upon him: French author Gérard de Sède – a man who would later go on to bring the story of Rennes-le-Château and Bérenger Saunière to the attention of the general public in France. Plantard also worked with Philippe de Chérisey and together these three men seem to have created the story that was to make up the Priory Documents. De Sède published a book in 1962 called *Les Templiers sont parmi nous* (The Templars are Amongst Us). Plantard had helped with its publication and in the pages of this book there are many of the themes that we later find in the Priory Documents, evidence perhaps that they were about to incorporate these ideas into another work of fiction: the Priory Documents themselves.

It is reported that there are letters in existence dating from this time between Plantard, de Chérisey and de Sède that detail their elaborate fraud and their plans for maintaining the fabric of their invention. French researcher Jean-Luc Chaumeil claims to own these letters and it is hoped that one day they will be published in full.

These revelations become more disturbing when we recall that we only know about certain features of the Rennes-le-Château mystery, such as the second tombstone of Marie de Nègre d'Ables and the Coume-Sourde Stone, through the books of de Sède. If it turns out that he invented large parts of the story, then the authenticity of all his claims is in serious doubt and this weakens the foundation of many of the other elements in the mystery.

In order to firmly establish the fraud, Plantard and de Chérisey came up with the brilliant plan of depositing forged documents in the Bibliothèque Nationale in Paris and in one fell swoop the Priory Documents were born. The idea was to create a false trail of evidence that would be stumbled upon by later researchers.

Along with de Sède, Plantard met with all three authors of the book that would eventually become *The Holy Blood and the Holy Grail* and appears to have fed them information which they received in good faith. As soon as this book was published in 1982, the Priory of Sion was instantly launched onto an unsuspecting world and the title became an international bestseller. Overnight, the Priory of Sion went from being mainly a French phenomenon to a worldwide sensation and today it is a minor industry all of its own, with a catalogue of books to its name in a dozen languages, as well as hundreds of websites devoted to the cause of solving the mystery.

The next few years saw a spate of books heavily criticising the story that was presented in *The Holy Blood and the Holy Grail*. Chief amongst those French authors out gunning for Plantard were Jean-Luc Chaumeil and Pierre Jarnac. It was Chaumeil who investigated the origins of the Priory of Sion and he concluded that:

> The Priory of Sion was created in 1956. We were able to contact former members of this office, who all burst out laughing when we mentioned Rennes-le-Château. According to its former President, the association was at the time a 'club for boy scouts' and NOTHING MORE!

Years later, one of the four founding members of the Priory of Sion, André Bonhomme, would go on record to state that the whole thing had been a hoax right from the start. He provided the following insight to the BBC in 1996:

It was four friends who came together to have fun. We called ourselves the Priory of Sion because there was a mountain by the same name close by. I haven't seen Pierre Plantard in over 20 years and I don't know what he's up to but he always had a great imagination. I don't know why people try to make such a big thing out of nothing.

In his book *The Archives of the Treasure of Rennes-le-Château*, Pierre Jarnac cast further doubt on the authenticity of the Priory Documents:

After their quarrel, Plantard made it known that the parchments in de Sède's book were fakes. In 1971, I received a letter from Phillipe de Cherissy implying that he was the author of the two parchments published by Gérard de Sède.

The many books that criticised Plantard and *The Holy Blood and the Holy Grail* seemed to present a very strong case that Plantard had created the Priory of Sion single-handedly and it even appeared that he had made up the Priory Documents, albeit with some help. Plantard's reputation was in tatters.

However, in 1989, as a new museum and visitor centre was opened in Rennes-le-Château, Plantard again crawled out of the woodwork and tried to graft new legends onto the battered tale of the Priory of Sion. Suddenly, he was claiming that the order had been founded in Rennes-le-Château in the year 1681, not in Jerusalem, as the fabricated Priory Documents had stated. Furthermore, he now claimed that while he still believed that he was descended from Dagobert II, it turned out that this was only an indirect lineage and he now believed that the real direct descendant was actually Otto von Habsburg.

Another change was revealed in the form of a new Grand Masters list. It was this that proved to be Plantard's downfall. On the new list was the name of Roger-Patrice Pelat, once an old friend of François Mitterrand and, unfortunately for Plantard, a man whose affairs were being investigated posthumously in 1993 by Judge Thierry Jean-Pierre after a financial scandal. Remarkably, Plantard was called to testify in court and under oath he admitted once and for all that he had made up the story of the Priory of Sion, including the so-called Grand Master list that had included Pelat's name.

Plantard received a severe reprimand and after the hearing he was never to revive the Priory of Sion again. He died in the year 2000 in Paris.

Now that we have heard the full story of Plantard's inventions, what are we to make of the mystery of that famous French village?

The Priory of Sion appears everywhere in the mystery of Rennes-le-Château. The organisation is intriguing and its list of Grand Masters is extremely alluring. But there is one problem. What we know about the Priory of Sion stems largely from a single source: the Priory Documents. And what we have learned about these Priory Documents is that they appear to be fabricated and many of those who supposedly deposited them in the French National Library were already dead before the documents were placed there.

If the Priory of Sion and the Priory Documents appear to be fakes, then one must ask who would benefit from such a deceit? Once more the answer appears to be Pierre Plantard, and possibly another name closely connected with the mystery.

Gérard de Sède, who collaborated with Plantard on his book *The Gold of Rennes* as well as other titles, also appears to have benefited greatly from the acceptance of the idea of the Priory of Sion. His books were bestsellers in France and introduced the parchments discovered by Saunière for the first time.

The authors of *The Holy Blood and the Holy Grail* make the strongest case for the Priory of Sion being a real historical society but again this is largely predicated on the Priory Documents being factual. So the theme continues – what appears to be a fabricated secret society is based on fabricated documents that in turn are based on fabricated artefacts. It would therefore seem that the Priory of Sion is a fraud and nothing else, although it is claimed by some that the almost-farce of Pierre Plantard is simply a bluff within a bluff, designed to divert our attention from the real order.

That there is a mystery surrounding the village of Rennes-le-Château and the Abbé Saunière is beyond doubt. There also seems to be some truth in the claim that an order known as the Priory of Sion did exist a long time ago in France. However, what now seems more likely, given the testimony of Plantard himself as well as that of a whole host of authors and researchers, is that all of these disparate threads cannot be woven into a single fabric that resembles anything like that of the Priory of Sion which Dan Brown uses to wrap around his novel *The Da Vinci Code*.

On the surface this is a disappointment; however, there are possibly even more alluring mysteries lurking at the fringes of the story of the Priory of Sion, and the tale of Plantard's colourful imaginings could just be hiding far greater enigmas and conundrums.

Maybe it is time to ask ourselves, does Dan Brown know more about the mystery of Rennes-le-Château than he has revealed? Indeed, it seems he might, because the mystery of nineteenth-century Rennes-le-Château is merely the tip of a much greater enigma. For nestled in the foothills of the French Pyrenees, aligned on the Rose Line with St Sulpice in Paris and Rosslyn Chapel in Scotland, there exists a location with an epic legend associated with it. The region is known as the Languedoc and it contains secrets that religious orders have savagely fought to possess, and protect, since time immemorial.

With such overt references to Paris, London and Edinburgh, why has Dan Brown chosen to conceal what is arguably the true inspiration of *The Da Vinci Code*?

He does make a further connection to the area surrounding Rennes-le-Château with the character Bezu Fache, captain of the French police team responsible for investigating the death of Jacques Saunière. Not far from Rennes-le-Château are the remains of an old Knights Templar fortress named Bezu.

The intrigue is reinforced by a strange counterfeiting incident in the year 1314 when coins minted with a higher than standard measure of gold were traced to Bezu. Additionally, Bezu figures in the sacred geometry of the Rennes-le-Château mystery. The rocky outcrop on which the fortress perches forms part of a spectacular natural pentagram of mountains in the landscape encircling Rennes-le-Château. Treasure and sacred geometry are two of the recurring themes of the Rennes-le-Château mystery and both also feature in *The Da Vinci Code*.

Cutting to the chase, the question we really have to ask ourselves is a big one: is the Languedoc home to the tombs of Mary Magdalene and Jesus Christ?

In order to be able to answer this satisfactorily, let us take a moment to reflect on the history of the region and the many secrets hidden there, including persistent tales of a treasure, either material or spiritual – or both – and the mysteries it has germinated through the ages.

THE ANCIENT VINEYARDS OF GNOSTICISM

The area extending from the north of Spain to the south-east of France is steeped like no other in religious secrets. To this day, the area known as the Languedoc – the sprawling, mountainous landscape to the south, east and west of the medieval fortress of Carcassonne –is imprinted with the memory of Gnosticism, Mary Magdalene and the Holy Grail. The region has been the focus of grail hunters for hundreds of years. But what was the nature of the treasure they sought?

The sacred painted caves of Lascaux, east of Bordeaux and just north of what would later become Cathar country, are thought to be over 15,000 years old. The first chamber in the caves, the Hall of Bulls, as it became known after its discovery in 1940, features several examples of what scholars call therianthropism: the representation of figures with both human and animal characteristics. These figures, such as the Unicorn Man at Lascaux, are now believed to represent a shared memory amongst shamans the world over, who used natural chemicals such as plants and mushrooms to produce man's earliest religious images.

The megalithic monuments of France are renowned for their grandeur, complexity and proportion, especially those in the region of Brittany in the north-west. Like the sacred caves of Lascaux, they speak in a tongue whose dialect has long been forgotten.

There are also abundant signs of megalithic settlement in the south of France, where they form a particularly dense corridor along the El Camino de Santiago (The Way of St James), or, as it is known today, the pilgrims' path to Santiago de Compostela. Here, according to legend, a Spanish peasant was guided by a falling star – a *campus stellae* – and discovered the tomb of St James, who had been martyred in Jerusalem in AD 44. The saint had frequented the region and his followers are said to have returned his body to Spain after his death. His shrine quickly became one of the most sacred sites in all of Christendom and countless thousands continue to walk the hallowed path to this day.

To the west, in what was ancient Roman Gaul, there exists another account of biblical figures travelling to the region from Jerusalem. Legend tells the story of Mary Magdalene and her daughter Sarah, a young Hebrew princess, who arrived on the shores of the French Mediterranean around AD 42 near present-day Marseille. Mary

Magdalene, her daughter Sarah, and Mary's brother and sister, Martha and Lazarus, had apparently fled to Alexandria from the Holy Land to escape persecution by the Romans. From Alexandria, they are said to have set sail for France.

Memories of Sarah, the 'dark queen', so-called due to her alleged Egyptian origin, are imprinted all across Europe. This is especially so in the south of France, where black Madonnas and churches dedicated to the Magdalene abound. Additionally, festivals in honour of Sarah are held across the south of France each year, such as the annual spring festival in Les Saintes-Maries-de-la-Mer. Many believe that Mary Magdalene was buried near St Maximin-la-Ste-Baume in Provence, where a mausoleum was constructed for her remains.

Memories of long-distance journeys also exist elsewhere in Europe. In England, for instance, folklore tells of the travels of Joseph of Arimathea, the wealthy uncle of Jesus Christ. As an established tin merchant, Joseph of Arimathea would have journeyed to the tin-trading capitals of his day, namely Cornwall in south-west England and Anglesey in north-west Wales. Legend states that on occasion he travelled with his nephew, Jesus. The memory is preserved in William Blake's poem, 'Jerusalem': 'And did those feet in ancient time/Walk upon England's mountains green?/And was the holy Lamb of God/On England's pleasant pastures seen?. . ./And was Jerusalem builded here/Among these dark Satanic mills?'

Located in the English county of Somerset, Glastonbury is commonly referred to as England's Jerusalem, although it is more famous today for its outdoor music festival than its holiness. Glastonbury was once a site of considerable pilgrimage, much like Santiago de Compostela. It is said to have boasted the burial site of King Arthur and his wife, Guinevere, as well as the first Christian chapel outside Jerusalem, founded by none other than Joseph of Arimathea.

THE MEROVINGIAN MYTHOS

Back in the Languedoc, the next group we need to look at are the Visigoths. Around the third century AD, Germanic invaders began to weaken Rome's empire and in 410 the Visigoths sacked Rome. The renowned sixth-century historian Procopius, famed for his eight-volume work *History of the Wars*, would have us believe that they seized the treasure the Romans had previously looted from Herod's Temple. And the Languedoc is where they appear to have taken it, for that is where the Visigoths established their new kingdom.

Did the Visigoths in fact lay their hands on the treasure of Solomon when they occupied Rome? Could these sacred relics and riches have been secreted in the Languedoc? To answer these questions, we need to briefly trace the history of the hoard from Solomon's Temple.

The Old Testament account of the construction of Solomon's Temple confirms that it was built to house the Ark of the Covenant. Its treasures are also said to include riches of gold, silver and precious gems, many of which were given to Solomon by the Queen of Sheba.

In 586 BC, the Babylonian King Nebuchadnezzar sacked the temple and burned its contents. Ezra chapters 1–3 indicate that Cyrus, the King of Persia, reconstructed the temple and restored a large majority of its original booty, which had been reclaimed. In and around 35 BC, Herod then rebuilt Cyrus's temple, minus the Ark of the Covenant, which by this time had gone missing from the historical record.

The first-century Jewish historian Flavius Josephus, author of *Jewish Antiquities* and *The Jewish War*, informs us that the Roman General Titus sacked Jerusalem in AD 70, including the Temple of Solomon. Josephus, who was born in AD 37, was alive at the time and recounts how Titus paraded the treasures of Solomon in a victory procession. He specifically mentions the seven-branched menorah, which, after the Ark of the Covenant, was the most sacred relic in the temple.

It is entirely plausible, therefore, that after seizing them from the Romans in 410, the Visigoths could have brought the treasures of Solomon to what would later become southern France.

In their book *Sacred Treasure, Secret Power: The True History of the Web of Gold*, authors Guy Patton and Robin Mackness state:

> Having settled in their new kingdom, straddling the Pyrenees, the Visigoths established their capital at Toulouse and created well-fortified centres of power at Toledo, Carcassonne and Rhédae, the little hilltop village of Rennes-le-Château. Evidence that the Visigoths had possession of an immense treasure is borne out not only by the Guarrazar artifacts, but from commentators and historians including Procopius, El Macin, Fredegaire, and the Englishman, Gibbon. That this included the spoils of Rome is confirmed by their references made to the Missorium, a magnificent jewel-encrusted golden plate weighing about 100 pounds, and also to the Emerald Table with its gold stands and pearl inlay.

As it is the Priory Documents that make reference to Rennes-le-Château as Rhédae, this theory must be subject to doubt. However, within view of the Tour Magdala lies the village of Coustaussa. On the hillside above the village are the remains of what appears to have been an ancient settlement. It is known locally as the Grand Camp and consists of roughly carved stone walls over six feet high as well as dozens of stone houses known as Capitelles. The structures are in a state of decay and somewhat surprisingly they have yet to be dated and in fact seem to defy classification. There is nothing else like them in the surrounding area. Until archaeologists can satisfactorily date the structures we cannot be sure if they are an anomaly or something more tangible and significant, such as evidence of the ancient settlement of Rhédae.

To the west of Rennes-le-Château are a number of archaeologically rich caves and grottos. They lie in the immediate vicinity of what would later become the Cathar fortress of Montségur. Academia has largely ignored them but their former glory has been preserved in myth and legend.

One such cave is that of Lombrives, which is purported to be the largest underground grotto in Europe. In their book *In Search of the Holy Grail and the Precious Blood*, Ean and Deike Begg state:

> Legend attributes the discovery of Lombrives to Roderic, King of the Goths, who sought in the grotto an emerald table brought from Rome by the Visigoths and which eventually ended up in the safe keeping of the hermit of Trevrizent.

Grail romance enthusiasts will recall Trevrizent as the hermit in Wolfram von Eschenbach's *Parzival*. By all accounts, Trevrizent sounds suspiciously similar to a Cathar. Legend encourages us to believe that the Visigoth king Roderic discovered the emerald table of Solomon as well as a treasure chest containing three cups. Here we have a record of the treasure of Solomon in the vicinity of Rennes-le-Château. We also have the first account of a cup, or chalice. Could it possibly be the Holy Grail, as some believe?

The Frankish Merovingian dynasty (476–750) is another mysterious group connected with the Languedoc, founded by King Merovich. The Merovingians were known as the 'long-haired kings' due to their belief that hair was the source of their strength. Clovis I, the grandson of Merovich, became king of the Franks in 481 and was responsible for much expansionism. Several generations later, he would ultimately be succeeded by Dagobert, who would banish his son Dagobert II to Ireland due to political pressures, only to see him return 14 years later and claim the throne of Austrasie in north-east France. Dagobert I was assassinated near Stenay in 679 and a cult of Dagobert rapidly grew.

Dagobert II is believed to have joined the Merovingian and Visigoth bloodlines with his marriage to the Visigoth princess Gisele de Razès. Centuries later, Bérenger Saunière would apparently discover parchments in Rennes-le-Château that, when decoded, revealed the inscription TO KING DAGOBERT II AND TO SION BELONGS THE TREASURE AND HE IS THERE DEAD.

The story goes that Dagobert II's infant son, Sigebert IV, was taken to his mother's home in Rennes-le-Château, or Rhédae, as it was allegedly known in those days. There he reigned as the Count of Razès. Many believe that his journey is depicted on the Knight's Stone, the four-foot slab preserved in the museum in Rennes-le-Château.

The Visigoths, who had battled with the neighbouring Merovingians for some time, were finally defeated at the battle of Jerez de la Frontera in 711 by the Moorish Islamic invasion. Had the Visigoths secured their much-travelled treasure or had the relics of Solomon passed once more to a new master, the Muslims?

THE LANGUEDOC - HOME OF THE GOOD MEN

The Merovingian dynasty would soon be usurped by the Carolingians, who were lords of the Languedoc from 751 to 987. The most famous of their rulers was Charlemagne, who would unite the kingdom, albeit for a brief time. The Carolingians were renowned for their patronage of the arts and literature and are said to have inspired a true Renaissance. Much of the early architecture of the village of Rennes-le-Château dates from this period.

The Cathars were the next order to preside over the Languedoc. With their base in Albi, they were known as the Albigenses, hence the Albigensian Crusade, a campaign initiated by Pope Innocent III in 1209 to extinguish his fellow Christians. The Cathars, or 'pure ones' as the ancient derivative of their name implies, were pacifists and referred to themselves as 'Good Men'. So why were they regarded as heretics?

For a start, the Cathars were dualists, which is a belief system far older than Christianity, and that alone was considered threatening to the Catholic Church. Central to the concept of dualism is the existence of two Gods: one good and one bad. Although this is not dissimilar to the concept of God and Satan in contemporary Christianity, the essence of the Cathars' dualist beliefs was that the good God was immaterial and the bad God was all things material, including every person and object. The domain of the good God was heaven, where purified souls resided. The domain of the bad God was earth, where Rex Mundi reigned.

Thus, in the dualist paradigm, the Cathars believed that Christ was symbolic of the good god, not the actual son of God. If Christ was the son of God, they argued, then he was born of flesh and this would make him inherently evil.

The Cathars were passionate about their faith, which was clearly incongruous with that of the Catholic Church, and it appears that when challenged they frequently took their own lives by walking off cliffs or into fires rather than compromise their beliefs. Their legacy is the spectacular fortresses they constructed on inhospitable mountain tops, such as Peyrepetuse, Queribus and Montségur.

Built at an altitude of 1,207 metres, the first fortifications of Montségur were constructed in 1204. Counter-intuitively, the dramatic cliff-side edifice had not been constructed for military purposes but rather as a refuge, a place of meditation. Nevertheless, invading forces in the name of God advanced on Montségur in 1243 and laid siege to the fortress for the next ten months. When Montségur finally fell, legend has it that over 200 Cathars were led hand in hand to the base of the cliff, where they were burned at the stake for their heretical beliefs. We are told that they sang joyfully in unison as they marched to their inevitable death.

But did the Cathars manage to hide their treasure before this massacre? Something curious is said to have happened the previous night. Allegedly, four Cathar priests climbed down the rugged mountainside cliff face, a vertical drop of hundreds of metres, carrying a treasure. The names of three of the priests have been preserved as Aicart, Highes and Paytavi. Other accounts support this idea but also purport that the Cathars anticipated the siege and hid more of their treasure in a nearby forest, where it would be safe for future transport.

In his *Histoire des Albigeois* of 1870, Napoléon Peyrat, the pastor of Saint Germain-en-Laye, tells us that Bishop Amiel Aicart, one of the four Cathar priests who climbed down the mountain and escaped from Montségur in 1244, was still practising his faith in the great grotto of Lombrives some years later. Sadly, however, the siege of Montségur marked the successful and bloody conclusion to the Albigensian Crusade. For all practical purposes, the Cathars were no more.

THE FALL OF THE TROUBADOURS AND RISE OF THE GRAIL ROMANCES

From the eleventh to the thirteenth centuries, the south of France was home to the aristocratic poet-musician known as the troubadour. Over 400 troubadours, many of whom were also noblemen and crusader knights, were known to have lived between 1090 and 1292. With the end of the Albigensian Crusade, many fled to the north of France or to Germany, due to the fact that their patrons had been sympathetic to the Cathars. The toil of the troubadours was preserved in the grail romances of the day, most notably *Perceval* (1180) by Chrétien de Troyes, *Romance of the History of the Grail* (1200) by Robert de Boron and, last but not least, Wolfram von Eschenbach's *Parzival* (1210).

Many historians believe that Munsalvaesche (Mountain of Salvation), the grail castle in Eschenbach's *Parzival*, is Montségur. Still others believe that Munsalvaesche is actually San Juan de la Peña, outside of Huesca in northern Spain. Legend says that San Juan de la Peña was in fact the fortified monastery that housed the grail for over three centuries. It was also the burial place of the kings of Aragon. The truth is, one is spoiled for choice when it comes to grail castles in Spain. Tradition maintains that the grail was simply moved from one castle to the next for safe-keeping. Another school of thought argues that the grail of San Juan de la Peña is one and the same as the cup of St Laurence, which can be traced to first-century Rome and resides in Valencia Cathedral to this day.

The Nazi Otto Rahn spent considerable time in and around the area of Montségur. The Germans were obsessed with the Holy Grail and were convinced by the theory that Montségur was Munsalvaesche. Hitler had even planned to celebrate the victory of the Third Reich with a command performance of Wagner's *Parzival*. But it was the caves that fascinated Rahn most. He was particularly interested in Lombrives, where Roderic, the king of the Goths, is said to have discovered the Table of Solomon and the chest with three cups. In Rahn's book, *Lucifer's Court*, he writes:

> Naturally I was most moved by the evidence from the Albigensian era. There are quite a few, but they are hard to find. I spent an entire year not seeing one that was right before my eyes, one that a Cathar hand had drawn upon the marble wall in charcoal and in the cavern's eternal night some even centuries earlier. It depicts a boat of the dead with the sun as its tail, the sun, giver of life that is reborn each winter! I saw a tree as well – the tree of life – also drawn in charcoal, and last, within a very mysterious crevice, the outline of a dove carved onto a stone, which was claimed to have been the symbol of the Holy Grail and which figured on the coat of the arms of the knights of the Grail.

Not far from Lombrives is the cave of Montreal. Here, beneath the remains of Castel de Montreal-de-Sos, is an ancient wall painting that includes each and every component of Chrétien de Troye's grail procession.

It's no wonder that the grail romances all point to this region and that further to the south-west, in the vicinity of Huesca and San Juan de la Peña. This is grail country. Those who wrote about it, notably Wolfram von Eschenbach, never wrote fiction, only history.

Another peculiar twist in the tale occurred in the middle of the thirteenth century. Blanche de Castile, the mother of St Louis, king of France, was alleged to have travelled to Rennes-le-Château at this time with a treasure. Legend informs us that she commissioned a team of men to transport the treasure to an underground vault. To preserve the secret, she is said to have buried the men alive with the treasure.

Blanche de France, the daughter of St Louis, also visited Rennes-le-Château. In honour of her visit, the castle formerly occupied by the Templars was renovated and renamed 'Blanchfort'. Legend claims that the region around Blanchfort is rich with underground mines containing millions in gold and other assorted treasure. Many believe that it was a part of these treasures that Saunière discovered.

THE MYSTERY OF LOURDES

Gothic France slowly transitioned into the Renaissance era, assisted by France's invasion of Italy in 1494. The Wars of Religion (1562–98) divided France once more, and not for the last time. The eighteenth century would bring both enlightenment and revolution, then in 1858, just when the Church appeared completely separated from the state, a miracle occurred: the Virgin Mary visited the Languedoc.

Over a five-month period, the Virgin Mary appeared eighteen times to fourteen-year-old Bernadette Soubiroux. The visions, along with the appearance of a spring and accounts of miraculous healing, brought worldwide attention to Lourdes, a previously quiet and unassuming French town. France was transfixed by the news and Bérenger Saunière, who was a boy of six years old, is likely to have heard the story, especially as Lourdes is only 100 miles or so west of Rennes-le-Château. The first apparition occurred on 11 February 1858 and is recorded on the official Lourdes website as follows:

> Accompanied by her sister and a friend, Bernadette went to Massabielle on the banks of the Gave to collect bones and dead wood. Removing her socks in order to cross the stream, she heard a noise like a gust of wind, she looked up towards the Grotto: 'I saw a lady dressed in white, she wore a white dress, an equally white veil, a blue belt and a yellow rose on each foot.' Bernadette made the Sign of the Cross and said the Rosary with the lady. When the prayer ended the Lady suddenly vanished.

The eighth apparition has an interesting relevance to our story, as Bérenger Saunière would pay homage to it some 22 years later when he renovated his church following his apparent discovery of the treasure. The Lourdes website describes the eighth apparition, which took place on 24 February 1858, as follows: 'The message of the Lady: "Penance! Penance! Penance! Pray to God for sinners. Kiss the ground as an act of penance for sinners!"'

The first of several miracles occurred shortly thereafter. Much debate would follow and Bishop Laurence, the bishop of Tarbes at the time, headed a commission to examine the merits of the apparitions. After four years of deliberations and extensive questioning of Bernadette, the commission made its decision on 17 January 1862 and published its findings the following day. The bishop concluded:

> There is thus a direct link between the cures and the Apparitions, the Apparitions are of divine origin, since the

cures carry a divine stamp. But what comes from God is the truth! As a result, the Apparition, calling herself the Immaculate Conception, that Bernadette saw and heard, is the Most Holy Virgin Mary! Thus we write: the finger of God is here.

The stage had been set. The die cast. Could a single region have spawned more obsession with the holy family, particularly the Virgin Mary, Mary Magdalene and the bloodline of Jesus Christ, not to mention copious amounts of treasure? As we shall see, this is only the beginning.

THE HOLY COUPLE IN THE SOUTH OF FRANCE

There is no denying the mysterious history of the south of France. However, is there proof that Mary Magdalene and her daughter sailed to Gaul in the first century AD? Well, there is plenty of circumstantial evidence if not an actual smoking gun.

The legends of James travelling to Spain, Joseph of Arimathea to England and Mary Magdalene to France should not be met with undue scepticism. For a precedent, one need look no further than the Phoenicians, who by 600 BC had turned the Mediterranean into an established network of ports and commerce, including Marseille and Narbonne. The Romans had established a presence in Gaul, along with trade routes, many years before Mary is said to have set sail. In fact, Roman Gaul was first established around 125 BC and expanded by Julius Caesar in the Gallic Wars of 58–51 BC.

In *The Coming of the Saints* (1969), John Taylor states that: 'Mary Magdalene died in AD 63, aged sixty, at the place now called Saint Baume in Southern France.'

The Archbishop Mayence (Mainz) and Abbé of Fuld, Raban Marr, wrote in his ninth-century epic *The Life of Mary Magdalene*:

They traveled on across the [Mediterranean] Sea between Europe and Africa, leaving the city of Rome and all the land of Italy to the right. Then, happily changing course to the right, they came to the city of Marseilles in the Gaulish province of Vienne, where the River Rhone meets the coast. There – once they had called upon God, the great King of all the world – they parted.

Many believe that the hundreds of churches dedicated to the Magdalene in the south of France, and across the rest of Europe, serve as testament to the oral tradition that Mary arrived on Gaul's shores in ancient times. Likewise, the black Madonnas appear to commemorate Sarah, the 'dark queen', the legendary daughter of Mary and Jesus. In his 1985 book *The Cult of the Black Virgin*, Ean Begg recounts a strange tale:

In AD 633, during the reign of Dagobert I, the King of all France, who may have been attending Sunday mass there at the time, a ship sailed into the harbor, without oars or sails, containing nothing but a statue, three feet high, of the Black Virgin and a copy of the Gospels in Syriac.

In a similar vein, in his 1996 book *Bloodline of the Holy Grail: The Hidden Lineage of Jesus Revealed*, Laurence Gardner states that:

The Black Madonna of Boulogne reinforced the connection between Mary and 'the sea' in the popular mind. The 'Mary of the Sea' emblem was used on pilgrims' badges before the time of Charlemagne, and a version of the same device found its way into Scotland before armorial seals were common in Britain.

Paintings of the Madonna of the Sea continue to flourish today. They pay homage to the legend of Mary arriving in Gaul and many serve to further the symbiotic relationship between France and Scotland, as recounted by Dan Brown in *The Da Vinci Code*. Take, for example, the strange twelfth-century seal of Leith, the sea port of Edinburgh. Here, Mary Magdalene is pictured travelling in a boat to a far-off destination.

But what about Jesus? How could the Son of God end up being buried in the Languedoc, as some of these theories suggest? Kersey Graves' 1875 book, *The World's Sixteen Crucified Saviors,* recalls 15 saviours who were crucified before Christ. Many of these figures share the same characteristics: immaculate conception, born under a significant constellation of stars, crucifixion and resurrection on or around the 25 December. This has led underground schools of thought to believe that Christ was an archetype, not a real historical figure. Or, if he was a man, then he was re-enacting the saviour archetype, in which case his resurrection was spiritual. It would appear that many key biblical figures may have been archetypes. For instance, the comparison has been made between the iconography of the goddess Isis and the Virgin Mary.

Other accounts speak of Christ's twin, Thomas, who may have been switched with Christ and crucified in his place. This is alluded to in the church in Rennes-le-Château, where an image depicts baby Jesus with a twin. Additionally, a Station of the Cross in the church was modified by the priest in a very unusual way.

Saunière added a night sky and a moon to a scene that is traditionally believed to have taken place during the day: the burial of Christ. As Roman/Jewish tradition would not allow for a burial at night, the image has been interpreted as symbolic of the fact that Christ never really died on the Cross.

Still further accounts purport that Christ's uncle, Joseph of Arimathea, created a chemical reaction that simulated death when he placed a cloth over Christ's face while on the Cross. Proponents of the theory cite the presence of the conspicuous amounts of myrrh and aloe that were readied in preparation for his body being returned to the tomb. In John 19:39, Nicodemus is said to bring 'a mixture of myrrh and aloes' that weighed about 100 pounds. As a sedative, the function of myrrh is understood but sceptics question the role of aloe, the strong fast-acting properties of which are of help to the living, especially those who are wounded, but not the dead.

There is little written about the life of Christ from the time of his adolescence until he appears later in the New Testament at the age of 30. He is said to have travelled to places such as India, where local tradition also says he is buried. Clearly the 'missing years', as they are termed, leave open the possibility that Christ travelled to England, France or just about anywhere. And if the missing years are expanded to include the period after his alleged Crucifixion, then the mystery deepens even further.

With respect to the idea that Jesus and Mary were man and wife, again little can be said with much confidence. The historical record is ambiguous but does contain some clues. The word used to describe Mary in the Coptic texts is *'koinonos'*, which has been translated as 'partner'. In the Gnostic scriptures, Mary is known as 'beloved'. Early Christian texts speak of Mary being the one 'Christ loved more than all the disciples'. Others believe that the marriage feast at Cana, as described in the New Testament, is actually describing the marriage of Jesus and Mary, which is why Christ plays such a prominent role, i.e. turning water into wine.

We cannot therefore rule out the distinct possibility that Mary Magdalene, her daughter Sarah and other members of the holy family could have travelled to the south of France in the first century AD. In the attempt to answer the question once and for all, it is time, finally, to reveal one of the secrets that Saunière took with him to his grave, although he left clues scattered all over the village of Rennes-le-

Château. It could be the greatest secret of all and it has been hiding in the shadow of Rennes-le-Château for centuries.

THE MAGDALENE

Let us return to the village of Rennes-le-Château and the Church of St Mary Magdalene, for it is here that we pick up the first clue.

Researcher Andrew Gough directs our attention towards the altar painting that Saunière personally designed and had commissioned. Astonishingly, this is perhaps the clue that has received least attention.

The painting depicts Mary Magdalene in a grotto. She is on her knees, her eyes fixed on a long wooden cross, or X. Her hands are crossed in an unusual fashion and appear to form the ancient sacred sign of the swastika. Over her shoulder, in the distance beyond the grotto, are the silhouettes of three structures. Gough believes that the skyline in the background represents real features of the village of Rennes-le-Château. Starting from the viewer's right, these include (1) a mountain – Pech Cardou, (2) a castle – the Hautpoul residence and (3) a tower – the Tour Magdala.

Dozens of books have applied sacred geometry in the attempt to pinpoint the location of the grotto in Saunière's altar painting. Many believe that, if discovered, the grotto will reveal Saunière's treasure. After much complicated conjecture, most researchers have ultimately placed the grotto in some distant part of the countryside. However, the truth is that the grotto depicted by Saunière is not very far away at all.

The Magdalene kneeling in the grotto with a skull is a relatively common form of symbolism. Many classical artists have portrayed such a scene. But what about her hands? Her fingers appear unnaturally crossed. Closer inspection indicates that they reveal three Xs, which are in the direct line of sight of a skull that rests at her knees. Is this significant? What are these Xs meant to portray?

As one of the few acknowledged references in Dan Brown's *The Da Vinci Code*, Margaret Starbird is a recognised expert on Mary Magdalene and the lost wisdom of the sacred feminine. Throughout her book, *The Woman with the Alabaster Jar*, Starbird discusses the significance of the X in classical paintings, recognising it as a sign of concealed mystical knowledge. Literally, X marks the spot. In Saunière's painting, Gough observes four Xs. The Magdalene is staring at one and her crossed hands form another three (which the skull is gazing at). Is Saunière trying to tell us that he has uncovered concealed knowledge? Is he indicating that his discovery is somehow related to the grotto in the painting?

Earlier in this chapter we alluded to the appearance in the mystery of Rennes-le-Château of the numbers 17 and 22. These numbers crop up time and time again and they seem to hold the key to much of the mystery.

For example:

- 17 January is the feast day of St Antoine the hermit, who is associated with grottos and whose statue stands opposite that of Mary Magdalene in Saunière's church;
- Mary Magdalene's feast day is 22 July;
- Marie de Nègre d'Ables, whose tombstone Saunière is said to have defaced, died on 17 January 1781;
- the feast day of St Sulpice is 17 January (St Sulpice is associated with the story via 'Le Serpent Rouge', the mysterious work that references Rennes-le-Château and the Church of St Sulpice in Paris, each of which is located on or near the Paris Rose Line);
- Nicolas Flamel was said to have achieved the great work of alchemy on 17 January 1381 and many documents and letters attributed to the Priory of Sion were written on 17 January;

- Sigebert VI, son of Dagobert II, is purported to have visited Rennes-le-Château on 17 January 681;
- the lost body of Dagobert II was supposedly rediscovered on 17 January 872;
- Saunière himself suffered a heart attack on 17 January 1917 and he died a few days later on 22 January.

This brings us conveniently to the number 22, which seems even more significant in the mystery.

- The feast day of Mary Magdalene is 22 July;
- Marie Denarnaud, the 'priest's Madonna' sold her estate (formerly Saunière's) to Noël Corbu on 22 July 1946;
- the Tour Magdala and the other buildings that Saunière left for posterity are encoded with the number 22. There are a total of 22 steps leading from Saunière's gardens to the observatory that overlooks the countryside below. Both the gazebo at one end of the garden and the Tour Magdala itself have a total of 22 steps each. As Saunière dedicated this building to the Magdalene, it should come as no surprise to find the number 22, her feast day, encoded within the construction.

However, it does not end there and we have yet to follow all of Saunière's clues. It is researcher Andrew Gough who has put the final few pieces together.

When you enter the Tour Magdala, you are faced with a tiled floor. There just happens to be one anomalous tile at the foot of the stone spiral staircase, a tile that is highlighted with a red dot whereas every other tile has black dots. This red dot points to the staircase, with its total of 22 steps, which winds up to the top of the tower. Along the way, a single window just happens to point unambiguously towards a grotto across the valley below, one mile in the distance.

It transpires that the name of this grotto is Grotte du Fournet – dite de la Magdeleine, which translates as 'the burial site of the Mary Magdalene'. Is this what Saunière has been drawing our attention to with his life's work?

Gough recounts having made an interesting discovery as he set out on the arduous walk to the grotto a couple of years ago. The villagers warned him to take a compass reading or he would never find the grotto as he approached through the winding valley. From the aforementioned window in the Tour Magdala, and facing the burial site of the Mary Magdalene, Gough recorded a compass reading of 22 degrees, south of west. It seems that Saunière may have sited the Tour Magdala precisely to line up with the grotto.

The visual of this highly symbiotic relationship between 22 and the Magdalene is highlighted in the diagram on page 207 of the gazetteer section of this book, along with photographs that will highlight many of the points made here.

Concealed in the back of the burial site of the Mary Magdalene grotto, Gough found an imprint in the shape of a coffin that had recently been adorned with candles and flowers, as well as a recess that appears to resemble a shallow grave. As shocking as this may sound, could this possibly be where Saunière discovered the remains of the Magdalene? The very name of the grotto seems to confirm as much.

In truth, we simply cannot say what Saunière discovered. All the evidence seems to be demonstrating that he stumbled upon something to do with Mary Magdalene. Furthermore, there is little disputing the fact that his creation, the Tour Magdala, pays homage to this discovery.

If Saunière did not discover the bones of Mary Magdalene or her daughter, he at least appears intent on commemorating her, like several local priests before him. But why go to all that effort for a memorial? Unless of course, there was a discovery of a tomb, as his diary indicated on the autumn equinox of 1891.

So, we end this chapter in much the same vein as Dan Brown ends *The Da Vinci Code*, with the alluring suggestion that the true resting place of Mary Magdalene and the secret behind the Holy Grail could finally have been revealed to us.

On the other hand, perhaps only Bérenger Saunière knows the full story.

SUGGESTED READING LIST

Baigent, Michael, Lincoln, Henry and Leigh, Richard, *The Holy Blood and the Holy Grail* (Jonathan Cape, 1982)

Bradley, Michael, *The Secret Societies Handbook: The Truth Behind the World's Most Sinister Secret Brotherhoods Including: Illuminati, Priory of Sion, Opus Dei* (Cassell Illustrated, 2005)

Douzet, André, *Saunière's Model and the Secret of Rennes-le-Château* (Frontier Sciences Foundation, 2001)

Fanthorpe, Lionel and Patricia *Secrets of Rennes-le-Château* (Red Wheel/Weiser, 1999)

Gardner, Laurence, *The Magdalene Legacy: The Jesus and Mary Bloodline Conspiracy – Revelations Beyond The Da Vinci Code* (Harper Element, 2005)

Hall, Manly P., *The Secret Teachings of All Ages* (Philosophical Research Society, 1988)

Lincoln, Henry, *The Holy Place: The Decoding of the Mystery of Rennes-le-Château* (Jonathan Cape, 1991)

Lincoln, Henry, *Key to the Sacred Pattern: The Untold Story of Rennes-le-Château* (Windrush Press, 1997)

Patton, Guy and Mackness, Robin, W*eb of Gold: The Secret History of Sacred Treasures* (Sidgwick & Jackson, 2000)

Picknett, Lynn and Prince, Clive, *The Sion Revelation: Inside the Shadowy World of Europe's Secret Masters* (Time Warner Books, 2006)

Picknett, Lynn and Prince, Clive, *The Templar Revelation: Secret Guardians of the True Identity of Christ* (Corgi, 1997)

Putnam, Bill and Wood, John E., *The Treasure of Rennes-le-Château: A Mystery Solved* (Sutton Publishing, 2003)

Robin, Jean-Luc, *Rennes-le-Château: The Secret of Saunière* (Sud-Ouest Editions, 2005)

Sède, Gérard de, *The Accursed Treasure of Rennes-le-Château* (DEK Publishing, 1967)

Starbird, Margaret, *The Woman with the Alabaster Jar* (Bear & Company, 1993)

THE DEATH OF POPES

... thou art Peter, and upon this rock I will build my church; and
the gates of hell shall not prevail against it.

Matthew 16:18

A CONGREGATION OF OVER A BILLION

Living in palatial surroundings, in his own sovereign state, guarded
by a fiercely loyal private army, it is difficult to imagine how the head
of a church with over one billion members could be murdered. This,
however, is the premise of the plotline in *Angels and Demons*, in
which Dan Brown has the previous pope killed off by a man it
transpires is his son. In the novel, this introduces two themes: that of
a pope being assassinated and that of a supposedly celibate pontiff
having a child whom he has patronised and raised to an office within
the Vatican. Could there be any precedent for either of these
outrageous suggestions – has Mr Brown been inspired by real events?

To understand the turmoil that has often accompanied the office of pope, we need to examine what the position actually entails. It is sometimes difficult for us to grasp that in earlier times popes were not only seen as the representatives of Christ on earth and inheritors of the spiritual authority of St Peter, they were also the vastly wealthy temporal rulers of huge areas of Italy. As medieval potentates, their lands often excited the envy of rival princes and at times popes fought wars of aggression or defence when they felt their interests threatened. Other rulers sought to use papal influence to their own advantage.

Threats came not only from rival states within Italy itself but sometimes from outside. The French for many years had political interests in Italy, making claims at different times to the Kingdom of Naples, the Duchy of Milan and the Republic of Genoa. They also protected the Duchy of Savoy in order to safeguard the Alpine routes between the two countries.

Between 1494 and 1495, having first ensured the neutrality of Henry VII of England, Maximilian of Austria and Ferdinand of Aragon by bribery and diplomacy, Charles VIII of France led a powerful army to capture Florence, Rome and Naples. Styling himself 'King of Sicily and Jerusalem' and, worse, 'Emperor' (referring to the now defunct Eastern Roman Byzantine Empire), he rapidly alienated the Germans, who believed he might be claiming the Holy Roman Empire; the Aragonese, since Ferdinand had his own claims in Naples; and the Borgia pope, Alexander VI. An alliance called the Venetian Holy League was formed to coordinate opposition to the over-ambitious king and an army was raised. Charles himself retreated quite rapidly into France, leaving most of his army to continue the occupation in his absence. While they won set-piece battles, the French could find no answer to the guerrilla war that was waged against them and they were forced eventually into abject surrender.

The intriguing aspect of all this is that the Catholic French were relaxed about the prospect of attacking land belonging to the holy father. Their fellow Catholics, who formed the Holy Alliance to thwart their ambitions, did not do so primarily in order to defend the pope, although no doubt they will have believed that this end sanctified their cause. They took up arms with the papal forces to defend their own territorial interests and political ambitions. At the heart of medieval politics was a perceived necessity to preserve, and if possible to enlarge, one's power, wealth, prestige and standing. Princes and popes alike fought with all the means at their disposal to that end.

THE EXERCISE OF PAPAL AUTHORITY

Popes had weapons in their armoury that were spiritual rather than physical. During the reign of Stephen of England (1135–54), the king offended the pope, who retaliated by putting the country under an interdict. This forbade the performance of all church services, including burial and the sacrament of marriage, and effectively paralysed many aspects of normal life. Priests who feared the authority of the pope more than that of the king were obliged to comply. During his dispute with Archbishop Thomas Becket, Stephen's successor, Henry II (1154–89), was forced to have all ports and coastline closely watched to prevent any messenger bringing a new interdict into the country from Rome, where Becket's cause was receiving support. After his succession to the throne, Henry's son John (1199–1216) alienated the Church and not only did the pope lay an interdict on the country but he also had John excommunicated and declared him deposed. This effectively gave his subjects carte blanche to rebel, so John was forced into a humiliating climb-down in which he agreed to hold his land by the pope's permission and to pay an annual fee for the privilege.

The duties of the reigning pontiff therefore included not only ruling on doctrinal matters and making senior clerical appointments but also balancing the finances of his territories, deciding on foreign alliances and ensuring the defence of his realm. The temporal rulers of Europe made conflicting demands on the ruling pope, the balancing of which required a deft and diplomatic hand.

One of the most spectacular examples of this occurred during the pontificate of Pope Clement VII, who was faced with the demands of Henry VIII for a divorce from his wife Catherine of Aragon, while her family put pressure on him to refuse to grant the annulment. Catherine's nephew, the Emperor Charles V, had previously attacked and overrun the city of Rome in 1527, imprisoning Clement VII for six months over a previous dispute, so the pope's reluctance to grant the divorce is understandable. A papal dispensation had already been necessary (granted by Pope Julius II) for Henry to marry Catherine, as she was his brother's widow and this was normally prohibited.

Henry VIII thought of himself as a good Catholic monarch and after publishing a stout defence of the established Church and attacking Martin Luther in his work *Defence of the Seven Sacraments*, Henry was granted the title 'Defender of the Faith' by Pope Leo X. This title is still held by Henry's successors, including Her Majesty Queen Elizabeth II, despite the fact that the faith they are defending is now the Church of England rather than that of the Catholic Church. When Henry VIII finally realised that he was not going to prevail with Rome, he found a solution by devolving the Church in England from papal control. When Henry divorced Catherine in 1533 to marry the already pregnant Anne Boleyn, he was excommunicated and England became a Protestant country. It has remained so apart from a brief period in the reign of Henry and Catherine of Aragon's daughter Mary, demonstrating the profound importance of the decisions made by the pope.

FAMILY CONNECTIONS

The Vicar of Rome, or pope, holds an office that is believed to have originated with St Peter, one of Christ's apostles. In the gospel of

Matthew 8:14, we discover: 'And when Jesus was come into Peter's house, he saw his wife's mother laid, and sick of a fever.' This clearly indicates that Peter was married and suggests that being married was no impediment to his ministry. The much more contentious issue of whether Jesus was also married is a theme developed in Dan Brown's *The Da Vinci Code*, where he suggests that a bloodline exists as a result of a union between Jesus and Mary Magdalene.

In the early Christian Church, there was no requirement for priests to be celibate and, although commended by St Paul, there was no rigorous enforcement of the policy. After the first and second Lateran Councils in AD 1123 and 1139, clerical celibacy was made part of Church doctrine and remains so to this day. In the twentieth century, there were calls to review the policy but both Pope Paul VI in 1967 and John Paul II upheld the traditional position.

St Peter was reputedly martyred by crucifixion around AD 67 but, in contrast to his Lord, he was crucified upside down, apparently because he felt that he was not worthy of sharing Jesus's fate. After St Peter, there followed a succession of popes over the next 300 years, nearly all of whom are traditionally believed to have been martyred for their faith but about whom little evidence exists.

Miltiades (311–14) was the pope who had the distinction of ruling the Church at the time when the Emperor Constantine decided that his victory at the battle of the Milvian Bridge had been assisted by the Christian God. Approval was extended to Christians, the emperor no doubt influenced by the fact that his mother, St Helena, was a Christian. In AD 380, the Emperor Theodosius I decreed that all the inhabitants of the empire should follow 'the form of religion handed down by the Apostle Peter to the Romans . . .'

Despite now having official endorsement, the early Church was engaged in a perpetual struggle with groups who held different, i.e. heretical, views. The split with the Eastern Orthodox Church, for example, resulted in repeated strife between Rome and Constantinople.

Given the huge influence and prestige associated with the office of pope, the desire to hold on to this power by creating ruling dynasties is understandable. Let us therefore look at the issue of the possibility of a pope having a child and then using his influence to promote his offspring. An early example is that of Pope Anastasius I (399–401), believed to be the father of his successor Innocent I, who reigned from 401 to 417. Just over 100 years later, Pope Hormisdas (514–23) was the father of Pope Silverius (536–7), who sadly did not enjoy the fruits of his father's patronage for long and was first forced to abdicate before then starving to death. Pope John XI (931–5) was the son of a lady called Marozia, who was thought to be the mistress of his predecessor Sergius III (904–11).

The period starting with the pontificate of Sergius III and ending with the death – or more precisely murder – of John XII has been dubbed the 'Pornocracy'. This alludes to the fact that the popes were being influenced by powerful Roman families – in particular by some very forceful women, of whom Marozia was a striking example.

After the death of her first husband, Marozia married Guy of Tuscany and one of their acts was to imprison Pope John X in Castel Sant'Angelo, where he was murdered. In 929, when Guy died, the indomitable Marozia selected his half-brother Hugh of Arles as her next husband. Inconveniently, he was already married but once her son John XI had been manoeuvred onto the papal throne he arranged an annulment of Hugh's marriage and the couple were wed. Fate finally caught up with Marozia when in 932 her son Alberic II, by her first husband, imprisoned her. Alberic II then married his stepsister and fathered the future Pope John XII. Marozia therefore has the distinction of having both a son and grandson elevated to the papacy.

If election was not to be secured by being the son of a former pope, there were other close family ties that would suffice, as shown in the following examples. Benedict VIII was succeeded by his brother John XIX in 1024, despite the fact that John was a layman and had to be ordained as a bishop before he could take office. The family line was further extended when, after John XIX died, his nephew (also a layman and according to some sources only aged 12) ascended to the papacy as Benedict IX. Given his inauspicious start, it is not surprising that he abdicated, allegedly for financial gain, in favour of his godfather Gregory VI in 1045. A confusing series of events then resulted in Benedict IX being restored twice before his eventual deposition and excommunication, with Gregory also being deposed.

Innocent III (1198–1216) was the nephew of Clement III, Gregory XI (1370–8), the nephew of Clement VI, while Pius III (who reigned for 27 days in 1503) was the nephew of Pius II. A sequence of Eugenius IV (1431–47), who was the nephew of Gregory XII and himself the uncle of Paul II, can be traced. The first Borgia pope, Callixtus III, was the uncle of Alexander VI (1492–1503), who established the Borgias as a powerful influence in Europe. Alexander VI had several children, the most famous being Lucrezia and Cesare, both of whom enjoy colourful reputations. At one stage, Cesare was ordained as a cardinal, presenting the possibility of his own eventual succession to the papacy, but the Church was spared this prospect when it suited Alexander's ambitions more to arrange a marriage for his son, and Cesare became the Duke of Valentinois. Alexander's acclaimed mistress Guilia Farnese, however, had a brother Alessandro, who was given a cardinal's hat by Alexander. This fortunate young man later became Pope Paul III but only after fathering four illegitimate children, and he was then able to make two of his teenage grandsons cardinals in 1534.

It is clear from some of the examples already mentioned that the fathering of children was no impediment to becoming pope in the Middle Ages or Renaissance. Adrian II had been married before taking orders and had a daughter from his marriage; Clement IV had also produced legitimate children from a marriage pre-dating his ordination. Popes Pius II, Innocent VIII and Julius II produced numerous illegitimate children, as did the formidable Medici Pope Clement VII, who was widely believed to be the father of Alessandro de Medici. Clement VII was certainly the uncle of Catherine de Medici, who through his influence married into the French royal family and became queen. The pattern continued with Pius IV (1559–65) having several illegitimate children and Gregory XIII having just one son, who was born before Gregory's ordination.

ASSASSINATION ATTEMPTS

It is perhaps not surprising, given the influence and power of the position as previously explained, that there have been attempts on the lives of some of the Supreme Fathers. One of the most notable examples in modern times took place in 1981 when Pope John Paul II survived an assassination attempt after being shot in St Peter's Square by Mehmet Ali Agca. Famously, John Paul II visited his attacker in prison and forgave him for the shooting. Another attempt was made on the life of John Paul II on 12 May 1982, when an aggrieved priest, Juan Maria Fernández y Krohn, attacked him with a bayonet in Fatima, Portugal.

Pope Paul VI (1963–78) was also the victim of an assassination attempt. On a visit to the Philippines in 1970, he was attacked by a Bolivian painter, who attempted to stab him with a dagger. It is a matter of speculation as to whether or not the pope received a stab wound during the incident, something that the Vatican denied. Certainly Paul VI was more fortunate than Leo III, who in 799 was attacked by thugs at the behest of some of the Roman elite who were displeased with him. The gang attempted to cut out his tongue and gouge out his eyes before leaving him on the streets to die. Leo III was able to escape and continued to reign under the patronage of the Emperor Charlemagne until his death in 816.

A RELUCTANT POPE

So much for assassination attempts – is it possible that a reigning pope could actually have been murdered?

Originally named Pietro di Morrone, the future Celestine V, whose fate is discussed in *Angels and Demons*, was a Benedictine monk from a peasant family and had lived much of his life as a hermit. He had a reputation for saintliness and had founded a new monastic order, the members of which dedicated themselves to caring for the poor and sick.

For an unambitious man of 79 years of age, the prospect of becoming pope was very daunting, if not disagreeable. He tried to refuse the office but was persuaded to take up the role under the title Celestine V. Once he assumed office, it very quickly became obvious that not only was he unsuited to the responsibilities but that the role also prevented him from devoting himself to prayer as he wished. He consulted his cardinals about the possibility of resignation and was given careful advice in the matter by Benedict Caetani. On 13 December 1294, after an unhappy five months in office, Celestine announced his resignation and presumably looked forward to a peaceful retreat to his former life.

The election of none other than Benedict Caetani as his successor, as Pope Boniface VIII, however, resulted instead in Celestine being held in custody. Clearly Boniface was not prepared to risk his saintly predecessor being used as a pawn by anybody seeking to undermine his own authority. Celestine tried in vain to flee but was detained in the Castel Fumone, where he suffered harsh treatment and died in 1296. Until recently, when a controversial new theory was advanced, it was supposed that he had died from an infected abscess. In 1998, however, claims were made by Rev. Quirino Salomone that a CT scan carried out on the skull of Celestine V had revealed a half-inch hole in the temple that could have been caused by a nail being driven into the skull.

Whether or not he hastened his predecessor's end, Boniface himself was soon confronted by powerful enemies. He came into conflict with the French King Philip IV and sought to underline his authority in a papal bull called *Unam Sanctam*, which stated that none could enjoy salvation unless they were subjects of the Roman pope. A French minister was dispatched to demand that Boniface resigned, which he refused to do, and the pope was then captured and suffered physical abuse. Perhaps realising that they had overstepped the mark, after two or three days Boniface was released and he returned to Rome. When Boniface died a month later, it was assumed that he had died either from injuries sustained in the attack or from shock. Both Celestine V and his successor were therefore possible candidates for meeting their deaths as a result of violence.

'THEY HAVE ASSASSINATED HIM'

In *The Vatican Exposed: Money, Murder and the Mafia*, Paul L. Williams raises suspicion over the death of Pope Pius XI in 1939. Much of the material he uses was provided by Cardinal Tisserant, who in his journal recorded the words, '*Ils l'ont assassiné*' (They have assassinated him). Any accusation of murder requires the existence of a motive and it is the diplomatic manoeuvrings of Pius XI that provide a possible incentive to remove him.

Pope Pius XI was elected in 1922, with the Vatican still in conflict with the state of Italy over the seizure of the Papal States in 1870. From this time, the modern country of Italy had an uncomfortable relationship with the papacy, which now had its temporal power curtailed. After detailed negotiations, the Lateran Treaty was signed in 1929 by Pius XI and Benito Mussolini, the dictator of Italy. This treaty established the Vatican as a sovereign state within Italy and guaranteed certain rights and privileges to the Church. It was also as a result of this agreement that the finances of the Church were improved with the establishment of the Vatican Bank – although this sowed the seeds of later discontent.

The Church also entered into proceedings with Nazi Germany, with Cardinal Eugenio Pacelli acting on behalf of the pope. A concordat was drawn up in 1933 by which Hitler guaranteed independence for Catholic organisations and the provision of religious teaching in schools. It became apparent, however, that these conditions were not being met and concern grew in the Vatican that, contrary to the agreement, the cults of the Reich and of Hitler as the Führer were replacing the Church's place in society in the new state of Germany. The pope was concerned enough to issue an encyclical, *Mit brennender Sorge* (With Great Sorrow), in 1937 that denounced Nazi totalitarianism and the breaches to the concordat.

As further evidence reached the Vatican of the persecution of Catholic institutions and the violent tactics employed against citizens in Germany, Pius XI prepared another encyclical. The text of this included a condemnation of the struggle for racial purity and denounced violence of innocent persons '. . . branded as outlaws by the very fact of their parentage'. A meeting had been called for 11 February 1939 at which the pope was planning to meet with Church hierarchy and the encyclical was on his desk awaiting signature.

Pope Pius XI died on 10 February and the existence of the encyclical was not made public until 1972, thus preventing a rift at the time with the Nazi government. While this staggering coincidence invites conspiracy theories, it must be stated that Pius XI was an elderly man, over 80 years old, who had been in poor health for some time, suffering from heart disease.

The journals of Cardinal Tisserant contain the details of his suspicions concerning the death, or in his opinion murder, of Pius XI. A doctor who had recently started to treat the pope was Dr Petacci, who, according to Tisserant, was the only person with access to the pope's apartments immediately prior to his death. Pius XI's death was

THE DAN BROWN COMPANION

recorded as having occurred at 5.30 a.m. on the morning of 10 February but when Tisserant asked about the health of the pope at 6.19 a.m. (he claimed to have recorded the time carefully), he was told that the pope's condition was 'serious'. Tisserant also claims that only Dr Petacci and Cardinal Pacelli entered the bedroom of the dead pope for the next two hours until, finally, other cardinals were admitted and the pope was officially pronounced dead.

Cardinal Pacelli had the role of camerlengo. In *Angels and Demons*, the camerlengo is correctly portrayed by Dan Brown as being the authority figure in the Vatican during the period between the death of the incumbent and the election of a new pope. In this capacity, Pacelli refused Tisserant's calls for there to be an autopsy on Pius XI. Tisserant's request was prompted by his observation that the body of Pius XI had 'strange bluish markings' on it and that the face was 'distorted'. As events unfolded, the next pope to be elected was in fact Cardinal Pacelli, who chose the papal name Pius XII.

Interestingly, Dr Petacci had a daughter, Claretta Petacci, who is far better known than her father. Claretta was the mistress of the Italian dictator Mussolini and was with him at the time of his capture in April 1945 when they were both shot and their bodies later displayed to the public. Could this connection, in addition to the soon-to-be-published encyclical, have provided a potential motive for the murder of Pope Pius XI?

The role of Pope Pius XII during the Second World War is very controversial, with many critics claiming that he did not act decisively to assist the victims of the Holocaust. In his book *Hitler's Pope*, John Cornwell states that: 'Pacelli's failure to respond to the enormity of the Holocaust was more than a personal failure, it was a failure of the papal office itself and the prevailing culture of Catholicism.'

In contrast to this, many Jewish leaders such as Golda Meir, Rabbi Louis Finkelstein and Rabbi Isaac Herzog praised the efforts of Pius

XII and the Catholic Church in helping thousands of Jews to escape persecution. In *The Myth of Hitler's Pope*, Rabbi David G. Dalin refutes the claims made by John Cornwell and argues that Pius XII should be considered as a 'righteous gentile' for his efforts to reduce the suffering of the Jewish people.

THE PASTORAL POPE

While it is impossible to be certain whether the claims of Cardinal Tisserant that Pius XI had been assassinated are true, there is an even more recent example of an allegation of foul play in the Vatican. This relates to the death of Pope John Paul I, who died after only 33 days in office.

There have been many other popes who held office for a short period, which is perhaps inevitable given the fact that many men have been very elderly when elected to the papacy. The shortest reign was that of Stephen II, who died only three days after his election and before he could be enthroned. For this reason he is not included in some lists as a bona fide pope, thus creating a problem with the numbering of all subsequent popes who took the name Stephen. There have been ten other popes who did not survive their election by more than a month, thereby forcing the cardinals to re-enter conclave and choose again.

The death of Pope John Paul I has been the subject of a great deal of speculation and has been written about extensively. Here we examine some of the key features of his life and look at the theories about his possible murder. The financial scandals that engulfed the Vatican in the 1970s and 1980s are also inextricably bound up in the story.

Pope John Paul I was born in 1912 and was ordained as a priest in 1935, working as the vice-rector in a seminary in Belluno for ten years. He was recognised as a learned scholar and good teacher, and seems to have enjoyed his time there very much. Between 1948 and

1958, he worked within the diocese of Belluno, publishing a book on the Catechism, before being made bishop of Vittorio Veneto. In 1958, Pope John XXIII ordained Luciani as a bishop in St Peter's Basilica and read from *The Imitation of Christ* by Thomas à Kempis on the subject of living a peaceful life. As a bishop, Luciani worked in a pastoral role and spent much of his time visiting local parishes and making time to talk to the parish priests. This very approachable style was in contrast to that of most bishops, who were remote authority figures occupied with ceremonial duties and official business. Luciani would visit the sick in hospital unannounced, often arriving on his bicycle.

When the patriarch of Venice died in 1969, Luciani was persuaded after initial reluctance to accept the position. Once again, he tried to maintain a modest lifestyle and departed from the usual lavish ceremonies associated with the arrival of a new patriarch. But he was faced with more difficult and complex issues, including a financial scandal involving the Banca Cattolica del Veneto. This bank had traditionally been used by priests and bishops to raise funds needed for their work and churchmen had received specially discounted rates of interest. The dioceses held around 5 per cent of the bank's shares, and the majority shareholding was in the hands of the Instituto per le Opere di Religione, commonly (and henceforth here) known as the Vatican Bank.

In 1972, however, the special treatment stopped and the clergy learnt that they would have to pay the standard rates. There was outrage among the clergy and this was heightened when they discovered that, despite an understanding that the Banca Cattolica del Veneto would not be sold to a third party, with the 51 per cent shareholding of the Vatican Bank used to guarantee this, there was a new owner – the Banco Ambrosiano in Milan. The Banco Ambrosiano had been allowed to purchase shares owned by the Vatican Bank, including those held as security against loans taken out by the clergy. The two men involved in this transaction would feature prominently in the speculation about the later death of Luciani, as Pope John Paul I: Bishop Paul Marcinkus, who as president of the Vatican Bank authorised the sale, and Roberto Calvi from the Banco Ambrosiano.

Concerned at what had happened, and after meetings with his disgruntled colleagues, Luciani started to investigate the circumstances surrounding the takeover. He visited Rome, where he talked to Monsignor Giovanni Benelli, a senior official in the Vatican Secretariat, and discovered that the Church was aware of the transaction. As Pope Paul VI was unwilling to remove Marcinkus from his position, there was nothing that could be done. Luciani removed the official diocesan accounts as well as his personal account from the Banca Cattolica and was forced to accept the situation.

Pope Paul VI elevated Luciani to cardinal in 1973 and seems to have appreciated the loyalty and discretion of his Venetian patriarch. On doctrinal matters, including the position of the Church on artificial birth control, Luciani was always careful to support the teachings of the current pope, even when his personal views differed from the official line.

After the death of Paul VI in 1978, the cardinals were faced with several candidates for the vacant papacy. Cardinal Siri was seen as a conservative who would uphold the teachings of the Church on family issues. In contrast, Giovanni Benelli, now also a cardinal, was considered likely to be receptive to reforms and was seen as a more liberal candidate. Among the many names considered as Rome waited for the conclave to start, there was virtually no mention made of the quiet man from Venice. And so as the cardinals were sealed up in the Sistine Chapel on 26 August 1978, during an intense heatwave that must have made the conclave very uncomfortable, very few would have anticipated the outcome.

The voting that takes place during the conclave is supposed to remain secret, with severe penalties for any cardinal who speaks about the election. However, in his book *In God's Name*, the author

THE DAN BROWN COMPANION

David Yallop gives figures from the four ballots that are believed to have taken place. At the conclusion of the fourth ballot, and within the first day of their deliberations, the cardinals had elected Luciani as pope, which he accepted, although with reported reservations. In tribute to his two predecessors, he chose the name John Paul, the first double name used by a pope, and compounded this unique situation by adding 'the first'. No pope had previously chosen to use the appellation 'first', it had always been added retrospectively on the election of a second pope with the same name.

The new pope was now in a position to introduce his own style and ideas into the very traditional world of the Vatican. Instead of the customary papal coronation with the papal tiara, a three-tiered jewelled crown that had been used by his predecessors, John Paul I opted for a papal inauguration mass. He also discouraged the use of the *sedia gestatoria*, or portable throne, on which popes were usually carried, and when he spoke he used the singular form of 'I' rather than 'we' to describe himself.

Following his coronation, John Paul I established a routine in his Vatican apartments but after just 33 days in office this was shattered when his body was found on 29 September 1978. It would appear that Sister Vincenza, one of the nuns who looked after the pope, noticed that the coffee she had left outside his room earlier was untouched. She entered his bedroom and found him sitting up in bed, unresponsive. She called his secretaries, who slept nearby, and Fathers John Magee and Diego Lorenzi arrived to find the pope dead. The secretary of state, Cardinal Villot, was then summoned and a strange series of events followed.

The official statement issued at 7.27 a.m. on 29 September on Vatican Radio gave the following information:

> This morning, September 29th 1978, about 5.30, the private
> secretary of the pope, contrary to custom not having found the

holy father in the chapel of his private apartment, looked for him in his room and found him dead in bed with the light on, like one who was intent on reading. The physician, Dr Renato Buzzonetti, who hastened at once, verified the death, which took place presumably towards eleven o'clock yesterday evening, as 'sudden death that could be related to acute myocardial infarction'.

There was more detail released suggesting that the secretary was Father Magee, an Irish priest who had been in the Vatican as a secretary to Pope Paul VI and was then retained by John Paul I. The spiritual work that was said to have been found with the pope, which he had been reading at the time of his death, was *The Imitation of Christ* by Thomas à Kempis, in a strange echo of his ordination as a bishop.

The Vatican maintained the fiction that it had been Magee who found the body of the pope until 2 October when, after much speculation and pressure, it was admitted that Sister Vincenza had made the discovery.

Sister Vincenza had worked for Luciani for 19 years and was in the habit of taking him a pot of coffee at 4.30 a.m. when he normally rose. The name of the book given was presumably chosen as a sound ecclesiastical work that would be a fitting subject for the pope to be reading as he sat up in bed. The problem with this story was that Luciani's own copy of the book was still in Venice, with other of his personal belongings that had not yet been transported to Rome. Not only was his personal copy not present but the papal apartments in fact contained no copy of Thomas à Kempis's work. On 2 October, the Vatican was forced to correct this error by stating that there had been papers relating to personal writings, speeches and various notes. This was further clarified on 5 October with the explanation that the papers related to 'nominations in the Roman Curia and in the Italian episcopate'.

As camerlengo, it would presumably have been Cardinal Villot who decided that it was somehow improper for a nun, in this case Sister Vincenza, to have been in the papal bedroom and therefore the first one to find the body of the dead pope. The cause of death had been announced as a myocardial infarction, or heart attack, on the basis of an external examination only. A further explanation was added when it was hinted that the pope might have taken an accidental overdose of the medicine that he was taking to treat his low blood pressure. Those in the papal apartments immediately after the body was discovered claimed that Villot had removed the bottle of medicine from beside the bed and put it in his pocket.

The doctor who had prescribed the medication for Luciani was Professor Giovanni Rama, and he had been treating his patient for three years. He stated, 'An accidental overdose is not credible. He was a very conscientious patient.'

While he was patriarch of Venice, the doctor attending to Luciani was Dr Giuseppe Da Ros, who used to visit him every fortnight. Dr Da Ros made three visits to his patient after Luciani's elevation to the papacy, the last of which was on 23 September. He was sufficiently pleased with Luciani's health that he advised one of the pope's secretaries, Father Lorenzi, that he would not come again for three weeks. When asked about the health of Pope John Paul I at the time of this visit, Dr Da Ros is reported as saying, 'He's not well but very well.' This confidence in the health of his patient and friend explains his reaction to the news of the sudden death, which was shock and mystification.

Dr Buzzonetti, who provided the opinion that John Paul I had died of a heart attack, had not examined his patient while alive. This was confirmed in an interview with David Yallop. When asked about the medicines that the pope had been taking, he answered, 'I don't know what medicines he was taking. I was not his doctor. The first time I saw him on a doctor/patient basis he was dead.'

This is an extraordinary statement from a physician who then, on the basis of an external examination alone, determined the time and cause of death and signed the death certificate of the patient. Buzzonetti was a Vatican physician but his actions do not present a case for the official cause of death to be accepted with any confidence.

'WHY SAY NO TO AN AUTOPSY?'

Another huge controversy erupted when news of the embalming of the body of Pope John Paul I became known. On 1 October, the front page of the Milan newspaper *Corriere della Sera* carried the question, 'Why say no to an autopsy?' The argument was made that the cause of death of the pope was a matter of legitimate public interest and that the Church had nothing to fear and nothing to lose. The momentum calling for an autopsy grew until Cardinal Villot stated that it was forbidden under canon law and the funeral was planned for 4 October. The fact, however, that the body had already been embalmed meant that even if an autopsy had been performed, evidence would have been compromised. The chemicals used for embalming would change the composition of any blood samples taken and make detecting untoward compounds in the body very unlikely.

Italian law states that a body cannot be embalmed less than 24 hours after death unless a magistrate has given permission. The body of Pope Paul VI had been embalmed after the 24 hours had elapsed but just less than two months later the same officials disregarded the procedure and embalmed Pope John Paul I on the day of his death. The morticians Arnaldo and Ernesto Signoracci were called to perform the embalming that, according to Father Lorenzi, took place after 6 p.m. on 29 September. Also present were Professor Marracino, who carried out the actual work with Ernesto Signoracci, and Professor Cesare Gerin, who was supervising.

The Signoracci brothers had been summoned to the Vatican much earlier in the day, as early as 5 a.m. according to some reports. This would have meant that before the dean of the sacred college, the captain of the Swiss Guard or Dr Buzzonetti had been informed of the news, a telephone call had been made to the embalmers. The exact time of this call and the observations of the brothers as they arranged the body of the dead pope are very significant. According to David Yallop, he has spoken to the brothers on three separate occasions and their opinion was that the pope had only recently died when they saw him. This places the time of death at between 4 a.m. and 5 a.m. on 29 September and implies that when Sister Vincenza found John Paul I he was only very recently deceased. This contrasts with the official time of death estimated as 11 p.m. the previous evening.

The manner of the embalming was as curious as the speed with which it was conducted. It is customary to drain the blood from the body and then introduce the embalming fluid into the circulatory system; however, in the case of Pope John Paul I, no blood was drained. This made it more difficult to inject the embalming fluid but also ensured that there were no blood samples available for later analysis. Once the process had been completed, any toxicology samples taken would be contaminated with the preserving fluid.

The body of John Paul I lay in state while an enormous number of people came to pay their last respects. Despite his short tenure at the Vatican, the warm nature of Albino Luciani had endeared him to his followers and they filed past his body in unexpectedly large numbers. On the evening of 3 October, the night before the funeral, the doors closed to the public at 7 p.m. and a group of officials and doctors approached the body. Depending on how sympathetic one is to the Vatican hierarchy, the subsequent examination of the body was either a routine check of the status of the embalming prior to the funeral or a secret autopsy. While the previous embalming of the body would make an accurate cause of death more difficult to establish if such an autopsy were performed, the lack of any subsequent publication of a conclusion of natural death perhaps lends weight to the theory that the pope had been murdered.

The way in which this could have been achieved has been suggested as poisoning, specifically by digitalis, a drug that acts on the heart. Those favouring the idea of a conspiracy suggest that the digitalis could have been added to the pope's regular medication so that it became a self-administered poison. As this would require access to the papal apartments, it would mean that someone very close to John Paul I either directly added the poison or facilitated a substitution of the medicine.

At this stage, we need to look at who would have had a motive to remove John Paul I; again, David Yallop provides some startling suggestions.

THE ROLE OF THE CAMERLENGO

Cardinal Villot, who had been Vatican secretary of state since 1970, had acted as camerlengo during the interregnum following the death of Pope Paul VI and performed the duty again after the demise of John Paul I. In this capacity, he was responsible for the clearing of the papal apartments, the erroneous statements about how the body had been found and making the arrangements to have the body embalmed.

On the afternoon of 28 September, Villot had attended a two-hour interview with John Paul I at which the pope had given very clear instructions about changes he was about to implement. There were a large number of dismissals to be made, including the removal of Villot himself, and the appointment of new men to important roles. The pope had told Villot that he must resign the following morning and, out of regard for his frail health, return to France, where he could enjoy a contemplative retirement.

Jean Villot would have known that many of those on the list to be dismissed were Vatican officials whose names had appeared in a document presented to John Paul I on 12 September. This document identified them as members of a Masonic Lodge called P2. It had long been accepted that priests and Church officials could not also become Masons due to the potential for a conflict of interest. A papal bull entitled *In eminenti* had been published by Pope Clement XII in 1738 making the position of the Church clear: that membership of both organisations was incompatible and would lead to excommunication.

As secretary of state, Villot would also have known about a forthcoming meeting between John Paul I and a delegation from the USA, planned for 24 October, to discuss population control. Knowing that Luciani had written a memorandum to Pope Paul VI on the subject of birth control prior to the publication of *Humanae Vitae*, and was sympathetic to reform, Villot may have suspected that Church policy was about to be relaxed.

THE CARDINAL FROM CHICAGO

Another prominent name to feature in the proposed ecclesiastical re-shuffle was Cardinal John Patrick Cody of Chicago, an extremely controversial character. Cody had been archbishop of Chicago since 1965, after moving from New Orleans, and he was elevated to cardinal in 1967. He inspired strong feelings in many of the priests who worked with him. For example, in *In God's Name* David Yallop reports the comments of one priest from New Orleans when he heard that Cody was moving on: 'When that son of a bitch was given Chicago, we threw a party and sang the *Te Deum*.'

Pope Paul VI had received numerous complaints about Cody from clergy within the diocese of Chicago but Cody had retained his post. In contrast, Pope John Paul I had discussed the problem of the Chicago cardinal with Vatican officials and the consensus was that Cody should be moved. If Cody knew that his position was vulnerable, he must have been relieved when John Paul I died before carrying out his plan to unseat him. Under the next pontiff, John Paul II, Cody was left to run his empire in Chicago unimpeded by the

Church hierarchy, although the lay authorities eventually tried to step in.

The Chicago archdiocese consists of some two and a half million Catholics, making it a very rich patrimony with an annual income of $250 million. Under Cody's charge, mounting speculation over the financial affairs of the diocese led to an investigation by US attorneys and in January 1981 Cody was subpoenaed by a federal grand jury to provide details of his financial affairs.

In September 1981, the *Chicago Sun Times* published the allegations against Cody, who responded by saying, 'This is not an attack on me. It is an attack on the entire Church.' Cody stalled and failed to comply with the requirements of the subpoena. When he died in April 1982, he effectively ended the investigation.

In his 1978 book *The Making of the Popes*, Father Andrew Greeley describes Cardinal Cody's survival:

> Cardinal Cody parlayed his past financial contributions to Poland (and some new contributions, according to Chicago sources), the size of the Polish population in Chicago, and his alleged friendship with the Pope, into a successful counter offensive against his enemies.

The pope referred to here is, of course, the Polish pope Karol Wojtyla, Pope John Paul II, who maintained the status quo within the Church and did not implement any of John Paul I's planned changes.

A BISHOP AS HEAD OF THE VATICAN BANK

Another of the names John Paul I discussed with Villot as someone to be removed from his position was Bishop Paul Marcinkus, the head of the Vatican Bank. John Paul I had begun an investigation into Vatican finances in his first days in office but was of course familiar with the role of Marcinkus as a result of the Banca Cattolica del Veneto affair some years earlier. Just five days into his pontificate, on 31 August 1978, an Italian economic journal *Il Mondo* published an open letter to the new pope asking very awkward questions:

> Is it right for the Vatican to operate in markets like a speculator? Is it right for the Vatican to have a bank whose operations help the illegal transfer of capital from Italy to other countries? . . . Why does the Church tolerate investments in companies, national and multi-national, whose only aim is profit: companies which, when necessary, are ready to violate and trample upon the human rights of millions of the poor, especially in that Third World which is so close to Your Holiness's heart?

Specifically on the subject of Bishop Marcinkus it said:

> He is the only bishop who is on the board of a lay bank, which incidentally has a branch in one of the great tax havens of the capitalistic world. We mean the Cisalpine Overseas Bank at Nassau in the Bahamas. Using tax havens is permitted by earthly law, and no lay banker can be hauled into court for taking advantage of that situation; but perhaps it is not licit under God's law, which should mark every act of the Church.

With questions as explicit as these being asked of the pope, it is not surprising that he was considering major changes to the personnel responsible for Vatican finances.

The man who had been president of the Vatican bank since 1971, Paul Marcinkus, was an American born in Cicero, Illinois, a suburb of Chicago, and it was in Chicago that he was ordained as a priest in 1947. Initially he worked as a parish priest but he later held a number of jobs for the Vatican equivalent of the diplomatic service. His ability to speak English, Spanish and Italian was valuable in appointments in Bolivia and Canada, for example.

Marcinkus was also physically formidable, being 6 ft 3 in. tall and weighing 16 st. It was his size that ensured further promotion when he dramatically came to the assistance of Pope Paul VI in 1964. Paul VI was making a visit in Rome when a surge of eager followers threatened to trample him. Marcinkus pushed a path through the crowds for the pope and protected him. This marked the beginning of Marcinkus's unofficial role as bodyguard to the pope and he gained the nickname of 'the Gorilla'.

In 1969, Marcinkus was ordained as a bishop, with the title and role of archbishop of Horta. He also, despite having no banking experience, became secretary of the Vatican Bank and effectively its head, since Cardinal di Jorio, the official head, was 84 years of age and did not take part in the daily administration.

In 1971, Michele Sindona, a Sicilian banker, introduced Marcinkus to Roberto Calvi. This was to have far-reaching implications and the acquaintance of the two men led to the movement of billions of dollars through the international banking system.

The sale of Banca Cattolica del Veneto to Calvi's bank, the Banco Ambrosiano, has already been discussed. This sale was made public in 1972, despite the fact that the transaction actually occurred in 1971. Also in 1971, the Banco Ambrosiano Overseas Ltd, Nassau, was set up in the tax haven of the Bahamas with Bishop Marcinkus on the board of directors. The new enterprise was originally called the Cisalpine Overseas Bank and was the institution referred to in the *Il Mondo* article quoted earlier.

One of Calvi's business associates, Flavio Carboni, recorded several of their conversations in 1981 and 1982, and David Yallop has reproduced these in *In God's Name*. Speaking about Marcinkus and the Banca Cattolica affair, Calvi said:

Marcinkus, who is a rough type, born in a suburb of Chicago of poor parents, wanted to carry out the operation without even telling the boss. That is the pope. I had three meetings with Marcinkus regarding Banca Cattolica del Veneto. He wanted to sell it to me. I asked him: 'Are you sure? Is it available to you? Is the boss in agreement with it?' It was I who insisted and told him, 'Go to the boss; tell him.' Marcinkus took my advice. Later Marcinkus told me, yes, he had spoken with Paul VI and had his assent. Some time later Marcinkus got me an audience with Paul VI, who thanked me because in the meantime I had sorted out some problems of the Ambrosiano Library. In reality I understood he was thanking me for buying Banca Cattolica del Veneto.

This not only reinforces the image of Marcinkus as a confidant of Pope Paul VI and someone who could arrange audiences with the pope but also explains why Albino Luciani found that nothing could be done about the sale of the bank.

The Vatican Bank was estimated by Roberto Calvi in 1982 to be worth at least US$10 billion, suggesting that its manoeuvrings had been successful in financial terms. On 25 May 1986, *The Observer* (London) quoted Bishop Marcinkus as having said, 'You can't run the Church on Hail Marys' and this pragmatic approach to the business world may explain his willingness to deal with businessmen of a certain reputation.

IL CRACK SINDONA

Michele Sindona had come to the attention of Pope Paul VI while the latter was archbishop of Milan, as he had proved very effective in raising funds for charitable causes. In 1969, when the Italian government decided to revoke the Vatican's tax-exempt status and the amount due to be paid was US$720 million, Paul VI turned to Sindona for help. They agreed to move assets out of Italy and it was agreed that Sindona would work closely with Bishop Marcinkus to protect the Church's wealth.

Sindona was very well connected for anyone wanting to operate clandestinely in international money markets. He had become a trusted banker for the Mafia and was also a member of P2, the Masonic lodge that boasted cabinet ministers, generals, judges and business executives on its roll. He began to purchase from the Vatican large share-holdings in major Italian companies involved in construction, water and chemicals. The Church's investment in Sereno, the pharmaceutical company that made oral contraceptive tablets, was also sold, removing a potential cause of embarrassment. Networks of banks across Europe were used by Sindona to conceal the true value of his investments and to confuse banking regulators in individual countries.

A scandal erupted when it was discovered that bonds deposited on behalf of the Vatican in banks in Rome and Zurich were counterfeit. A trail of evidence led back to the Vatican Bank and investigators managed to gain an interview with Paul Marcinkus. According to their report, Marcinkus admitted knowing Michele Sindona but would not confirm any details of transactions involving private accounts in Nassau. US investigators considered indicting Marcinkus but reportedly decided that the matter was too delicate given the involvement of the Catholic Church.

The net was tightening around Sindona, however, and when the Banca Privata was liquidated with losses of $300 million in September 1974 and the Franklin National Bank in the USA collapsed in October despite frantic efforts to shore them up, exposure of his activities became inevitable. During investigations into the collapse of the Franklin National, Sindona's illegal pilfering of $45 million, money he was using to try and keep other business interests afloat, was discovered. As other banks collapsed and billions of dollars of losses were uncovered, the affair became known as *Il Crack Sindona*, a cruel reference to money disappearing into a chasm. The Italian authorities issued an arrest warrant for Sindona and from New York he tried to avoid deportation to face charges in Italy.

Estimates vary as to how much the Vatican lost as a result of *Il Crack*. It claimed not to have suffered but the loss was probably between $50 million and $240 million. Despite this setback, Bishop Marcinkus retained both his position at the Vatican Bank and the confidence of the pope.

It was not until 1976 that Sindona was arrested in America and released on $3 million bail. He successfully resisted attempts to return him to Italy, although this looked like a hollow victory when the American Justice Department charged him in connection with the collapse of the Franklin Bank.

On 27 March 1980, Sindona was convicted in the USA of over 60 charges of fraud, perjury and misappropriation of funds. He was sentenced to 25 years in prison and began both his sentence and a vigorous campaign to petition senior American officials for leniency. Then, in July 1981, the Italian authorities charged Sindona with ordering the execution of Giorgio Ambrosoli, a bank investigator who had traced the connections between the Mafia and the Vatican and been shot in 1979. Further charges followed in 1982, connecting Sindona with various Mafia families accused of running a lucrative heroin trade between Italy and the USA.

The American authorities extradited Sindona to Milan in 1984 and he received a life sentence for murder and bank fraud. He had served two years of this new sentence when he was poisoned with cyanide in his solitary confinement cell in a maximum-security prison. It is not clear how this murder was achieved but the man known as 'St Peter's Banker' was now silenced.

GOD'S BANKER

Of course, with Sindona unavailable, the Vatican needed an alternative 'financial adviser' and this vacancy was filled by Roberto Calvi, who proved equally adept at undertaking complex share dealings for apparently vast profit. Unfortunately, some of these financial miracles later transpired to be illusory and this partnership was to cost the Vatican Bank dearly – both financially and in reputation.

Roberto Calvi had become the general manager of Banco Ambrosiano in 1971 and its chairman in 1975. A complex web of companies, many based in countries such as Panama and Luxembourg and including the Cisalpine Overseas Bank (later to become Banco Ambrosiano Overseas Ltd, Nassau), bought and sold shares, often in other parts of the Calvi business empire. It was the cooperation of the Vatican Bank that gave apparent legitimacy to these transactions and reassured creditors that there were sufficient funds available to repay loans taken out by Calvi's network of companies. Calvi himself gained the nickname of 'God's Banker'.

Despite the careful attempts of Calvi and Marcinkus to evade suspicion regarding these transactions, the Italian banking authorities began an investigation into Banco Ambrosiano in the late 1970s. In 1981, the two men exchanged letters that were to become infamous after the affair became public knowledge. Marcinkus provided Calvi with a letter falsely stating that the Vatican bank controlled eight companies involved in the emerging conspiracy. In exchange, Calvi wrote a disclaimer to the effect that there would be no liability or loss suffered by the Vatican Bank as a result of its involvement with these companies. Also in 1981, Pope John Paul II demonstrated his confidence in Marcinkus by elevating him to the status of archbishop and making him president of the Vatican City state.

The investigation into the affairs of Banco Ambrosiano continued and Roberto Calvi was arrested, tried for currency offences and sentenced to four years in prison. He managed to obtain his release on bail while an appeal was prepared and he used the opportunity to try and raise more funds to cover up the rapidly widening gap in the finances at Banco Ambrosiano.

Unfortunately for him, some of the money that Calvi was unable to repay belonged to the Mafia and it is claimed by David Yallop that several Mafia families were using Calvi to launder money obtained from illegal activities. Calvi was also a member of the Masonic Lodge P2, to which Michele Sindona had belonged and to which Paul Marcinkus as well as Cardinal Villot appeared to be connected.

In his efforts to raise money, Calvi, despite being on bail in Italy, travelled to London, one of the world's main money markets. It has been suggested that he was seeking help from Opus Dei, the Catholic organisation that features heavily in Dan Brown's *The Da Vinci Code*. Subsequent events suggest that if Calvi did meet with the treasurer of Opus Dei in London, he did not receive the lifeline that he needed.

The body of Roberto Calvi was discovered on the morning of 18 June 1982, hanging from scaffolding under Blackfriars Bridge in London. There were several unusual elements noted by police, including the fact that a large amount of money was found on the body, along with an expensive wristwatch. There were heavy stones placed in the pockets of the suit Calvi was wearing and, when the body was discovered, his feet were trailing in the muddy water of the River Thames. The first inquest in July 1982 recorded a verdict of suicide, which was contested by his family (who, apart from any other motives, would not be able to claim on insurance policies if suicide was the cause of death).

A second inquest in July 1983 recorded an open verdict, as it was questioned whether Calvi would have been able to climb along the scaffolding to hang himself. There were also other suspicious elements, for example there was no trace of rust or paint on his shoes from the scaffolding pole.

There was enormous speculation surrounding the case and significance was attached to the apparent Masonic connections. An Italian nickname for the Masons is *fratelli neri* (Blackfriars) and the Masonic oath provides for traitors to be roped down in the proximity of the rising tide – which can easily be compared to a man hanging with his feet in a tidal river.

In 1998, the body of Roberto Calvi was exhumed for further examination and in October 2002 a forensic report concluded that Calvi had been murdered, as had always been claimed by his family. Carlo Calvi, Roberto's son, has said, 'I believe the killers were sending a message by killing him in public in the heart of the city – there was something theatrical about it.'

In July 2003, the Italian authorities named four suspects for the killing and murder charges were brought in April 2005. The suspects were Flavio Carboni, Manuela Kleinzig, Ernesto Diotallevi and a man already in prison for Mafia offences, Pippo Calo. The trial of these four, along with Silvano Vittor, who was Calvi's driver on his fateful visit to London, opened in Rome in October 2005.

The story of Roberto Calvi has been dramatised in an Italian film called *I Banchieri di Dio* (God's Bankers), which portrays the links between Calvi and the Vatican in unflattering terms. Rutger Hauer plays the role of Bishop Marcinkus, who provides the letters of guarantee for the debts of Banco Ambrosiano. The film also provides a platform for allegations that money was channelled to Poland and other parts of Eastern Europe to undermine Communism, with the support of Pope John Paul II. This is the same suggestion made by Father Greeley, who referred to funds reaching Poland.

There is also a character in *The Godfather Part III*, Frederick Keinszig, who is regarded as being based on Roberto Calvi and who suffers the same fate – ending up hanging beneath a bridge. This film also portrays a fictional Pope John Paul I, who is discovered dead in his bed after a brief reign, and other characters who could be likened to Marcinkus and Licio Gelli, the head of P2.

Roberto Calvi was quoted as having said, 'The only book you've got to read is *The Godfather*. That's the only one that tells how the world is really run.' In another sad reflection of the way that the world is run, Graziella Corrocher, Calvi's secretary, fell, or was pushed, to her death from a fourth-floor office at Banco Ambrosiano in Milan on the same day that her boss died.

With Calvi dead, investigators into the affairs of Banco Ambrosiano very quickly confirmed earlier suspicions that the bank was insolvent. The bank collapsed with a deficit of $1.3 billion and liquidators were appointed to try to recover money owed to creditors. Despite evidence of the close involvement of the Vatican Bank in the affairs of Banco Ambrosiano, and the 'letters of comfort' supplied to Calvi by Marcinkus, the Vatican was not willing to cooperate with the investigation into the collapse. As evidence of corruption mounted, and documents began to emerge that confirmed Vatican knowledge of fraudulent transactions, the Church looked for a compromise. A payment of around $250 million was made to creditors of Banco Ambrosiano by the Vatican as a gesture of 'goodwill' with no admission of liability.

If Archbishop Marcinkus had hoped that the payment would end the investigation into the Vatican Bank's involvement in corruption he was to be disappointed. In 1987, a warrant was issued for his arrest in connection with conspiracy and fraud but the Italian police were unable to execute the warrant. Under the terms of the Lateran Treaty, signed by Pius XI in 1933, the Vatican State is a sovereign country. Archbishop Marcinkus had a Vatican passport that made it impossible for the Italian authorities to arrest him, much to the frustration of those who would have liked to establish his responsibility for fraud.

To the incredulity of many, Paul Marcinkus retained his position at the Vatican Bank until 1989 and his presidency of the Vatican state until 1990. He then moved to Sun City, Arizona, still with his Vatican passport and, despite approaches from journalists and researchers, he continued to maintain his silence over the banking scandals. Following his death in February 2006, it seems that he has taken his secrets to the grave.

This study of the shady dealings of the Vatican Bank and its financial partners provides an understanding of why in 1978 a papal investigation into the financial activities of the Vatican Bank would have been very unwelcome. The people with the most to lose from disclosure of their activities were Bishop Marcinkus, Roberto Calvi, Licio Gelli and Michele Sindona, all members of the P2 Masonic lodge along with Cardinal Villot.

THE PUPPET MASTER

P2 stands for Propaganda Due and is a lodge that was originally founded in 1877 in Italy. It had relatively few members until Licio Gelli took over as its head and began recruiting influential people from many walks of Italian life, including the army, the judiciary and commerce. Gelli was a man who fought for Franco during the Spanish Civil War, spent the Second World War treading a delicate path between the Nazis and partisans, and emerged to help fleeing Nazis reach South America. His connections with South America continued with his claims to be a confidant of president Juan Peron of Argentina and the involvement of members of the Argentine military junta in P2.

Gelli has been referred to as the 'Puppet Master' and it is believed that he controlled the activities of Michele Sindona, Roberto Calvi and others through his P2 lodge. As a result of the Banco Ambrosiano scandal, he received a 12-year prison sentence for fraud but went on the run, initially to Switzerland. He was captured but subsequently escaped from his Swiss prison and fled to South America, where he remained until he gave himself up to the Italian authorities in 1987.

While on parole at his home in Arrezo, Tuscany, he absconded again and was finally recaptured on the French Riviera in 1998. It was reported that gold ingots worth $2 million had been found at his villa after documents were seized from his Cannes apartment.

Mino Pecorelli exposed a list of P2 members in a journal called *L'Osservatore Politico* in 1978 and was subsequently murdered on 20 March 1979. Following a search of Gelli's house in 1981, a list with over 900 names of members of P2 was discovered, confirming Pecorelli's disclosure. It is the list produced by Pecorelli that would have been available to John Paul I as he contemplated whom to involve in his papal administration.

DEATH BY NEGLECT?

In *A Thief in the Night: The Death of Pope John Paul I*, the author John Cornwell refutes the suggestion that the pope was murdered and challenges some of the evidence produced by David Yallop. Cornwell provides another explanation for the death of John Paul I and the apparent Vatican cover-up, namely neglect.

Cornwell suggests that Albino Luciano was already in failing health, having poor circulation, when he was elected pope. His theory is that on the afternoon before his death, the pope began to display symptoms of a pulmonary embolism, such as breathlessness and pain, but that neither John Paul I nor those around him called for medical attention. After retiring for the night, a more severe embolism killed the pope before he could sound the alarm. Cornwell believes that the subsequent variation in the accounts issued by the Vatican about the pope's death can be explained as an attempt at cover-up after those responsible for the well-being of the pope realised that they had let him down.

The fatal embolism postulated by Cornwell could have been brought on by Luciani neglecting to take anti-coagulant drugs, possibly prescribed for him following a blood clot in one eye that he suffered in December 1975. Other accounts, however, do not mention him being prescribed anti-coagulant drugs for long-term use.

According to a poll quoted by Father Jesus Lopez Saez, who wrote a book, *Se pedira cuenta* (Ask for Justification), about the death of Luciani, 30 per cent of Italians believe that Pope John Paul I was murdered, a considerable number to subscribe to such an unpalatable theory. In *Angels and Demons*, Dan Brown has his fictitious pope murdered with an overdose of the anti-coagulant drug heparin that he is already being prescribed. If John Cornwell's theory about the death of John Paul I is correct, the fact and fiction would be mirror images of each other, with one man dying for the lack of anti-coagulant and the other from an overdose.

SUGGESTED READING LIST

Cornwell, John, *A Thief in the Night: The Death of Pope John Paul I* (Penguin, 1990)

Cornwell, John, *Hitler's Pope: The Secret History of Pius XII* (Penguin, 2000)

Dalin, David G., *The Myth of Hitler's Pope: How Pope Pius XII Rescued Jews from the Nazis* (Regnery Publishing, 2005)

Kelly, J.N.D. and Walsh, Michael, *Oxford Dictionary of Popes* (Oxford University Press, 2006)

Maxwell-Stuart, Peter G., *Chronicle of the Popes: The Reign-by-Reign Record of the Papacy from St Peter to the Present* (Thames & Hudson, 1997)

McBrien, Richard, *Lives of the Popes: The Pontiffs from St Peter to John Paul II* (HarperSanFrancisco, 2000)

Williams, Paul L., *The Vatican Exposed: Money, Murder, and the Mafia* (Prometheus Books, 2003)

Yallop, David, *In God's Name: An Investigation into the Murder of John Paul I* (Corgi, 1985)

THE CHURCH V. SCIENCE

ARTISTS OR SUBVERSIVES?

In his novel *Angels and Demons*, Dan Brown puts the following words into the mouth of one of his characters:

> For centuries the church has stood by while science picked away at religion bit by bit. Debunking miracles. Training the mind to overcome the heart. Condemning religion as the opiate of the masses. They denounce God as a hallucination – a delusional crutch for those too weak to accept that life is meaningless. I could not stand by while science presumed to harness the power of God himself!

In this impassioned outburst, Brown gives a flavour of the conflict that exists between the world of belief and that of experiment and proof. It has been an issue for hundreds of years and is plainly visible today in the division of opinion over advances in science such as stem-cell research.

In both *The Da Vinci Code* and *Angels and Demons*, historical characters such as Leonardo da Vinci, Copernicus, Galileo and Bernini are introduced to the plotline and Brown implies that these men of science or the arts were opposed to the theological teachings of the Church. But is there any justification for suggesting that these individuals were trying to undermine the Church's authority through their involvement in subversive activities?

First under the spotlight is Leonardo da Vinci, whose work is also discussed in greater detail in the gazetteer section of this book. Da Vinci's position is somewhat contradictory: some of his greatest works have a religious theme but certain of his ideas and practices would appear to have clashed with the religious orthodoxy of the day.

For example, some of Leonardo's most remarkable drawings are his anatomical sketches. His famous depiction of Vitruvian Man, where a spread-eagled figure is contained within a square and a circle, was an important study of the proportions of the human body. The most successful way to get the information he required for such work was by dissecting bodies. But the Church was strongly opposed to dissection, considering it disrespectful towards the departed soul or spirit. The majority of knowledge about anatomy at the time was gained through treating wounds and observing living patients, and the only bodies usually available for study by surgeons or artists were those of executed criminals.

When a German servant of Leonardo's levelled an accusation of necromancy against him due to his activities at the San Spirito Hospital, the pope upheld the complaint and forbade Leonardo from carrying out any more dissections. The artist bitterly complained that the assistant had 'hindered me in anatomy, denouncing it before the Pope', suggesting that his pursuit of perfection in art was more important to him than the sensibilities of the Church. This would not automatically mean, however, that he was anti-Christian.

It was only when Andreas Vesalius published his *De humani corporis fabrica libri septem* (The Seven Books on the Structure of the Human Body) in 1543 that a comprehensive reference work on anatomy became available. Vesalius had carried out detailed dissections of the human body and was able to correct assumptions that had been made by the Roman physician Galen (*c.* AD 129–201), who up until this time was regarded as the authority on medicine. Vesalius had been court apothecary to Emperor Charles V before being employed at the Spanish court as physician to King Philip II but he was eventually condemned by the Inquisition for 'body snatching' and dissection.

THE COPERNICAN VIEW

For Copernicus, the situation is similarly complicated. His book *De revolutionibus orbium coelestium* (On the Revolutions of the Heavenly Spheres) was included on the list of banned publications by the Church in 1616; however, this was over 70 years after Copernicus's death.

The Julian calendar, established under Julius Caesar in 46 BC, was still the one in use at the time of Copernicus. However, it had become apparent that it was not accurate and during the Fifth Lateran Council (1512–17), the Church was looking for scholars to assist in improving it. Copernicus was asked to contribute to the discussion, suggesting that he was held in high regard by the Church authorities, but he excused himself on the grounds that his studies were not yet sufficiently advanced.

The problem of calendar reform was not settled at the Fifth Lateran Council and it was not until 1582 that the Gregorian calendar, named after Pope Gregory XIII, was adopted across the Catholic, but not Protestant, parts of Europe (Britain waited until 1752 to adopt this calendar). However, the Fifth Lateran Council did make some declarations that would have affected Copernicus. For example, in a specific section related to the printing of books, Pope Leo X pointed out that:

> Some printers have had the boldness to print and sell to the public, in different parts of the world, books . . . containing errors opposed to the faith as well as pernicious views contrary to the Christian religion and to the reputations of prominent persons of rank.

The statement goes on to instruct that no books must be printed unless a bishop, or someone delegated by him to do so, has approved them and issued a warrant. The penalties for not following this instruction included the seizure and burning of the books, payment of a large fine and excommunication – and if the offender continued in his error 'he is to be punished with all the sanctions of the law, by his bishop or by our vicar, in such a way that others will have no incentive to try to follow his example'.

In 1514, Copernicus's theory of heliocentricity had been described in a publication called *De hypothesibus motuum coelestium a se constitutis commentariolus* (A Commentary on the Theories of the Motions of Heavenly Objects from Their Arrangements). This is usually referred to simply as *The Commentary* and it was only distributed among a close circle of his friends. Over the next few years, in spite of this limited circulation, knowledge of Copernicus's theory spread across Europe and he received several invitations to publish his work. He was reluctant to do so, however, perhaps because of the possible consequences should the Church disapprove of his ideas.

In the early sixteenth century, astronomy was still rooted in the teachings of classical scholars such as Aristotle and Ptolemy. The basic model of the universe was geocentric, i.e. it was believed that the earth was at the centre of the universe and the other planets moved around it. This accorded with the belief that God had created the earth, had created man in his image, and that this world formed the centre of God's order. In Psalm 104, God is worshipped as he, 'who laid the foundations of the earth, that it should not be removed for ever'.

Copernicus, however, challenged this model when he deduced that it was the earth which revolved around the sun once a year, while completing a daily cycle around its axis. He was also able to correctly calculate the order in which the other planets orbited around the sun and he explained the phenomena of the precession of the equinoxes. The fact that in making his astronomical observations Copernicus was using the naked eye – the telescope was not yet available to him – confirms his brilliance as a scientist.

PUBLISH AND BE DAMNED?

Towards the end of his life, Copernicus was finally persuaded to let George Rheticus take the manuscript of *De revolutionibus* to Nuremberg, where it was prepared for publication in 1543. Copernicus credited two churchmen, Cardinal Schomberg and Tiedemann Giese, bishop of Culm, with encouraging him to publish the work. Andreas Osiander, a theologian from the city, added a preface to the book, explaining that the work was not intended to have implications beyond the scope of astronomy. This was intended to mitigate criticism of the ideas as counter to Church teaching. Copernicus himself had explained that his purpose in setting down his ideas was to enable more accurate astronomical predictions to be made. This would have a direct benefit for the Church in enabling more precise calculations of the calendar and the timing of festivals such as Easter to be made. Copernicus dedicated the book to Pope Paul III, stating in the dedication:

> For I am not so much in love with my conclusions as not to weigh what others will think about them, and although I know that the meditations of a philosopher are far removed from the judgement of the laity, because his endeavour is to seek out the truth in all things, so far as is permitted by God to the human reason, I still believe that one must avoid theories altogether foreign to orthodoxy.

In the preface to *De revolutionibus*, the plea is made:

> Therefore alongside the ancient hypotheses, which are no more probable, let us permit these new hypotheses also to become known, especially since they are admirable as well as simple and bring with them a huge treasure of very skilful observations.

Copernicus died shortly after the book was published, so it is difficult to judge the immediate reaction of the Church. Although his work was added to the *Index librorum prohibitorum* (Index of Forbidden Books), this was only after his ideas reached a wider audience and were expanded upon by other writers.

HELIOCENTRIC MODEL GATHERS MOMENTUM

Galileo, whose trial by the Inquisition is famous, or rather infamous, as an example of the suppression of ideas by the Catholic Church, is presented by Dan Brown in *Angels and Demons* as a member of a subversive group of scientists. While the scientific theory that he supported was radical, there is no evidence that Galileo was a member of the Illuminati or any other underground society.

The element of Galileo's work that distinguished him from other scientists was the emphasis that he placed on observation, consideration of the facts and doing experiments. In one observation, supposedly made when he watched a chandelier swinging in the cathedral in his hometown, he noted that it swung at a constant rate, regardless of the amplitude of the swing. This observation was later used to regulate the workings of clocks.

The breakthrough that accelerated Galileo's astronomical studies was the invention of the telescope in Holland in 1608. By improving on the original designs, he developed an instrument that could magnify by eight times the heavenly bodies he was viewing. In 1610, he observed the four moons of Jupiter and eventually deduced that they were orbiting their planet. This did not fit with the geocentric view that objects in the universe were all orbiting the earth.

Further evidence which challenged the geocentric model came when Galileo observed a full set of phases of the planet Venus, something that had been predicted by Copernicus. Galileo's observations and conclusions seemed to fit Copernicus's heliocentric (sun-centred) model.

Castelli, a former pupil of Galileo's, was openly defending the views of Copernicus and in a letter sent in 1613, Galileo told him: '. . . the task of wise interpreters is to strive to find the true meanings of scriptural passages agreeing with those physical conclusions of which we are already certain and sure from clear sensory experiences or from necessary demonstration'.

While Galileo can therefore be seen to be encouraging scientific progress and accuracy, he did not fundamentally disagree with the teachings of the Bible. He did not regard his actions as heretical but believed that he was correcting mistaken assumptions.

Copies of his letter to Castelli, some of them inaccurate, were passed to the authorities in Rome and Cardinal Bellarmine of the Inquisition began to study the matter. In an attempt to head off criticism of his work, Galileo went to Rome in 1616 and claimed that belief in the heliocentric model was not necessarily contrary to scriptural passages such as Psalms 93 and 104. But as a result of the examination of the so-called Copernican theory, it was at this time that Copernicus's book was placed on the list of prohibited texts.

THE TRIAL OF GALILEO

Following his appearance in front of the Inquisition, Galileo was instructed by Cardinal Bellarmine not to uphold or promote the heliocentric theory. He was not, however, forbidden to theorise on the subject and it was left open for hypotheses to be advanced. Galileo was encouraged when Pope Urban VIII was elected in 1623 because, before his elevation, the former Maffeo Barberini had appeared receptive to Galileo's ideas. In interviews with Galileo in 1624, the pope suggested that if a hypothetical case was made for the heliocentric theory, and the opinions of the pope were included in a book, such a publication would be acceptable to the Church.

Nearly ten years later, *Dialogo sopra i due massimi sistemi del mondo* (Dialogue Concerning the Two Chief World Systems) was finally published after permission was received from the Florence authorities. It had been Galileo's intention to obtain clearance of his book from Rome but this had not been possible due to poor communication links. When copies of the book reached the Vatican, the nature of the work provoked an outcry.

Galileo presents the material in the *Dialogue* in the form of discussions between three characters about the theories of Aristotle and Copernicus. One of the characters, Simplicio, is the defender of the geocentric model, the version approved by the Church. Since Simplicio is shown to be a fool, this had the effect of annoying the Church hierarchy and Galileo was summoned to Rome to stand trial for heresy.

Negotiations followed in which Galileo's ill health and the fact that he was 70 years of age were presented as reasons for the hearing to be conducted in Florence. These pleas were unsuccessful, however, and in 1633 he set off once more for Rome.

During his trial, Galileo was housed in comfortable apartments and treated well. He produced a letter from Cardinal Bellarmine confirming that he was allowed to discuss the heliocentric theory in hypothetical terms but it did not convince his judges that his actions were justified. The judgment against him declared:

> We say, pronounce, sentence and declare that you, the said Galileo, by reason of matters adduced in trial, and by you confessed as above, have rendered yourself in the judgement of this Holy Office vehemently suspected of heresy, namely of having believed and held the doctrine which is false and contrary to the sacred and divine Scriptures – that the sun is the centre of the world and does not move from east to west and that the earth moves and is not the centre of the world . . .

The *Dialogue* was prohibited and, after being ordered to recant his beliefs, Galileo was sentenced to remain in prison indefinitely. Fortunately, he was not confined to a prison cell and effectively spent the rest of his life under house arrest, at his own home or those of friends and patrons such as the archbishop of Siena.

A story has been passed down which alleges that at his trial Galileo muttered '*Eppur si muove*' (But it does move) in defiance at being made to recant his theories. While it makes a snappy quote and a good anecdote, it is now generally accepted that this story is apocryphal. Had Galileo made such a statement and been caught, the penalty imposed by the Inquisition could have been much more severe.

Despite the judgment against him, Galileo continued to work and in 1638 he published a book in Leiden (in the Netherlands) called *Discorsi e dimonstrazioni matematiche intorno a due nuove scienze* (Dialogues Concerning Two New Sciences). This new work, which had been smuggled out of Italy to ensure its publication, was a treatise on motion and the strength of materials, and is today regarded as possibly his most important scientific work.

Galileo died in 1642 and is now buried in the Church of Santa Croce in Florence, where his remains were moved in 1734 after being disinterred from his original simple grave. *The Dialogue Concerning the Two Chief World Systems* was removed from the *Index of Forbidden Books* in 1835 and his work was no longer considered to be in conflict with Church teaching.

Galileo has been further rehabilitated by the Catholic Church after a study was made into the matters surrounding his trial. When announcing in 1979 that the Galileo case would be looked at again, Pope John Paul II stated:

> Theologians, scholars and historians, animated by a spirit of sincere collaboration, will study the Galileo case more deeply and, in frank recognition of wrongs from whatever side they come, dispel the mistrust that still opposes, in many minds, a fruitful concord between science and faith.

Once the conclusions of the study were announced in 1992, the pope referred to the part the Galileo case had played in creating the 'myth' of a conflict between the Church and science:

> From the beginning of the age of Enlightenment down to our own day, the Galileo case has been a sort of 'myth', in which the image fabricated out of the events was quite far removed from reality. In this perspective, the Galileo case was the symbol of the Church's supposed rejection of scientific progress . . . This myth has played a considerable cultural role. It has helped to anchor a number of scientists of good faith in the idea that there was an incompatibility between the spirit of

science and its rules of research on the one hand and Christian faith on the other. A tragic mutual incomprehension has been interpreted as the reflection of a fundamental opposition between science and faith.

Despite the statements made by John Paul II, there can be no doubt that at the time they were published Galileo's ideas were firmly rejected by those in positions of power in the Church. His subsequent rehabilitation and the general acceptance of his theories today does not change the fact that he was denounced by the Church – his house arrest was no myth. But at the same time it is not possible to say that Galileo rejected religion. It seems more accurate to say that he was attempting to correct the errors of those who had interpreted the word of God. Indeed, in his letter to Castelli, he stated: 'If Scripture cannot err, certain of its interpreters and commentators can and do so in many ways.'

OBSTETRIC ANAESTHESIA

An instance where a rift between science and the Church may have been more mythical than real can be seen with the introduction of obstetric anaesthesia. The use of anaesthetics was introduced in the 1840s, with volatile gases such as ether being used to relieve the pain of tooth extractions and then amputations. The administration of the anaesthetic by placing a soaked sponge in a container over the patient's mouth was haphazard. The margin for error between giving sufficient to produce the desired effect without stopping the patient breathing completely was quite narrow. Common side effects included nausea and vomiting, so the post-operative recovery was itself often unpleasant.

While the risks associated with anaesthesia could be weighed against the awful prospect of limb amputations in its absence, there was a more delicate balance when it came to its use in childbirth. Queen Victoria famously, and controversially, allowed her doctor John

Snow to administer chloroform when she gave birth to her eighth child, Prince Leopold, in 1853.

Victoria, although devoted to her husband, clearly had reservations about giving birth. She wrote to her eldest daughter in 1858:

> What you say of the pride of giving life to an immortal soul is very fine, dear, but I own that I cannot enter into that; I think much more of our being like a cow or a dog at such moments; when our poor nature becomes so very animal and unecstatic.

It has been suggested that there was opposition to the use of obstetric anaesthesia based on religious grounds. In Genesis 3:16, after the Fall of Man in the Garden of Eden was attributed to Eve, we find God declaring: 'Unto the woman he said, I will greatly multiply thy sorrow and thy conception; in sorrow thou shalt bring forth children.'

This statement was interpreted by some as scriptural justification for not relieving the pain of childbirth and in December 1847, Sir James Young Simpson, who is credited with developing obstetric anaesthesia, wrote a paper entitled 'Answer to the Religious Objections Advanced against the Employment of Anaesthetic agents in Midwifery and Surgery'. In it, he stated that:

> Patients and others strongly object to the superinduction of anaesthesia in labour, by the inhalation of ether or chloroform, on the assumed ground that an immunity from pain during parturition was contrary to religion and the express command of the Scripture.

It would now appear, however, that this statement was intended as a direct appeal to the public to support his innovation, which women enthusiastically did, rather than to counter any determined religious resistance.

The story of Church opposition to the use of anaesthesia in childbirth appears to have started with the publication in 1896 of A.D. White's *History of the Warfare of Science with Theology and Christendom*. In his chapter on the opposition of theologians to medical advances, White claims that, 'From pulpit after pulpit Simpson's use of chloroform was denounced as impious and contrary to Holy Writ.' Modern writers, however, have failed to find evidence of a concerted Church campaign. In an article for the journal *Anaesthesia* in 1980, for example, A.D. Farr wrote: 'On examination, this particular "conflict" appears to be an artefact of historiography based on a contemporary defence prepared against an attack which never materialised.' While some individual clergy may have advised their nineteenth-century parishioners against obstetric anaesthesia, there does not appear to have been sustained opposition by organised religion against the practice.

CURIOSITY AND SPECULATION ABOUT ORIGINS

In contrast, there is a clear example of a clash between scientific advancement and religious dogma in the controversial debate that arose from the publication by Charles Darwin of *On the Origin of Species by Means of Natural Selection* (commonly known as *Origin of Species*) in 1859.

In the early nineteenth century, many scientists were studying the natural world and trying to determine the relationship between different species. The Swedish botanist Linnaeus had devised a system for classifying plant and animal species that formalised the study and reinforced a hierarchical view of species. In 1809, Frenchman Jean-Baptiste Lamarck had published *Philosophie Zoologique* (Zoological Philosophy) containing the hypothesis that all life forms are on a path from the simple to the complex, culminating ultimately in man. One of his two 'laws' stated that organs are improved with repeated use and weakened by disuse, the other that any alterations made 'are preserved by reproduction to the new individuals which arise'.

The concept of the environment altering creatures unilaterally was in conflict with the biblical description of how God had formed the world – Genesis 1:

> In the beginning God created the heaven and the earth . . . And God created great whales, and every living creature that moveth, which the waters brought forth abundantly, after their kind, and every winged fowl after his kind: and God saw that it was good.

Finally, mankind was created and the position of the human race as the dominant species on the earth was set out with divine purpose.

> And God said, Let us make man in our image, after our likeness: and let them have dominion over the fish of the sea, and over the fowl of the air, and over the cattle, and over all over the earth, and over every creeping thing that creepeth upon the earth.

Thomas Aquinas (1225–74) and other theologians after him had argued that the marvellous complexity of living organisms was proof of the existence of a creator. In one of his major works, *Summa theologica*, Aquinas derived five proofs of the existence of God, the fifth of which contends that many things in the world that lack intelligence act for an end; whatever acts for an end must be directed by an intelligent being, so the world must have an intelligent designer. This designer is God.

Alfred Wallace is a man whose role in the development of the theory of evolution has largely been overlooked. Wallace was a naturalist who had developed his own theory of natural selection very similar to that being worked on by Charles Darwin. He wrote to Darwin while on an expedition in what is now Malaysia and a paper outlining the work by both men was presented to the Linnean Society in London the year before *Origin of the Species* was published. It was called 'On the Tendency of Species to Form Varieties, and on the Perpetuation of Varieties and Species by Natural Means of Selection'.

The ideas of the two men differed in respect to mankind itself. Wallace held the opinion that divine intervention was necessary to create mankind, and that natural selection does not apply in this case. Darwin, on the other hand, went on to write *The Descent of Man and Selection in Relation to Sex.*

NATURAL SELECTION AND A FAITH IN CRISIS

Darwin had developed his theory of natural selection over 20 years and had initially been in no hurry to publish his thoughts. A 35-page outline of the theory was drafted in 1842 and this was expanded in 1844. He was aware that his views would be controversial and among those he was anxious not to upset was his wife, Emma, who was a deeply religious woman. The letter from Wallace in 1858 and their subsequent joint publication may have been the impetus for Darwin to publish *Origin of the Species* rather than risk Wallace or anyone else publishing first and taking the limelight.

The Darwin and Wedgwood families (his mother, Susannah, was the daughter of Josiah Wedgwood, founder of the famous pottery) were both supporters of the Unitarian Church. Until he was 16 years of age, Darwin attended Shrewsbury School, where he received a Church of England education, so his early religious credentials were impeccable. He later studied to become a clergyman and passed his final exams, at which point we must assume that his faith was still active. By the time he published *Origin of the Species*, however, he was not convinced that intelligent design, or God, could account for the wonderful variety of nature that he had studied. There were also some tragic events that may have weakened his faith, such as the death of his ten-year-old daughter Annie in 1851, which affected him deeply. It seems that it was after this event that he stopped accompanying his family to church. By the end of his life, he was agnostic but was buried in Westminster Abbey because of his enormous service to science. In his autobiography, he said:

> I cannot pretend to throw the least light on such abstruse problems [i.e. why man should believe in God]. The mystery of the beginning of all things is insoluble to us; and I for one must be content to remain an agnostic . . .
>
> Another source of conviction in the existence of God connected with the reason and not the feelings, impresses me as having much more weight. This follows from the extreme difficulty or rather impossibility of conceiving this immense and wonderful universe, including man with his capability of looking far backwards and far into futurity, as being the result of blind chance or necessity. When thus reflecting I feel compelled to look at a first cause having an intelligent mind in some degree analogous to that of man: and I deserve to be called a theist.
>
> This conclusion was strong in my mind about the time, as far as I can remember, when I wrote the Origin of Species; and it is since that time that it has very gradually with many fluctuations become weaker.

He is also quoted as writing: 'Man in his arrogance thinks himself a great work, worthy of the interposition of a deity, more humble & I believe true to consider him created from animals.'

Contemporary defence of the biblical interpretation of creation was exemplified by the Protestant Charles Hodge, who published *What is*

Darwinism? in 1874. He described the theory of natural selection as 'the most thoroughly naturalistic that can be imagined and far more atheistic than that of his predecessor Lamarck'.

An alternative approach taken by theologians was to interpret evolution as a process that was being used by God to implement his divine plan. In *Systematic Theology*, written in 1885, A.H. Strong wrote, 'We grant the principle of evolution, but we regard it as only the method of divine intelligence.'

HOW HEREDITY WORKS

At the same time as Darwin was working in England, in Austria-Hungary a monk called Gregor Mendel was unravelling another missing link in the understanding of evolution. From 1856, Mendel began conducting a series of experiments using pea plants in his Augustinian monastery garden. He studied the offspring of different varieties of the garden pea and the extent to which characteristics such as seed colour and shape, tallness of the plants and the shape of the pods was expressed in the next generation. His conclusion was that the different combinations were due to the presence of pairs of elementary units of heredity. He was describing what we know today as genes and his work was published in a 1866 paper entitled 'Versuche über Pflanzenhybriden' (Experiments in Plant Hybridisation).

In 1868, Mendel was elected as abbot of his monastery. This meant that, while he continued to pursue his scientific interests, he had less time and opportunity to develop his ideas. In 1900, other botanists duplicated Mendel's research – and when they explored the history of their discovery they encountered the earlier work of Mendel, thus bringing him belated recognition.

As the twentieth century progressed, the synthetic theory of evolution was developed, which combined the genetic change in populations with natural selection. Following the discovery of the mechanism of DNA by James Watson and Francis Crick in 1953, science has advanced to the point where it is now possible to manipulate human genes, a practice that raises many ethical issues.

THEORY OF EVOLUTION GAINS ACCEPTANCE

The theory of evolution has now been accepted by both the majority of scientists and theologians, and many interpreted the 1950 papal encyclical by Pius XII, *Humani Generis*, as confirming the approval of the Catholic Church. Pius XII stated that the teaching of evolution was '. . . in conformity with the present state of human sciences and sacred theology, research and discussions, on the part of men experienced in both fields'. The proviso was, however, that while the human body may have its existence through evolution, the soul must be created by God, and he went on to say that:

> Both opinions, that is, those favourable and those unfavourable to evolution [must] be weighed and judged with the necessary seriousness, moderation and measure, and provided that all are prepared to submit to the judgment of the Church, to whom Christ has given the mission of interpreting authentically the Sacred Scripture and of defending the dogmas of faith.

In a statement made to the Pontifical Academy of Sciences in 1981, Pope John Paul II refuted the ideas of the minority of biblical fundamentalists who believe that the world was created exactly as stated in Genesis in six days:

> The Bible speaks to us of the origin of the universe and its make-up, not in order to provide us with a scientific treatise but in order to state the correct relationships of man with God and with the universe. Sacred scripture wishes simply to declare that the world was created by God, and in order to

teach this truth it expresses itself in the terms of the cosmology
in use at the time of the writer . . .

The teaching of evolution has been a volatile topic over a number of
decades and it is one that is still being hotly debated today. In the
1920s, some southern states of the USA passed laws prohibiting the
teaching of evolution in public schools. The controversy raged
backwards and forwards, with proposals in various state legislatures
that any teaching of evolution be balanced by study of creation, with
the biblical explanation as the template. In 1925, there was a famous
court case over the issue, which has become known as the Scopes
'monkey trial'.

MONKEY TRIAL

John T. Scopes, a teacher in Dayton, Tennessee, was charged with
unlawfully teaching his students the theory of evolution. He admitted
to having taught Darwin's theory and was consequently found guilty
and fined $100, although on appeal it was judged that the fine was
excessive and he was acquitted on this technicality. The prosecution
was led by the prominent figure William Jennings Bryan, who
secured the Democratic Party nomination in the presidential elections
of 1896, 1900 and 1908. The epithet of the 'monkey trial' was a
reference to the theory of evolution itself and to nineteenth-century
cartoons of Darwin showing him as a monkey with a human head.

All the resources of the press were devoted to covering the Scopes
trial and it was front-page news not only in America but around the
world. Edward Larson wrote about the trial in *Summer for the Gods*,
as did L. Sprague de Camp in *The Great Monkey Trial*. A play called
Inherit The Wind, by Jerome Lawrence and Robert E. Lee is a
fictionalised account of a court case that has a lot of parallels with the
Scopes trial.

The Supreme Court of the United States passed legislation in 1968 making it unconstitutional to ban the teaching of evolution. The USA has a constitutional requirement to ensure separation between the Church and the state, and it was ruled that teaching creationism instead of evolution contravened this principle.

Those who believe in the literal explanation of the earth's creation given in Genesis are known as biblical creationists to distinguish them from scientific creationists. The latter group believe that a creator is responsible for existence but that the biblical narrative is not a historically accurate account of the process. In addition to the creationist principle, a system has emerged to challenge evolution from a scientific basis: this is known as Intelligent Design (ID).

EVOLUTION ON TRIAL

The concept of Intelligent Design is described by Dr William Dembski, one of its leading supporters, as that 'there are natural systems that cannot be adequately explained in terms of undirected natural forces and that exhibit features that in any other circumstances we would attribute to intelligence'.

The National Academy of Sciences takes the view that ID is pseudoscience – a conclusion also reached by Judge John Jones in his ruling in *Kitzmiller et al*. v. *Dover Area District* re the Teaching of Natural Design in Biology Lessons on 20 December 2005. The case was brought by 11 parents of children from Dover, Pennsylvania, who complained that their children were going to be taught that evolution was only a theory not a fact, and that as a theory it was on a par with Intelligent Design. Judge Jones concluded that ID was not science and that the purpose of the school board who wished to introduce its teaching was to promote religion: 'We conclude that the religious nature of ID would be readily apparent to an objective observer, adult or child.'

The effect of this ruling was to uphold the complaint of the parents and to prevent the teaching of ID as part of the science curriculum.

One of the witnesses called in the Pennsylvania case was Michael Behe, who gave evidence on the concept of irreducible complexity. Behe is a professor of biochemistry and a fellow of the Discovery Institute, a non-profit educational organisation to which many supporters of ID belong. Behe has conducted studies on bacterial flagellum, a complex device that gives a bacterium its mobility. After considering the multiple components, all of which need to be present for the flagellum to function, Behe was convinced that it could not have evolved by natural selection. In a paper entitled 'Molecular Machines: Experimental Support for the Design Inference', Behe describes irreducible complexity as: 'A single system which is composed of several well-matched interacting parts that contribute to the basic function, wherein the removal of any one of the parts causes the system to effectively cease functioning.'

Another member of the Discovery Institute's Center for Science and Culture is Philip E. Johnson, who is recognised as one of the founders of the Intelligent Design movement. Johnson's 1991 book *Darwin on Trial* refuted the basis for evolution being considered as a proven scientific fact and instead described it as 'an imaginative story . . . a creation myth'. The Discovery Institute also promotes a campaign called *Teach the Controversy*, which aims to encourage the presentation of evolution and ID as two competing theories in schools.

The Vatican, through its official publication *L'Osservatore Romano*, has entered the debate and asserted its view that ID should not be taught in schools. In an article of 16 January 2006, Professor Fiorenzo Facchini stated:

If the model presented by Darwin is not considered sufficient, one should search for another. But it is not correct from a methodological point of view to stray from the field of science while pretending to do science . . . It only creates confusion between the scientific plane and those that are philosophical or religious.

Another prominent voice to endorse the view that ID should be considered part of the religious studies curriculum rather than that of biology is that of Father George Coyne, the Jesuit director of the Vatican Observatory. At a conference in Florence in 2005, he said: 'If you want to teach it in schools, intelligent design should be taught when religion or cultural history is taught, not science.'

Father Coyne had also written about the issue in the British Catholic publication *The Tablet* on 6 August 2005:

> So why does there seem to be a persistent retreat in the Church from attempts to establish a dialogue with the community of scientists, religious believers or otherwise? There appears to exist a nagging fear in the Church that a universe, which science has established as evolving for 13.7 x 1 billion years since the Big Bang and in which life, beginning in its most primitive forms at about 12 x 1 billion years from the Big Bang, evolved through a process of random genetic mutations and natural selection, escapes God's dominion. That fear is groundless.

The intervention of Father Coyne, who is a Jesuit priest as well as holding a doctorate in astronomy from Georgetown University, is a significant step and his position as priest and scientist is reminiscent of that of the original murder victim, Leonardo Vetra, in *Angels and Demons*.

It may be that Coyne was moving to counter statements made by Cardinal Christoph Schönborn in the *New York Times* in July 2005 that seemed to question the Catholic Church's acceptance of evolution:

Defenders of neo-Darwinism dogma have often invoked the supposed acceptance – or at least acquiescence – of the Roman Catholic Church when they defend their theory as somehow compatible with Christian faith.

But this is not true. The Catholic Church, while leaving to science many details about the history of life on earth, proclaims that by the light of reason the human intellect can readily and clearly discern purpose and design in the natural world, including the world of living things.

BIG BANG THEORY

The article written by Father Coyne in *The Tablet* raised another interesting subject that is covered in *Angels and Demons*, namely that of the Big Bang. The Big Bang theory, which provides an explanation for the initial expansion of the universe and its current state, was proposed by a Catholic priest, Georges Lemaître, in 1927. Essentially, the theory suggests that the universe was originally a very dense mass at extremely high temperature and that it has been expanding and cooling ever since.

It has been calculated that 13.7 billion years have passed since the initial expansion started. This calculation is based on the observations of Edwin Hubble, who was able to measure the expansion in 1929, confirming Lemaître's theory.

When Hubble measured the rate at which galaxies were expanding, it called into question the previously held understanding of a static universe. Albert Einstein had postulated a cosmological constant to calculate a static universe but when he understood the implications of Hubble's measurements, he visited the Mount Wilson Observatory to congratulate Hubble on his work.

There are still aspects of the Big Bang theory that scientists are seeking to refine. For example, there is something known as the baryon asymmetry problem, which refers to the apparent fact that the baryons in the universe are overwhelmingly matter as opposed to antimatter. The destructive potential of antimatter was described in *Angels and Demons* and as a layperson the whereabouts of the 'missing' antimatter seems a legitimate concern. Attempts to resolve this question using a hadron collider are being made by scientists at the CERN laboratory in Switzerland. CERN is the institution of which Leonardo Vetra was a member in *Angels and Demons*. It is the European Organization for Nuclear Research and undertakes research on behalf of the 20 member countries. When construction is finished in 2007, the hadron collider will consist of a circular tunnel 27 kilometres in length and will enable scientists to re-create conditions similar to those that existed just after the Big Bang.

The acceptance of the Big Bang theory as an explanation of the processes at work in the universe is not incompatible with religious faith as there is still a role for a creator of the matter and energy involved. The Catholic Church has accepted that the Big Bang theory is a valid explanation for the physical status of the universe and Pius XII in particular spoke enthusiastically about it. In an address to the Pontifical Academy of Sciences on 22 November 1951, he said that 'everything seems to indicate that the universe has in finite times a mighty beginning'.

There is a principle known as 'First Cause argument' that places God as the prime mover in the process. The First Cause argument is based on another of the proofs of God derived by Thomas Aquinas and goes like this: everything has a cause; nothing can cause itself; everything is caused by another thing; the causal chain must have a beginning; there must be a first cause; this is God.

There are, however, those who disagree with the Big Bang theory on religious grounds. One such movement is called Young Earth Creationism. The beliefs of its members are based on study of the text in Genesis and an interpretation of the events described there as fact. They hold that this means that life on earth was created by God a relatively short time ago.

Many early Jewish scholars such as Josephus believed that the days of creation as described in Genesis were 24-hour days and Abraham Ibn Ezra (1092–1167) expanded on this belief in his commentary on the books of the Torah. In a book he published in 1650, James Ussher, the archbishop of Armagh, continued on from the first books in the Bible and, after adding up the genealogies described, calculated the date of creation as 4004 BC. To be precise, Ussher dated the first day of creation as 23 October 4004 BC.

One key event in the Bible dated on this timeline is the Great Flood, defined as 2348 BC. When confronted with fossil evidence of the existence of dinosaurs, modern Young Earth creationists argue that these are the remains of creatures that died in the Great Flood or, alternatively, that Noah took dinosaurs on to the ark and that they have since become extinct.

The question of the antiquity of the earth was also raised in the eighteenth and nineteenth centuries when geologists such as James Hutton and Charles Lyell were studying rock strata and publishing their work. With ideas such as those of Ussher being prevalent at the time, the suggestion that the earth was millions of years old was a controversial one. Hutton presented a paper to the Royal Society of Edinburgh in 1785 that explained how erosion, sedimentation and the formation and cooling of rocks such as granite required the earth to be considerably older than currently thought. This notion was criticised by Richard Kirwan in his 1799 book *Geological Essays*, where he described Hutton's theory as atheist. Charles Lyell's book, *Principles of Geology*, published in parts between 1830 and 1833, explained that slow gradual processes had produced the state of the earth. Interestingly, *Principles of Geology* was one of the books that Charles Darwin took with him on HMS *Beagle*.

STEM-CELL CONTROVERSY

Another area of scientific investigation that is causing controversy in religious circles is stem-cell research. The possibility of curing diseases such as Parkinson's, Alzheimer's and diabetes by using cells that have the ability to develop into any required cells or organs is a prize that pharmaceutical companies and research groups value highly. There are claims and counter claims about the current state of research in this field and the subject is fraught with moral dilemmas, since the majority of human stem cells are derived from aborted foetuses. In a meeting at Castel Gandolfo, the papal retreat in Italy, the subject was discussed by President George Bush of the USA and Pope John Paul II in 2001. John Paul II made his disapproval of President Bush's agreement to funding for stem-cell research clear, saying:

> Another area in which political and moral choices have the gravest consequences for the future of civilisation concerns the most fundamental of human rights, the right to life itself. Experience is already showing how a tragic coarsening of consciences accompanies the assault on innocent human life in the womb, leading to accommodation and acquiescence in the face of other related evils such as euthanasia, infanticide and, most recently, proposals for the creation for research purposes of human embryos, destined to destruction in the process.

This is a principled statement, derived from belief, spoken by a man who in 2001 was already displaying symptoms of the Parkinson's disease that would eventually destroy his health.

In August 2001, however, President Bush agreed to release funds to support stem-cell research, despite the advice he had been given by the pope just weeks earlier. The proviso in his approval was that the research should be confined to existing stem-cell lines, as this 'allows us to explore the promise and potential of stem cell research without crossing a fundamental moral line by providing taxpayer funding that would sanction or encourage further destruction of human embryos that have at least the potential for life'.

The British government announced in December 2005 that it would make £100 million available for research into stem-cell research over the following two years. A poll for the ABC news organisation in 2001 showed that 60 per cent of Catholics favoured the research, despite the Church's teaching. This acceptance on behalf of lay Catholics may be part of a larger divergance from Church teaching on moral issues such as contraception and in vitro fertilisation (IVF). Apart from the Catholic Church, other religious groups are also defining their positions on this difficult issue.

ASSISTED FERTILITY

The ability of science to help couples struggling to come to terms with infertility has provided yet another dilemma for the Church. Is it wrong to condemn a loving couple who want to bring a child into the world but are unable to do so naturally? Albino Luciani, the future Pope John Paul I, spoke of the moral dilemma when asked to comment on the birth of Louise Brown, the first 'test-tube' baby in 1978:

> Following the example of God, who desires and loves human life, I too send my best wishes to the baby. As for her parents, I have no right to condemn them; subjectively, if they acted with good intentions and in good faith, they may even have great merit before God for what they have decided and asked the doctors to do.

The Catholic Church gave a more considered, and less positive, verdict on IVF in *Donum vitae* (Respect for Human Life) in 1987. *Donum vitae* considered not only the prospect of interference in the process of creating life but also the consequences of producing embryos that are not implanted and might be destroyed. In a complex examination of the issues raised, it condemned practices such as surrogate motherhood or the insemination of a woman with the sperm of a deceased partner. It also makes clear that while recognising that many couples will have a strong desire to be parents, there is no 'right' to have a child.

It can only be imagined what further ethical considerations will be raised by future advances in the fields of genetic and medical research. The opinions of theologians and scientists are sure to interact, if not to clash, with each other for the foreseeable future.

SUGGESTED READING LIST

Aydon, Cyril, *Charles Darwin: The Story of the Amateur Naturalist who Created a Scientific Revolution and Changed the World* (Constable & Robinson, 2003)

Bramly, Serge, *Leonardo: The Artist and the Man*, trans. Sian Reynolds (Penguin Books, 1995)

Cropper, William H., *Great Physicists: The Life and Times of Leading Physicists from Galileo to Hawking* (Oxford University Press, 2004)

Desmond, Adrian and Moore, James, *Darwin* (Penguin, 1992)

Gassendi, Pierre and Thill, Oliver, *The Life of Copernicus (1473–1543): The Man Who Did Not Change the World* (Xulon Press, 2002)

Scott, Eugenie C., *Evolution vs. Creationism: An Introduction* (Greenwood Press, 2004)

Shea, William R. and Artigas, Mariano, *Galileo in Rome: The Rise and Fall of a Troublesome Genius* (Oxford University Press, 2003)

White, Michael, *Leonardo: The First Scientist* (Abacus, 2001)

THE ILLUMINATI

ORIGINS

In *Angels and Demons*, Dan Brown introduces us to the idea of the Illuminati, a powerful and mysterious brotherhood – long thought to be defunct – that is bent on the destruction of the Catholic Church. The two main characters in the novel, Robert Langdon and his accomplice, Vittoria Vetra, race around Rome in an attempt to prevent the Illuminati from destroying the Vatican with stolen antimatter.

The questions that those who have read the novel must be asking themselves are these: was the Illuminati a real organisation, did it truly exist and, more importantly, is it still around today, influencing world events?

On investigation, it is possible to find historical references to the Illuminati, suggesting that it did indeed exist. However, it must be stated from the start that Dan Brown seems to have used a fair amount of artistic licence in creating the order that we find on the pages of *Angels and Demons*. For example, in Chapter 9 he tells us:

In the 1500s, a group of men in Rome fought back against the church. Some of Italy's most enlightened men – physicists, mathematicians, astronomers – began meeting secretly to share their concerns about the church's inaccurate teachings. They feared that the church's monopoly on 'truth' threatened academic enlightenment around the world. They founded the world's first scientific think tank, calling themselves 'the enlightened ones'.

Is this fact? As there are no records of such a group being formed in Rome in the sixteenth century, it would appear not. So when do we first encounter the Illuminati in history?

The first recorded use of the term by an organised group was made by a sect in Spain in the late fifteenth century who called themselves Los Alumbrados (the Illumined – or enlightened – Ones). Disparate strands calling themselves the Illuminati were known as early as the fourteenth century but it is not until the appearance of the Alumbrados that the term is used to refer to a distinct group of believers.

Rather than being the sinister order that we might expect to find after reading *Angels and Demons*, the Alumbrados were instead a Gnostic sect who believed that it was possible for the human soul to attain such a level of perfection that it could comprehend fully the mysteries of the Trinity until finally it became one with its maker: God.

The Alumbrados believed that this religious unity would be achieved through trances, ecstasies and visions. One of their fundamental beliefs was that the illuminating light came from inside the individual and not from outside. They did not need the presence of priests to minister the word of God or even the sacraments of the Catholic Church; God came from within.

It was this conviction which ultimately led to their downfall. The Catholic Church declared the Alumbrados to be heretics and many of the group's members were subject to the attentions of the Inquisition. By 1620, the movement had lost its momentum and begun to dissolve.

Certain elements of the Alumbrados survived, fleeing Seville in 1623 for France, where the group became known as the Illuminés. They were suppressed in 1635 but almost a century later, around 1722, another group known by the same name sprang up in the south of the country and appears to have survived until almost the nineteenth century.

Around this time, the name Illuminati was adopted by an order who were to grow into an organisation that truly did possess the power to influence world events. They were known as the Bavarian Illuminati.

THE BAVARIAN ILLUMINATI

It is the year 1785 and a man is riding on horseback through the town of Regensburg in Bavaria. The man in question is Johann Jakob Lanz and he is on his way to Frankfurt on a vital mission. It is raining hard but Johann is eager to press on, so he continues despite the weather.

Suddenly, he is struck by a bolt of lightning and killed outright. Bavarian officials arrive to examine the body and they find on his person papers and documents belonging to an order known as the Illuminati. One of these documents is a tract written by Adam Weishaupt, the founder of the order, called *Original Shift in Days of Illuminations*. This text contains full details of the secret society's long-term plans for Europe and for 'the New World Order through revolution'.

It is not possible to gain access to all the documents that were found after Lanz was killed but sections of them have been quoted in other works. For example, Weishaupt has been quoted as saying: 'The true purpose of the order was to rule the world. To achieve this it was necessary for the order to destroy all religions, overthrow all governments and abolish private property . . .'

Imagine the storm this find caused. Bavaria was a conservative state dominated by the Catholic Church. Discovering that it had such an organisation in its midst must have generated much consternation and alarm.

The Bavarian government acted swiftly to outlaw the order. Then, in 1787, it published in full the details of the Illuminati conspiracy in a work titled *The Original Writings of the Order and Sect of the Illuminati* and, ironically, it is from this that most of our knowledge of the Illuminati is gleaned.

So much for the destruction of the order – what of its beginnings?

It is said that Adam Weishaupt grew up in a world of secret societies, having been a student at a Jesuit college in Ingolstadt. However, he later turned his back on Jesuit beliefs as he became attracted to the ideas of men like d'Holbach and Helvetius, who promoted atheism, rationalism, materialism and egalitarianism – all ideas that Weishaupt would later incorporate into the Illuminati.

Weishaupt had joined the Freemasons in 1774 but he soon became disillusioned and left to form the Illuminati in 1776. At first he named it the Order of Perfectibilists and it is thought that he was influenced by another famous order, this time a religious one, the members of which had practised their beliefs in Europe centuries before. They are known as the Cathars and their name means the 'perfect ones' or the 'pure ones'.

The devotees of the Cathar religion were split into two distinct groups: the smaller core of the *perfecti* (perfects) and the majority or *credentes* (believers). From his own writings, it seems that Weishaupt would certainly have had a lot in common with the beliefs of the Cathars, so his original name for the Illuminati, the Perfectibilists, seems fitting.

At first the order had just five members but this soon grew and by 1779 there were offices in five Bavarian cites. Their library contained many texts banned by the Catholic Church and initiates into the order began by reading the classical moralists such as Socrates and Plato before going on to study works by the rationalists and materialists, including Descartes and Leibniz, only taking on board more esoteric texts as they progressed. All of this was done in an atmosphere of the strictest secrecy, a precaution made all the more understandable when we learn that during Weishaupt's tenure as professor at Ingolstadt University – he was, incidentally, the first lay professor of natural and canon law at the university – one of the most controversial issues was whether the study of books written by a non-Catholic could even be entertained. Furthermore, all books by Enlightenment authors were banned outright. In such an atmosphere of censorship and religious dogma, it is easy to understand how the order of the Illuminati quickly flourished.

As the numbers swelled, Weishaupt re-entered the Freemasons and started to use the larger organisation as a vehicle to proliferate his own ideas. He realised that members of the Illuminati could penetrate the highest Masonic grades and so take control of the lodges. The first lodge to fall to the Illuminati in this way was in Munich and, as Weishaupt's plan progressed, so the order grew into a much larger and more organised society.

Weishaupt was apparently obsessed with the Great Pyramid of Giza in Egypt and he fashioned his order in this very form, dividing the members into three main classes. The more numerous lower classes contained novices, minervals and lesser Illuminati; the second class, ordinary and Scottish knights; and, finally, at the top of the pyramid, there were the priests, regent, magus and finally king, or Illuminatus Rex. Within the order, Weishaupt was himself known as Brother Spartacus, the name taken in honour of the Roman slave who had led a large uprising in Rome.

From the outset, Weishaupt's vision was of establishing a New World Order through the abolition of all governments and religions, and initially he seems to have been motivated by the altruistic desire to bring peace to the world and end oppression. The ultimate goals of the Order of the Perfectibilists, or the Illuminati, were to perfect human nature, to re-educate its initiates and achieve a communal state, free of bureaucratic interference: 'Princes and nations will disappear without violence from the earth, the human race will become one family and the world the abode of reasonable men. Morality alone will bring about this change imperceptibly.'

The five main principles of the Illuminati manifesto constructed by Weishaupt were therefore:

1. Abolition of monarchies and all ordered governments
2. Abolition of private property and inheritances
3. Abolition of patriotism and nationalism
4. Abolition of family life and the institution of marriage, and the establishment of communal education of children
5. Abolition of all religion

Weishaupt's stance on religion seems to have stemmed from his deist beliefs: in his view, God was above mere organised religion and the Roman Catholic Church was nothing more than the remnant of age-old superstitions. This did not mean, however, that he was above using the world's religions to enlarge his order. In his famous work on the Illuminati, *Proofs of a Conspiracy against all the Religions and Governments of Europe Carried on in the Secret Meetings of Freemasons, Illuminati and Reading Societies*, John Robison said of Weishaupt:

He employs the Christian religion which he thinks a falsehood, and which is afterwards to explode, as the means for inviting Christians of every denomination, and gradually cajoling them, by clearing up their Christian doubts in succession, till he lands them in Deism.

Dan Brown seems to have picked up on this antipathy towards the Catholic Church and incorporated the idea into *Angels and Demons* – even if he did move the location of the order of the Illuminati from Bavaria to Rome.

By 1782, the order is said to have numbered between 3,000 and 4,000, and reportedly included prominent members such as Herder, Goethe, Mozart and the reigning Duke of Gotha. It had also spread within Europe from Denmark to Portugal and even further afield. A lodge was founded in New York City in 1785 and one member even founded a chapter in Brazil, where he then proceeded to start an Illuminati uprising that was quickly quashed.

It all started to go wrong just as the order reached the height of its powers. Baron von Knigge had overseen a union between the Illuminati and European Freemasonry that further extended the order's influence; in return, he asked that he be made co-leader of the Illuminati. Weishaupt refused and Baron von Knigge left the order. There were other disgruntled parties and when the lightning bolt that killed Johann Jakob Lanz led to the discovery of the order by the Bavarian authorities, many of these individuals took the opportunity to come forward and denounce Weishaupt and the Illuminati.

Once the order had been proscribed, the members scattered. Weishaupt himself was charged with treason and his position at the University of Ingolstadt was stripped from him. He fled from the town on horseback and eventually found refuge in Gotha. Another of the order's associates, Dr Schwartz, loaded the entire contents of the Illuminati library, which included texts on the Kabbalah, Sufism and the Cathars as well as many other occult manuscripts, onto an ox-cart and headed for Moscow.

Many have suggested that the story ended there, with the

dissolution of the Illuminati and the banishment of Weishaupt – but was it really the end of attempts to establish a New World Order?

Looking back on what he had begun when he formed the order, Weishaupt wrote:

> I did not bring Deism into Bavaria, more than into Rome. I found it here, in great vigour, more abounding than in any of the neighbouring Protestant States. I am proud to be known to the world as the founder of the Illuminati.

NEW BEGINNINGS

The breaking up of the Order of the Illuminati in 1785 is unlikely to have been the end of the secret organisation. It is much more probable that its members simply went even further underground and that their ideas were disseminated throughout Europe. For example, just a few years after the Illuminati were outlawed, some believe that their plans to destroy Christianity and the world's governments finally began to bear fruit in the form of the French Revolution.

In 1797, a Jesuit priest, Abbé Augustin Barruél, caused a storm by writing a book called *Mémoires pour servir à l'histoire du Jacobinisme* (Memoirs Illustrating the History of Jacobinism), in which he claimed that the Illuminati were directly responsible for the French Revolution. This book has been considered by many to contain the world's first published conspiracy theory and even today is the primary source for much speculation regarding the Illuminati and a plan for a New World Order.

In Barruél's book, he went as far as to call Adam Weishaupt 'a human devil'. But were his accusations justified? There certainly seem to be a significant number of individuals at the time who believed so and were not shy about publicising their views. In 1789, before the fall of the Bastille, the Marquis de Luchet, for example, published his 'Essay on the Sect of the Illuminati' to warn the French people:

Deluded people: You must understand that there exists a conspiracy in favour of despotism and against liberty, incapacity against talent, of vice against virtue, of ignorance against light! It is formed in the depths of the most impenetrable darkness, a society is to rule the world, to appropriate the authority of sovereigns, to usurp their place . . . Every species of error which afflicts the earth, every half-baked idea, every invention serves to fit the doctrines of the Illuminati . . . I see that all great fundamentals which society has made good use of to retain the allegiance of man – such as religion and law – will be without power to destroy an organization which has made itself a cult, and put itself above all human legislation.

It may seem odd to some that Weishaupt would be involved in such a bloody conflict, especially as at the formation of the order the Illuminati seemed to hold such peaceful ideals. However, it is evident that, over the years, Weishaupt's vision of how the New World Order might be brought about changed drastically and later in life he was quoted as stating: 'Sin is only that which is hurtful, and if the profit is greater than the damage, it becomes a virtue.'

Furthermore, when the order was banished in Bavaria, several retired members had put together a document in which the order's secret rituals were revealed. One of the principles taught to Illuminees was said to be this: 'The end sanctifies the means. The welfare of the order will be a justification for calumnies, poisonings, assassinations, perjuries, treasons, rebellions; in short, for all that the prejudices of men lead them to call crimes.'

Freemasons, through their association with the Illuminati, and especially due to the fact that Weishaupt had penetrated their ranks with his own followers, were also blamed for the French Revolution. In *World Revolution: The Plot Against Civilisation*, Nesta H. Webster wrote:

> If, then, it is said that the [French] Revolution was prepared in the lodges of Freemasons – and many French Masons have boasted of the fact – let it always be added that it was Illuminized Freemasonry that made the Revolution, and that the Masons who acclaim it are Illuminized Masons, inheritors of the same tradition introduced into the lodges of France in 1787 by the disciples of Weishaupt, patriarch of the Jacobins.

The watchwords of Freemasonry in France before the revolution appear to have been liberty, equality and fraternity, and this same motto was taken up by the revolutionaries. Could this be mere coincidence?

A prominent figure involved in the French Revolution was the Marquis de Lafayette, a man who had also been involved in the American Revolution and who, it has been claimed, was introduced to Masonry by George Washington.

Lafayette was responsible for playing a role in the design of the French tricolour, the emblem of the French Revolution, and he said privately that it originated from George Washington's American flag design and the American Revolution itself. Such Masonic links to the French Revolution should perhaps not be surprising in the light of all that we know of the Illuminati and their plan for a New World Order.

An interesting footnote is that a ton of US soil was shipped over to Paris for Lafayette's burial in 1834, because he had expressed the wish to be buried in American soil. Legend also has it that during the First World War, when American soldiers landed on French soil and proceeded to Paris and Lafayette's tomb, General Pershing, or one of his staff, uttered the famous words, 'Lafayette, we are here!'

THE ILLUMINATI AFTER WEISHAUPT

The influence of the Illuminati does not appear to have ended with the French Revolution or indeed with Weishaupt's death, recorded by some sources as having occurred in 1830. We only have to look at his writings to appreciate what an organisation Weishaupt had started and how difficult it would be to stop such a force.

> Do you realize sufficiently what it means to rule – to rule in a secret society? Not only over the lesser or more important of the populace, but over the best of men, over men of all ranks, nations, and religions, to rule without external force, to unite them indissolubly, to breathe one spirit and soul into them, men distributed over all parts of the world? . . . And finally, do you know what secret societies are? What a place they occupy in the great kingdom of the world's events? Do you think they are unimportant, transitory appearances?

Just six years later, a new group suddenly rose to prominence – once again in Germany. Called the League of the Just, it soon had offices in London, Brussels, Paris and Switzerland. Interestingly, this group grew from an earlier incarnation that had been called the League of the Outlaws. Could this be a reference to its Illuminati connections? It certainly isn't the league's only link to the Illuminati and Weishaupt.

Karl Marx, the famous philosopher and political economist, joined the league in 1847 and, intriguingly, we find that he was also employed by them to update the writings of Adam Weishaupt, composed 70 years before. This would seem to suggest Weishaupt's beliefs must have been important to the League of the Just.

Karl Marx wrote his famous *Communist Manifesto* while a member of the League of the Just and shortly after this the group renamed itself the Communist League. It has been suggested that this important work was directly influenced by the works of Weishaupt that Marx had studied so closely. Just like Weishaupt, Marx believed that the family unit should be broken up and that all children should be raised by a central authority. As for God and religion, Marx had this to say: 'We must war against all prevailing ideas of religion, of the state, of country, of patriotism. The idea of God is the keynote of a perverted civilization. It must be destroyed.'

An interesting aside is that the Communists adopted 1 May as their primary holiday, which we find is also the date that Weishaupt founded the original Order of the Perfectibilists. Once again, is this coincidence or an indication of the links between the Illuminati and the Communist movement?

Another man who would go on to achieve worldwide recognition and notoriety joined the newly named Communist League in the 1890s. His name was Vladimir Ilyich Ulyanov – later changed to Lenin – and the ideas he went on to develop came directly from Karl Marx's *Manifesto*.

A strange, world-changing event happened in 1917. Lenin was in exile in Zurich, Switzerland, when news reached him of the Easter Revolution and the abdication of Tsar Nicholas II. Realising it was vital that he travel to Petrograd to steer the revolution, he started to wonder how he would reach Russia. The First World War was raging and Britain, France and Italy would not assist Lenin or allow him passage through their countries because of his anti-imperialist stance. So, Lenin came up with another plan: to ask the German authorities if they would allow him to pass through their borders and travel across Germany by train. At the time, Germany was at war with Russia but his request was granted, so long as Lenin travelled across Germany in a sealed train that would have extraterritorial status, just like a foreign embassy.

This incredible chain of events seems hard to comprehend but historians point out that the Kaiser was gambling that Lenin would fan the flames of the revolt in Russia, which in turn would eventually lead to a cessation of hostilities between Germany and Russia. Germany desperately needed to free up troops and resources, as they were struggling to fight a war on two fronts.

In the short term, the Kaiser's gamble paid off and the October Revolution took place a few months later. Lenin seized ultimate control of the government and later, in 1922, the Soviet Union was born. However, Lenin's mission was not just to overthrow imperialism in Russia but throughout Europe. If Germany had not aided Lenin then it is likely that history would have taken a very different path.

Winston Churchill was to comment on the dangerous nature of these events and the perilous game Germany had played, saying, 'They transported Lenin in a sealed train like a plague bacillus from Switzerland to Russia.'

We will never know to what extent if any the Illuminati were involved in Lenin's rise to power. However, Lenin himself hinted at the existence of powerful underground organisations that had more than a slight influence on Russian politics and the revolution: 'Behind the October Revolution there are more influential personalities than the thinkers and executors of Marxism.'

Aleksandr Solzhenitsyn, the Russian writer who was living in the USA after being expelled from the USSR, made the following statement in 1975 while delivering an address known as 'Words of Warning to the Western World'. Here he is commenting on the fact that the Russian Revolution received funding from many international sources, including financiers in New York and London:

There also exists another alliance – at first glance a strange one, a surprising one – but if you think about it, in fact, one which is well grounded and easy to understand, this is the alliance between our Communist leaders and your capitalists.

This alliance is not new. The very famous Armand Hammer, who is flourishing here today, laid the basis for this when he made the first exploratory trip into Russia, still in Lenin's time, in the very first years of the revolution. He was extremely successful in this intelligence mission and since that time, for all these 50 years, we observe continuous and steady support by the businessmen of the West of the Soviet Communist leaders.

People wanted to know what exactly was behind Lenin and his revolution, some of them prominent politicians. Three years after the October Revolution, Winston Churchill was to comment on the connection between the Bolsheviks and the Illuminati of Weishaupt, saying:

> From the days of Spartacus-Weishaupt to those of Karl Marx, to those of Trotsky, Bela Kun, Rosa Luxembourg, and Emma Goldman, this worldwide conspiracy for the overthrow of civilization and for the reconstitution of society on the basis of arrested development, of envious malevolence and impossible equality, has been steadily growing. It played a definitely recognizable role in the tragedy of the French Revolution. It has been the mainspring of every subversive movement during the nineteenth century, and now at last this band of extraordinary personalities from the underworld of the great cities of Europe and America have gripped the Russian people by the hair of their heads, and have become practically the undisputed masters of that enormous empire.

From this statement it is clear that Winston Churchill believed that the Illuminati had been in continuous existence since the late eighteenth century and was still influencing world affairs at the beginning of the twentieth century.

Furthermore, it almost didn't end there. If events in Eastern Europe had taken a different direction in 1919, we might be living in a very different world today and it is even possible that the Second World War would never have happened.

Buoyed up by his successes against the White Russian forces, Lenin decided in 1919 that it was time to spread the revolution to Western Europe. Germany was in tumoil at the time and a group called the Spartacist League was on the rise. It is surely no coincidence that Spartacus was the name that Adam Weishaupt, founder of the Illuminati, had adopted. We also shouldn't be surprised to discover that the Spartacist League was a left-wing Marxist group with views and policies similar to those of Weishaupt and the Illuminati.

The Spartacist League sought to incite a revolution in Germany similar to Russia's of October 1917 and by 1919 the League was trying to wrest control of Berlin. Lenin later commented on this period in history, saying: 'That was the time when everyone in Germany, including the blackest reactionaries and monarchists, declared that the Bolsheviks would be their salvation.'

Lenin knew that in order to join up with the Spartacist League and add support to a German revolution, he would have to cross Poland. At the time, there were clashes between Poland and the Bolshevik forces all along the borders of the newly formed Second Polish Republic as Poland sought to reclaim territory lost during the First World War. Lenin therefore decided that it was time for decisive action, writing in a telegram: 'We must direct all our attention to preparing and strengthening the Western Front. A new slogan must be announced: Prepare for war against Poland.'

The aim of the attack was not necessarily to crush Europe with the sheer weight of the Red Army, rather it was to be a tool to facilitate social change in the countries of the West. At the beginning of the campaign, the Russian general Tukhachevsky declared: 'To the West! Over the corpse of White Poland lies the road to worldwide conflagration. March on Vilno, Minsk, Warsaw!'

Lenin did not expect a stiff fight from the Poles but the war turned into a bitter and protracted conflict. It didn't help Lenin's cause that he was still fighting a civil war in Russia at the same time and many of his forces were diverted from the war with Poland, especially in the summer of 1919 as the White Russians marched on Moscow. In the end, after some dramatic advances, even up to the very gates of Warsaw, the Bolsheviks were forced back and in 1920, after a series of disastrous retreats, the Russians sued for peace and a ceasefire was agreed in October.

The attempt to reach Germany was therefore thwarted, the Spartacist League's uprising was quashed and the opportunity to install a Communist leadership in Germany was lost. If we believe that Lenin was attempting to bring about a New World Order, then we must acknowledge that, here in 1920, his cause had failed.

Just 13 years later, Hitler became Chancellor of Germany and one of the first things he did – according to many historians – was to have the Reichstag set alight and then blame the destruction on the Communists. This act of terrorism allowed him to suspend basic rights in Germany and at a stroke he had the entire membership of the Communist Party arrested or murdered.

From here on, after the defeat of Russia at Polish hands and the collapse of Lenin's plan to bring Communism to the West, the trail of the Illuminati becomes harder to follow. But there is one possible strand that seems to have taken root far from Bavaria, where it all began, yet one with apparent connections to the rise of Hitler and Nazism. The waters that hide the face of the Illuminati are just about to get even murkier.

Before we head there to pick up the trail, let us end this section with the words of Adam Weishaupt, in case we need reminding just how difficult the hidden trail of the Illuminati is to follow.

> The great strength of our Order lies in its concealment, let it
> never appear in any place in its own name, but always covered
> by another name, and another occupation. None is fitter than

the three lower degrees of Freemasonry; the public is accustomed to it, expects little from it, and therefore takes little notice of it.

SKULL AND BONES

One of the most notorious secret societies to hit the headlines over the last few years is Skull and Bones. Based at Yale University, its most famous member at the present time is US President George W. Bush.

Founded in 1832, Skull and Bones recruits by invitation only. In May each year, fifteen third-year students at Yale are 'tapped' and initiated into the order. Despite this small annual introduction of new blood, during the 2004 presidential race in the United States of America it transpired that both George W. Bush and his opponent John Kerry were members of Skull and Bones.

During his February 2004 appearance on NBC's *Meet the Press*, Bush was asked about his membership of this secret society but he declined to elaborate, saying, 'It's so secret I can't talk about it.'

When Kerry was asked what he could reveal, he was similarly elusive: 'Well, not much, because it's a secret . . . Sorry, I wish there was something I could manifest . . .'

Is the fact that both presidential candidates belong to the same secret organisation pure coincidence or an indication of something more sinister? Many proponents of conspiracy theories concerning the Illuminati and a New World Order have put forward the idea that elections in the USA and other countries are not truly free and democratic; that, instead, presidents are chosen by the Illuminati or other controlling bodies, the president elect being just a puppet.

While there is no hard evidence to support this idea, the fact that both Bush and Kerry are members of the same secret society does nothing to dispel the myth. More disturbing, it is reported that in his first term in office Bush appointed no less than 11 members of Skull and Bones to his administration. Is this merely an example of 'the old boys' network' or a symptom of something more ominous? It is time to do a little digging into the practices and history of the order.

Skull and Bones is also known as the Order of Death, the Order, the Eulogian Club and Lodge 322. Members of this secret society are known as Bonesmen, Knights of Eulogia and Boodle Boys.

The society's headquarters at Yale is known as the Tomb and it has all the appearance of a sepulchre or mausoleum. It is here that the Bonesmen meet and perform their secret rituals and where they are given secret names that they use amongst their ranks. Apparently, the members also call themselves 'knights' and refer to everyone else in the outside world as 'barbarians'.

William Huntingdon Russell founded Skull and Bones after a visit to Germany during the 1830s. In the late nineteenth century, an anonymous group calling themselves File and Claw – named after their unsubtle tools of the trade – broke into the Skull and Bones' Tomb and after finding documents and papers inside they revealed that, while in Germany, Russell had been initiated into a German secret society which had a skull and crossbones as its emblem:

> Bones is a chapter of corps of a German university. It should properly be called the Skull and Bones chapter. General Russell, its founder, was in Germany before his senior year and formed a warm friendship with a leading member of a German society. The meaning of the permanent number 322 in all Bones literature is that it was founded in '32 as the second chapter of the German society. But the Bonesman has a pleasing fiction that his fraternity is a descendant of an old Greek patriot society founded by Demosthenes, who died in 322 BC.

A 1933 Skull and Bones document mentions the 'birth of our Yale chapter'. This, coupled with the alternative name of the society, Lodge

322, suggests that Skull and Bones – however powerful and influential – is but a single chapter of a much larger, possibly worldwide, organisation.

Furthermore, we have some evidence that Skull and Bones could in fact be an arm of the Illuminati that began in Bavaria. The society is purportedly a direct descendant of an earlier order known as Phi Beta Kappa that had been created in 1776. This in turn has been shown to bear an uncanny resemblance to the Bavarian Illuminati, with many people declaring that Phi Beta Kappa was the 'Bavarian Illuminati . . . spread to America'.

In 1832, amid anti-Masonic hysteria and heavy campaigning by public figures such as John Quincy Adams, Phi Beta Kappa decided to turn its back on its secretive existence and became an open society. Later that same year, Skull and Bones was formed, and many historians claim it was a direct result of the changes in Phi Beta Kappa.

Returning again to the accounts of File and Claw, the clandestine group of burglars who broke into the Tomb, they describe a slogan painted onto the 'arched walls above the vault' of a sacred room 322. This reads: 'Who was the fool, who the wise man, beggar or king? Whether poor or rich, all's the same in death.'

Journalist Ron Rosenbaum – who also attended Yale – was shocked to discover very similar writings in a Scottish anti-Illuminist tract from 1798. This ancient document claimed to contain excerpts from Illuminist ritual manuals that were said to have been confiscated by the Bavarian state in 1785, at the time when the Illuminati were outlawed. Rosenbaum elaborates:

> Toward the end of the ceremony of initiation in the 'Regent degree' of Illuminism, according to the tract, 'a skeleton is pointed out to him [the initiate], at the feet of which are laid a crown and a sword. He is asked 'whether that is the skeleton of a king, nobleman or a beggar'. As he cannot decide, the

president of the meeting says to him, 'The character of being a
man is the only one that is [of] importance'.

The links to the Illuminati hinted at in these documents start to look
promising. Could we finally have evidence here that a modern-day
Illuminati does actually exist, one that has direct connections to the
mysterious order of the past and one that clearly has its operatives in
the policy-making powerhouse of the most influential nation on
earth? It is time to look more closely at the society today for further
clues.

Skull and Bones has some very odd rituals. Obviously the order's
emblem is strange enough, the skull and crossbones – a symbol that
has been used by pirates and the Nazis alike – but there is more than
just their emblem to link them to the Führer and Nazi Germany.

Several break-ins have occurred at Skull and Bones headquarters.
The first was by the aforementioned File and Claw. Those responsible
for later break-ins have reported finds such as human remains used
for ritualistic purposes and one room that contained nothing but Nazi
memorabilia. Now this may sound far fetched, and there is no
concrete evidence available to us to verify these claims; however, it
must be remembered that Prescott Bush (George W. Bush's
grandfather) and W. Averell Harriman – themselves Skull and Bones
members – were both supporters of the Nazi Party financial machine.
In fact, there is strong evidence that the New York banking house
Brown Brothers-Harriman – in which both these men were closely
involved – funded and directed the military-industrial machine that
powered both Hitler and the Nazi revolution. In the light of Skull and
Bones' German origins, these claims of a secret society based on, or at
the very least incorporating, the ideology of National Socialism no
longer sound as ludicrous as they might at first appear.

Hitler himself, along with many other high-ranking Nazis, has been
linked to a group known as the Thule Society. The Thule Society is

another order that uses the skull and bones as one of its emblems and commentators have raised the possibility that both the Thule Society and Skull and Bones are chapters linked to a larger organisation.

As a footnote, it should probably be mentioned that, again according to journalist Rosenbaum, the Skull and Bones' main rival at Yale, the Scroll and Key – a society that has also had members in key policy-making positions within Washington – is rumoured to hold the silverware of Adolf Hitler in its possession.

The stories just go on and on but one final account bears mentioning. During one break-in, it was alleged that human remains were found. There have also been accusations that Prescott Bush stole the mortal remains of Geronimo, the Apache leader, and stored them inside the Yale headquarters of Skull and Bones. It has been suggested that these, along with other bones held in the Tomb, are used in the initiation rites of the order. The whole episode came to light in 1988 and later Fitzhugh Green, a close ally of George Bush Snr, had this to say on the matter:

> Prescott Bush had a colourful side. In 1988, the press revealed the complaint of an Apache leader about Bush. This was Ned Anderson of San Carlos, Oklahoma, who charged that as a young army officer Bush stole the skull of Indian Chief Geronimo and had it hung on the wall of Yale's Skull and Bones Club. After exposure of 'true facts' by Anderson, and consideration by some representatives in Congress, the issue faded from public sight. Whether or not this alleged skulduggery actually occurred, the mere idea casts the senior Bush in an adventurous light.

Moving on from the peculiarities suggested by these revelations, we must address the bigger question. Should we be worried that the most powerful man in America at the present time is a member of Skull and

Bones, and, furthermore, that his father and grandfather were also members? Surely George W. Bush's loyalty is to his country and his people above all else? He would never place his allegiance to a secret society over that of his country, would he? Forgoing the good of the country and state – even the world – for that of a small group of individuals with an unknown agenda? Well, it would seem that on this point there are no guarantees. According to William Cooper in his book *Behold a Pale Horse*:

> Members of the Order [Skull and Bones] take an oath that absolves them from any allegiance to any nation or king or government or constitution, and that includes the negating of any subsequent oath which they may be required to take. They swear allegiance only to the Order and its goal of a New World Order . . . according to the oath Bush [George Bush Snr] took when he was initiated into Skull and Bones, his oath of office as President of the United States means nothing.

Is the pursuit of a New World Order really why Bush is in the White House? There is no evidence to back up such a theory, although his father, George Bush Snr, openly mentioned a New World Order in his speeches. The first incidence was in a State of the Union Address on 29 January 1991:

> We have within our reach the promise of a renewed America. We can find meaning and reward by serving some purpose higher than ourselves – a shining purpose, the illumination of a thousand points of light. And it is expressed by all who know the irresistible force of a child's hand, of a friend who stands by you and stays there, a volunteer's generous gesture, an idea that is simply right . . .
>
> The world can, therefore, seize this opportunity to fulfil the

long-held promise of a New World Order – where brutality will go unrewarded, and aggression will meet collective resistance.

Yes, the United States bears a major share of leadership in this effort. Among the nations of the world, only the United States of America has had both the moral standing, and the means to back it up. We are the only nation on this earth that could assemble the forces of peace.

Then, on 6 March 1991, he made a speech to Congress:

Until now, the world we've known has been a world divided – a world of barbed wire and concrete block, conflict and cold war.

Now, we can see a new world coming into view. A world in which there is the very real prospect of a New World Order. In the words of Winston Churchill, a 'world order' in which 'the principles of justice and fair play . . . protect the weak against the strong . . .' A world where the United Nations, freed from cold war stalemate, is poised to fulfil the historic vision of its founders. A world in which freedom and respect for human rights find a home among all nations. The Gulf war put this new world to its first test, and, my fellow Americans, we passed that test . . .

Tonight as our troops begin to come home, let us recognise that the hard work of freedom still calls us forward. We've learned the hard lessons of history. The victory over Iraq was not waged as 'a war to end all wars'. Even the New World Order cannot guarantee an era of perpetual peace. But enduring peace must be our mission.

Couched in such terms, a New World Order does not sound much to be feared; on the contrary, it sounds like something to which we would all aspire. But can we be sure that it is this kind of New World Order that is really being created?

We have examined Skull and Bones, now it is time to look elsewhere in the corridors of American power to search for more clues that might lead us to the modern-day Illuminati and allow us to discover just what their aims might be.

THE PROJECT FOR THE NEW AMERICAN CENTURY

It follows that if the Illuminati does exist, then for it to function it must have access to world governments in order for it to bring about the New World Order. Trying to achieve such a state merely through tireless lobbying would take millennia, if not eternity. So if the Illuminati does exist today, it would surely wish to place itself in a position of power and would try to control governments directly.

What would such a group look like? Unable to show its true face, it would surely hide behind other groups and fronts. Is there any evidence that such façades exist? What form would such operations take?

In 1997, a group of American conservatives formed a new think tank called the Project for the New American Century (PNAC). It has some political heavyweights behind it and some of the more well-known key players include Donald Rumsfeld, Dick Cheney, Jeb Bush, Paul Wolfowitz and George Weigel. Its manifesto sounds like a New World Order conspiracy theory right out of the pages of a novel. On its website it says:

Established in the spring of 1997, the Project for the New American Century is a non-profit, educational organization whose goal is to promote American global leadership . . .

The Project for the New American Century is . . . dedicated to a few fundamental propositions: that American leadership is good both for America and for the world; and that such leadership requires military strength, diplomatic energy and commitment to moral principle.

Furthermore, in its original statement of principles it states:

As the 20th century draws to a close, the United States stands as the world's pre-eminent power. Having led the West to victory in the Cold War, America faces an opportunity and a challenge: Does the United States have the vision to build upon the achievements of past decades? Does the United States have the resolve to shape a new century favorable to American principles and interests?

Back in 1998, Bill Clinton was in power and PNAC strongly urged him to take action against Iraq and Saddam Hussein, believing that his Democratic administration was not being proactive enough. The letter that was sent to Clinton went on to say:

We are writing you because we are convinced that current American policy toward Iraq is not succeeding, and that we may soon face a threat in the Middle East more serious than any we have known since the end of the Cold War. In your upcoming State of the Union Address, you have an opportunity to chart a clear and determined course for meeting this threat. We urge you to seize that opportunity, and to enunciate a new strategy that would secure the interests of the U.S. and our friends and allies around the world. That strategy should aim, above all, at the removal of Saddam Hussein's regime from power. We stand ready to offer our full support in this difficult but necessary endeavor.

PNAC makes no excuses for the fact that it was pushing for the invasion of Iraq back even before the dawn of the new millennium.

The 25 individuals who originally signed up to PNAC were a mix of academics and conservative politicians. After George W. Bush came to power in January 2001, several of these signatories found positions in the presidential administration. They found a much more favourable patch of soil into which to sow their ideas than that of Bill Clinton's administration and many critics of George W. Bush have made much of this eagerness to spoil for a fight, to turn to military arms when the negotiations fail.

It seems hard now, in the light of PNAC's involvement with George W. Bush, to see how the invasion of Iraq could ever have been prevented, with or without the events of 9/11.

Returning to the 1998 letter to Bill Clinton, one passage in particular makes it very clear that PNAC would be determined to see through its aims, whatever the international political climate:

> We urge you to articulate this aim, and to turn your Administration's attention to implementing a strategy for removing Saddam's regime from power. This will require a full complement of diplomatic, political and military efforts. Although we are fully aware of the dangers and difficulties in implementing this policy, we believe the dangers of failing to do so are far greater. We believe the U.S. has the authority under existing UN resolutions to take the necessary steps, including military steps, to protect our vital interests in the Gulf. In any case, American policy cannot continue to be crippled by a misguided insistence on unanimity in the UN Security Council.

We have to remember that just a few years later, some of the authors of this very letter would have positions of power within the White House.

Another quote that is often cited as evidence that something sinister has been developing in Washington can be found in a report released by PNAC during 2000, entitled *Rebuilding America's Defenses: Strategies, Forces, and Resources for a New Century*. In these post 9/11 days, the quote has taken on a disturbing significance in the eyes of some who believe that the US's role in the events of 2001 is not as straightforward as the official version of events on that fateful day: 'Further, the process of transformation, even if it brings revolutionary change, is likely to be a long one, absent some catastrophic and catalyzing event – like a new Pearl Harbor.'

Is the presence of this highly prescient line purely coincidental? Should we read anything into its appearance in such a report – one that was released for the following reasons, according to PNAC: 'From the belief that America should seek to preserve and extend its position of global leadership by maintaining the pre-eminence of U.S. military forces.'?

That was not the only controversial subject touched upon in the report. Other longer-term aims of PNAC seem to have been revealed in the pages of this document. Bear in mind again that this report was written in the year 2000, a year before the shocking events of 9/11:

> Over the long term, Iran may well prove as large a threat to U.S. interests in the Gulf as Iraq has. And even should U.S.–Iranian relations improve, retaining forward-based forces in the region would still be an essential element in U.S. security strategy given the longstanding American interests in the region.

Many have used these reports issued by PNAC to accuse George W. Bush's administration of planning military attacks in the Middle East, and elsewhere, well before September 2001. Should we read anything into these remarks? Could there be a conspiracy here, a plot that a hidden Illuminati might be developing with a view to developing a New World Order?

Journalist George Monbiot thinks so. Commenting on the original letter written by PNAC and sent to Bill Clinton in 1998, he said: 'To pretend that this battle begins and ends in Iraq requires a wilful denial of the context in which it occurs. That context is a blunt attempt by the superpower to reshape the world to suit itself.'

However, it seems that PNAC has its sights set on more than control of the world. It is pushing for control over the new frontiers of cyberspace and even space itself. Again in its own words, it believes that America should: 'Control the new "international commons" of space and "cyberspace", and pave the way for the creation of a new military service – U.S. Space Forces – with the mission of space control.'

What should we make of all this? Is it no worse than we should expect from any administration or is there just the slightest hint that what we are seeing here are signs that the Illuminati is tightening its grip on the reins of power? Once again, it is incredibly hard to discern from outside the corridors of power and probably only those at the top of the food chain really know what is going on.

At the beginning of this chapter we asked whether an organisation called the Illuminati was functioning in the modern world and whether it was trying to bring about a New World Order. Is it possible that in examining these powerful and secretive groups we have caught a brief glimpse of the Illuminati itself? Definitive proof is always going to be incredibly hard to track down and I think that if the Illuminati does exist, it is probably never going to be possible to say with conviction where and how it operates.

Maybe it is time that we went back to *Angels and Demons* and examined a facet of the Illuminati that we have yet to look at in any detail. Dan Brown says that the Illuminati's main opposition was the Catholic Church and that it accused the Illuminati of certain traits and beliefs. Perhaps here is a clue that we have overlooked. Is it possible to identify the Illuminati by their beliefs? Perhaps by following the clues, they will give away their identity.

SHAITAN

In *Angels and Demons*, Dan Brown states that the Illuminati were equated with Shaitan. At the beginning of the novel, Robert Langdon tells Kohler: 'The Vatican denounced the brotherhood as Shaitan . . . It's Islamic. It means "adversary" . . . God's adversary . . . Shaitan is the root of an English word . . . Satan.'

Many conspiracy theorists also accuse the Illuminati of being Satanists, especially those writers who would be considered part of the Christian Right. Is there any truth in this claim or is it a ploy to try and demonise the Illuminati?

Shaitan does indeed seem to relate to Satan and the term is found within the texts of Judaism, Christianity and Islam. The word's original meaning is 'adversary' or 'accuser'. This makes sense when we read some of the books from the Hebrew Bible, for example the Book of Job, where Satan appears as an angel, an instrument of God himself, sent to test mankind. It is interesting to note that in this context, Satan has no power to act alone; he needs God's permission. In the New Testament and the Hebrew Apocrypha, however, Satan plays a different role and is portrayed as a demon, an evil spirit who is the enemy of both God and man.

The Islamic view of Shaitan, or Iblis as he is also known, sees the convergence of these two distinct roles attributed to Satan. According to the Qur'an, Shaitan was created by Allah from pure fire but then disobeyed him and so was expelled from his court and damned for eternity. After being condemned, Shaitan responded by saying that he intended to bring all of mankind down with him. Allah decided to allow Shaitan to walk the earth, testing mankind wherever he went, whispering in the ear of whoever would listen. In this way, we see that Shaitan could be both accuser and devil at the same time.

There is no evidence that the Illuminati worshipped Shaitan. However, it is possible that this misconception was brought about by the fact that Adam Weishaupt, the founder of the Bavarian Illuminati, is often described as being a follower of Lucifer.

The name Lucifer comes from two Latin words and means literally 'to bring light' or 'to bear light'. In Greek mythology, Lucifer is the 'dawn-bringer', while in Roman astrology, the morning star, which we now call the planet Venus, was known as Lucifer.

It was only later, as the Christian tradition developed, that Lucifer's name took on a very different connotation. Lucifer became chief of the fallen angels and in turn the name became synonymous with that of Satan. Why or how exactly this happened is not entirely clear but it has been suggested that it was as a result of Lucifer's connection with the planet Venus.

Venus is the brightest object in the sky after the sun and the moon, yet because the planet's orbit lies between the earth and the sun, Venus can never rise high in the sky. Furthermore, Venus only appears just as the sun sets and as the sun rises. Therefore, it has been suggested that the myth of Lucifer being cast from heaven was created to explain why Venus could never be seen in the dead of night like the other stars.

A famous quote from the Book of Isaiah in the Old Testament clearly shows the old association with Venus, the morning star: 'How art thou fallen from heaven, O Lucifer, son of the morning! How art thou cut down to the ground, which didst weaken the nations!'

Other scholars attribute the association of Lucifer with Satan to mistranslations of the original biblical texts at the time of King James. To illustrate just how confusing matters have become, Jesus is also referred to as the 'morning star' or 'light bearer' in certain passages of the Bible.

John J. Robinson in *A Pilgrim's Path* sheds further light on these mistranslations:

To the point, the verse in the King James version (Isaiah 14:12) that begins 'How art thou fallen from heaven, O Lucifer . . .' has now been translated directly from the Hebrew in the New English Bible as 'How you have fallen from heaven, bright morning star . . .' There is no mention of Lucifer, no reference to any disobedient angel plunging to hell, nor should there be.

In the fourth century, there was even a Christian saint called Lucifer, suggesting that the name was not associated with Satan at this point in history. Lucifer Calaritanus was the bishop of Cagliari in Sardinia and he still has a feast day in the Catholic Church.

So, to be a follower of Lucifer might not be as bad as it would seem on first appraisal. In some instances, the name appears to relate to a 'god of light' not of darkness. Perhaps the Illuminati did find inspiration from Lucifer after all?

It is clear that Weishaupt was a follower of Gnostic tenets. He named the Illuminati the Order of the Perfectibilists, borrowing from the Cathars. The various Gnostic religions and sects of the early Christian era have common threads that can be traced right up to Catharism.

One of the most controversial beliefs of the Cathars was their dualist view of the world. Dualism describes not one god but two – one good and one evil. Furthermore, the Cathars believed that the gods of the Old and New Testaments were not the same god but opposite and very different deities. They were convinced that the god of the Old Testament could even be equated with that of the Demiurge himself – the equivalent to Satan. The true god, the god of the New Testament, was their god of immaterial things, such as souls and light.

It was Satan who had shaped the material world, the Cathars believed, and they taught their followers that he had captured the souls of man and imprisoned them on earth. It was mankind's task to resist all earthly temptations, to strengthen the soul through prayer and thereby escape the captivity that cloaked the divine spark of mankind's true nature.

Obviously, the views of the Cathars and the Catholic Church clashed. The Cathars called the Catholic Church the Church of Wolves, referring to the fact that priests and bishops lived in luxury and worshipped material objects such as relics and even the image of the Cross. Worse still, from the Cathar's standpoint, the Catholic Church worshipped the wrong god, the god of the Old Testament – the Demiurge himself. The Cathars referred to the works of Matthew and in their eyes this served to provide confirmation that they were right to hold the views they did on the Catholic Church: 'Watch out for the false prophets who come to you in the guise of lambs, when within lurk voracious wolves. Only their fruit will tell them apart.'

It has been argued that the Cathar's take on the world and the true nature of God is similar to the views held by Gnostic Luciferians (not to be confused with modern-day Luciferians), who believed that Lucifer was the true god and not the devil that the name is associated with today. Once again we see the reverse of long-held beliefs, the idea that Lucifer is the true god, the true 'bringer of light', whereas the god of the Old Testament is seen as the god of evil.

Weishaupt, as the founder of the Illuminati, held these beliefs and so labelling the Bavarian Illuminati and their followers as Satanists is more than likely incorrect and unfair. However, when viewed with our understanding of dualism, something strange is revealed. Remember Robert Langdon's words regarding Shaitan, 'It means "adversary" . . . God's adversary.'

If, as we suspect, Weishaupt believed, as the Cathars did, that the Roman Catholic Church was worshipping the wrong god, then of course the Illuminati really *were* God's adversary. But only because they viewed the Roman Catholic god as something evil, a god that it was their duty to resist and fight. It does not mean that they worshipped Satan, or any other dark god for that matter. It is simply a matter of perception.

Many people in the West are brought up believing that the Old Testament god of the Catholic Church is a benevolent and loving god; but to the Cathars, and to the Illuminati, this was certainly not the case. Also, if Lucifer meant anything to Weishaupt and the Illuminati, it certainly was not in terms of his modern role as Satan.

Of course, it does not help our cause to find that modern Luciferians differ in their view on Lucifer. Some accept that Lucifer is identified as Satan while others deny this and instead refer to the Lucifer of old, the 'bringer of light', the 'God of light'.

There is one final footnote to be added concerning Lucifer. A high-ranking Freemason, Albert Pike, wrote a book called *Morals and Dogma of the Ancient and Accepted Scottish Rite of Freemasonry* in the year 1872. This book is much respected but little understood in the world of mass-market Freemasonry. Excerpts from it talk of Lucifer in strange terms – at least, strange to anyone who has only heard of Lucifer in connection with Satan.

Lucifer, the Light-bearer! Strange and mysterious name to give to the Spirit of Darkness! Lucifer, the son of the morning! Is it he who bears the Light, and with its splendours intolerable blinds feeble, sensual or selfish Souls? Doubt it not!

When Albert Pike reveals some of Freemasonry's secret doctrines in this book, he is, like Lucifer himself, shedding light on the fact that Freemasonry, rather than worshipping Satan, is honouring the light bearer and talking about the light in terms of education and enlightenment. Pike and other Masonic scholars would talk about the 'Luciferian path' and the 'energies of Lucifer'. It should now be clear that, far from being a hidden satanic message, the inference is of spiritual enlightenment and sacred teachings.

This is what makes the task of searching for the Illuminati a long and arduous one. There are conspiracies wrapped within jealousies and prejudices, and the story becomes twisted and warped before we ever approach the truth.

THE ILLUMINATI TODAY

We have tracked down the original Illuminati, at home in the Bavarian secret societies, with its roots in Catharism and Gnostic religions. We have followed its trail to Karl Marx and Lenin and the birth of the Soviet Union. We have also followed its meandering course as it flows through the United States and picked up a whiff of its odour in the secret societies of Yale: Skull and Bones, Scroll and Key and countless others. But what of the Illuminati today?

The Bilderberg Group is often mentioned in the same breath as the Illuminati – but does it have any concrete links to a conspiracy for a New World Order?

The Bilderberg Conference is a yearly event that takes place with approximately 130 guests, all of whom meet to discuss economic and political issues concerning Western Europe and North America. The title of the conference comes from the location of the very first meeting in 1954, the Bilderberg Hotel in Arnhem in the Netherlands.

While this group is surrounded in controversy, it is hard to see how they could comprise a secret society when the members are known and the meetings take place in public. The media is not allowed into the conference and it is probably for this reason that claims are made about the discussion of nefarious and sinister topics.

There is no doubt that the Bilderberg Conference is designed to influence the balance of power in the Western world but perhaps we should view this group of individuals as a powerful lobbying body rather than a branch of the Illuminati. Of course, there is no firm evidence either way but I suspect that the Bilderberg Conference is not so much concerned with a New World Order as how to maintain its firm grip on the financial markets of the West.

Another organisation in the firing line when it comes to talk of a hidden Illuminati order directing world affairs is the Trilateral Commission. A private organisation founded in 1973 at the behest of David Rockefeller, the Trilateral Commission, like the Bilderberg Group, meets once a year and has members from North America, Western Europe and Japan (these three comprising the 'tri'- in trilateral). Its published aims are to facilitate close cooperation between the three groups and to develop business and political ties.

Members have included Jimmy Carter, Bill Clinton and Dick Cheney, who is also a prominent member of the Project for a New American Century.

We are unlikely ever to find out for sure whether the Bilderberg Group or the Trilateral Commission, or any of the other groups bandied about as Illuminati candidates, really are involved in a plot to create a New World Order. Of course, the argument put forward by conspiracy theorists is that these organisations are merely a front for a much more insidious and hidden elite that pulls the strings from behind the curtain. However, as it is impossible for us to verify that claim, we have to look at what is visible to us.

It is quite obvious that all of the groups that we have examined briefly – Bilderberg, the Trilateral Commission, Project for a New American Century, Skull and Bones and so on – have their own agendas, both secret or out in the open for all to see: we would expect nothing less from organisations with members who are so politically active. However, having considered some of the evidence, it seems more likely that what we are looking at is a series of disparate groups, each trying to bring about its own small victories. Looking across the broad sweep of history over the last 200 years, it would appear as if the Illuminati that was banished while under Weishaupt's leadership swiftly fragmented and broke up into a series of similar but distinct orders, some secret and some not so. We only have to look at the first half of the twentieth century for evidence of this. As we have seen,

Lenin's October Revolution in Russia appears to have been inspired from Illuminati origins. But less than two decades later, Soviet Russia met head-on with another candidate for Illuminati-sponsored leadership, the Nazis. Why would two groups who could claim Illuminati ancestry clash in the most destructive war ever known to man?

This could only have been the result of the fragmenting of the Illuminati leadership after the banishment of 1785. If one accepts that such a split occurred and separate cells were formed with diverging ideologies, then the Second World War can be seen as a clash not just of ideals and beliefs but also for the right to establish a New World Order – one made in the victor's image.

In the event, no all-encompassing New World Order was established in 1945; instead, the world was thrown into the Cold War and the long stand-off between East and West began. So, what now, after the collapse of the Soviet Union and the expansion of the United States' militaristic power? Will current events usher in a New World Order or will the concept of countries, of sovereign nations, of individual governments, of religions be with us for some time to come? We are about to find out.

Coming back to what started us off on this journey, the introduction of the Illuminati into *Angels and Demons*, it should be apparent by now that, as he has done with other subjects, Dan Brown has built up his fictional Illuminati around a factual base. The Illuminati clearly did exist at one time and we have followed the trail of their influence through powerful world events. They also did seem to wish to wage war on the Catholic Church, at the least on an ideological footing and at worst in an all-out conflict with the Vatican for power. However, the Illuminati as described in *Angels and Demons* is not, it seems, waiting to take over the world and thrust its New World Order upon us at any moment, though only those who climb the winding stair to the upper echelons of power will ever truly know.

At the end of the day, the conspiracy theorists will go on believing that the Illuminati still exists and the sceptics will continue to claim it is nothing more than fiction. I'll leave it to Adam Weishaupt, founder of the Illuminati, to have the last word concerning the eternal trait of man to believe what he will, despite all the evidence to the contrary:

> The most wonderful thing of all is that the distinguished Lutheran and Calvinist theologians who belong to our order really believe that they see in it the true and genuine sense of Christian religion. O mortal man, is there nothing you cannot be made to believe?

SUGGESTED READING LIST

Barruél, Abbé Augustin, *Mémoires pour servir à l'histoire du Jacobinisme* – Memoirs Illustrating the History of Jacobinism (originally published 1797–8)

Burnett, Thom (ed.), *Conspiracy Encyclopedia: The Encyclopedia of Conspiracy Theories* (Collins & Brown, 2005)

Halper, Stefan and Clarke, Jonathan, *America Alone: The Neo-Conservatives and the Global Order* (Cambridge University Press, 2005)

Marx, Karl, *The Communist Manifesto*

Mehring, Franz, *Karl Marx: The Story of His Life*, trans. Edward Fitzgerald (Covivi, Friede Publishers, 1935)

Millegan, Kris (ed.), *Fleshing Out Skull & Bones: Investigations into America's Most Powerful Secret Society* (Trine Day, 2003)

Payson, Seth, *Proof of the Illuminati* (originally published 1804)

Pearson, Michael, *The Sealed Train* (Putnam, 1975)

Picknett, Lynn, *The Secret History of Lucifer: Evil Angel or the Secret of Life Itself?* (Constable & Robinson, 2005)

Pike, Albert, *Morals and Dogma of the Ancient and Accepted Scottish Rite of Freemasonry* (R.A. Kessinger Publishing Co., 2004)

Robbins, Alexandra, *Secrets of the Tomb: Skull and Bones, the Ivy League and the Hidden Paths of Power* (Little, Brown, 2002)

Robinson, John J., *A Pilgrim's Path: Freemasonry and the Religious Right* (M. Evans & Co., 1993)

Robison, John, *Proofs of a Conspiracy Against All the Religions and Governments of Europe, Carried on in the Secret Meetings of Freemasons, Illuminati and Reading Societies* (originally published 1798)

Tarpley, Webster G. and Chaitkin, Anton, *George Bush: The Unauthorized Biography* (Executive Intelligence Review, 1992)

Webster, Nesta H., *World Revolution: The Plot against Civilisation* (originally published 1921)

Gazetteer

A guide to the people and places featured in Dan Brown's novels

Welcome to the gazetteer section of *The Dan Brown Companion*. In the following 108 lavish pages, you will find guides to the people and places featured in both *Angels and Demons* and *The Da Vinci Code*.

The aim of this section is twofold. First, it acts as a tourist guide for those of you who wish to visit the sites featured in the two novels. From the Vatican City to Rosslyn Chapel, Temple Church to Santa Maria della Vittoria, the Louvre to Piazza Navona – all are wonders and deserve a visit if you can.

Second, for the reader of the two novels who is unable to visit the sites, I hope that this section will bring to life many of the places and people that are mentioned and help them to visualise the myriad buildings, artworks and characters involved.

I have placed the people and sites mentioned in *The Da Vinci Code* first, followed by the people and places from *Angels and Demons*. All sites are accompanied by a 'Getting There' section to enable easier navigation and all details within this section are correct as of February 2006.

So turn the page. Rome, Paris, London and Edinburgh await.

CONTENTS

Characters – *Angels and Demons*

THE LOUVRE
Paris, France

The Louvre provides the backdrop for the murder at the heart of Dan Brown's novel *The Da Vinci Code*. The body of curator Jacques Saunière is discovered among the magnificent works of art in the Grand Gallery. Some of the priceless paintings from the collection have been used by the dying Saunière to leave clues for his granddaughter Sophie to help her unravel his fate and understand her destiny.

Originally a royal fortress, the Louvre has been through several transformations. Building started around 1190 and the foundations of this structure were uncovered as work began on the Grand Louvre project in 1985. As the city of Paris expanded, the Louvre became a royal palace rather than a fortified castle. The palace was the Paris home of the French royal family during the fifteenth and sixteenth centuries, and Francis I acquired works of art by Leonardo da Vinci among others. Once the Palace of Versailles was completed in the reign of Louis XIV and the French court relocated to the new residence in 1674, the Louvre buildings fell into disuse.

Given a new function and renamed as Museum Central des Arts, the Louvre was opened to the public in 1793 by the revolutionary government and provided an opportunity to display the newly acquired art collection of the state. Admission was free. Following his conquest of Italy, Napoleon Bonaparte enlarged the collection when he dispatched many of the treasures he had seized back to Paris.

GETTING THERE

Nearest Metro: Palais-Royal-Musée du Louvre

OPENING HOURS
Closed Tuesdays
Other days 9 a.m. to 6 p.m.
Late night opening until 9.45 p.m. on Wednesdays and Mondays (part only)
Admission: Adults €8.50 (€6 after 6 p.m.); under 18s free

Note: Separate tickets are required for temporary exhibitions
See official website www.louvre.fr for further details

PYRAMID INVERSÉE

The Da Vinci Code ends with the character Robert Langdon walking beneath the pyramid inversée, and realising that the search for the grail has led him to this location. The mainly glass pyramid inversée acts as a skylight in the underground Carrousel du Louvre and is positioned above a small stone pyramid, their tips almost meeting. It is these two shapes that Langdon interprets as symbols of the chalice and the blade, masculine and feminine, marking the end of his quest for the Holy Grail.

GLASS PYRAMID

Designed by the architect I.M. Pei, this controversial glass and steel structure has been greeted with dismay by those who feel that this modern addition looks out of place and jars with the rest of the building. The pyramid was added as part of the Grand Louvre project, a major remodelling including shops, transport links and public facilities that opened in 1989.

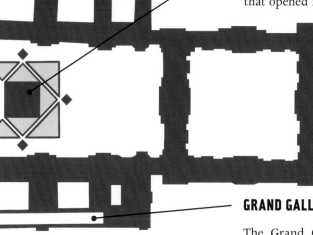

GRAND GALLERY

The Grand Gallery was originally built to link the royal apartments of the Louvre Palace with the Tuileries Palace nearby. It was constructed between 1595 and around 1606 and now holds some of the museum's most important Italian paintings. These include *The Madonna of the Rocks*, used by Dan Brown to conceal a key left by Saunière for Sophie. The gallery is now full of readers of *The Da Vinci Code* wondering how such a large and heavy picture could be lifted from the wall.

COLLECTION

Since its origins as a royal collection of paintings and antiquities, the Louvre has acquired some of the world's most notable masterpieces. Among the highlights that visitors traverse the vast building, often at a brisk pace, to see are the *Venus de Milo*, the *Mona Lisa* and the *Winged Victory of Samothrace*. The Egyptian antiquities section houses some exceptionally fine pieces, including the original Denderah Zodiac taken from the temple ceiling, and tomb paintings from the pharaoh Seti I. The first curator of the Egyptian collection was Jean-François Champollion, the man who played such a large role in the deciphering of hieroglyphic inscriptions.

MONA LISA

Arguably the most famous painting in the world, the image of the *Mona Lisa* by Leonardo da Vinci is immediately recognisable around the globe. An alternative name for the picture is *La Gioconda*, as the subject is believed to be the wife of Francesco del Giocondo. Every viewer of the painting is drawn to the enigmatic smile and art historians have speculated for centuries over what Leonardo was trying to convey. There has even been the suggestion that the facial features represent a self-portrait of Leonardo himself, due to similarities with a portrait of the artist in old age. The picture was produced between 1503 and 1506 and was obviously important to Leonardo since it is believed by many scholars to have still been in his possession when he died.

ST SULPICE
Paris, France

In *The Da Vinci Code*, after murdering the three sénéchaux and the Grand Master of the Priory of Sion, the character Silas visits the church of St Sulpice in Paris, believing he will find a keystone, or stone map, hidden there that will reveal the location of the order's most important secret. The two features of the church specifically mentioned by Dan Brown are a brass line on the floor marking a Rose Line and a gnomon. It is at the base of the gnomon that Silas breaks open the floor tiles and is then disappointed to find that, instead of the important keystone, there is only a reference to a verse from the book of Job, 'Hitherto shalt thou come and no further . . .'

As the church was built over a considerable period of years from 1646 to around 1780, the current structure is naturally the work of a number of architects. Dan Brown and others suggest that it was built over an earlier pagan temple, a claim that the church authorities vigorously deny. When the makers of the film of *The Da Vinci Code* were seeking locations, they were refused permission to film at St Sulpice. If you visit the church, you can see notices refuting claims made in the novel, a clear indication of the frustration that the church authorities feel over the notoriety St Sulpice has attracted through its inclusion in the book.

GETTING THERE

Nearest Metro: St Sulpice

OPENING HOURS
Daily 7.30 a.m. to 7.30 p.m.
Admission: free

GNOMON

A marble obelisk marked with signs representing dates and seasons through the year, the gnomon in St Sulpice seems an unusual structure to find in a church. It was actually commissioned in the eighteenth century by Jean-Baptiste Languet de Gergy, a pastor of St Sulpice, and its purpose was to help him accurately determine the dates of religious festivals such as Easter. The brass line that runs vertically down the centre of the gnomon is a continuation of the Rose Line mentioned earlier. There is a window in the south transept fitted with a system of lenses, and sunlight focused by the lenses falls on different points on the line on the gnomon as the year progresses. There are markers for the spring and autumn equinoxes and for the summer and winter solstices.

GNOMON ASTRONOMICUS
Ad Certam Paschalis
Æquinoctii Explorationem

QUOD. S. MARTYR ET EPISCOPUS HIPPOLYTUS
ADORSUS EST. QUOD. CONCIL. NICÆNUM
PATRIARCHÆ ALEXANDRINO DEMANDAVIT.
QUOD PATRES CONSTANTIENSES ET LATE-
RANENSES SOLLICITOS HABUIT. QUOD INTER
ROMANOS PONTIFICES GREGORIUS XIII.
ET CLEMENS XI. INCREDIBILI LABORE ET
ADHIBITÂ PERITIORUM ASTRONOMORUM
INDUSTRIÂ CONATI SUNT. HOC ÆMULATUR
STYLUS ISTE CUM SUBDUCTÂ LIN. MERI-
DIANÂ ET PUNCTO ÆQUINOCTIALI CERTIS
PERIODORUM SOLARIUM INDICIBUS.

THE ROSE LINE

The Rose Line that runs through the church, marked on the floor by a thin brass line, supposedly represents a meridian running from north to south through Paris. This Paris meridian was used for many years as the standard from which all degrees of longitude were measured, until it was superseded by the line in Greenwich, London. If the Paris line is continued south, it passes very close to the mysterious village of Rennes-le-Château, which is closely connected to *The Da Vinci Code*. It is also believed that Bérenger Saunière, the priest from Rennes-le-Château, visited St Sulpice to get assistance in deciphering some of the documents he discovered during the renovation of his church.

While visiting St Sulpice, it is well worth spending time in the Chapel of the Angels, on your right as you enter the church, where there are some splendid frescos by Delacroix. The most famous of these is *Jacob Wrestling with the Angel*.

WESTMINSTER ABBEY
London, England

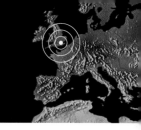

Standing proudly as a monument to kings and queens, Westminster Abbey is the final resting place for some of the most important individuals in the history of the British Isles and has been the setting for the coronation of every monarch since William the Conqueror.

There has been a church on this site since at least the 1040s, when Edward the Confessor, the final Anglo-Saxon king of Britain, built his royal palace close by on the banks of the Thames. At that time, the area was known as Thorney Island and there was a Benedictine monastery on the site that the abbey now occupies. King Edward took the monastery under his patronage, enlarging it and re-dedicating it to St Peter the Apostle. The church was called the west minster, to distinguish it from St Paul's (now the rebuilt Wren cathedral), which was then known as the east minster.

Edward also became the first king to be interred on the site when he was buried here soon after the church was consecrated on 28 December 1065.

The abbey of King Edward survived into the thirteenth century, until Henry III had it rebuilt in the then new Gothic style. It was under Henry III that the abbey became the site for royal coronations and he had the body of Edward the Confessor moved to a great tomb behind the high altar.

Right up until the present day, Westminster Abbey has remained a place of worship for commoner and royalty alike, becoming a symbol of Britain and the British people.

In *The Da Vinci Code*, it is in the Chapter House of Westminster Abbey that Sophie Neveu and Robert Langdon finally confront Leigh Teabing, who is revealed to be the Teacher.

GETTING THERE

Nearest Tube: Westminster or St James's Park

OPENING HOURS
The opening hours of the abbey vary and it is advisable to check the official website for up-to-date times before planning a visit: www.westminster-abbey.org. Sundays are reserved for worship with no tourist admission.
Admission: Adults £10, Concessions £6 (under 16, students and over 60), Family ticket £22 (two adults, two children)

ROSSLYN CHAPEL
Edinburgh, Scotland

osslyn Chapel is where all the clues finally lead Sophie and Langdon at the end of *The Da Vinci Code*. It is here that the two main characters learn the secret of what the Holy Grail is and, more importantly, where it is located.

Rosslyn Chapel has been the centre of mystery and speculation for a number of years now, with researchers and authors wildly proclaiming upon the 'truth' behind the chapel's many hidden charms and strange design. It is claimed that the chapel was built by the Knights Templar as a message in stone, concealing a great treasure or secret, and it is this mystery that Dan Bown has plugged into for his finale of *The Da Vinci Code*.

Building was started in 1446 by Sir William Sinclair and Rosslyn Chapel now stands as a truly marvellous example of the stonemason's art. Every inch of wall is covered with intricate and detailed carvings, both inside and out. Rosslyn Chapel really does deserve the epithet 'a book in stone'. Its official title is the Collegiate Chapel of St Matthew.

Over the past 25 years, dozens of books have speculated upon the so-called 'treasure' at Rosslyn. Theories have included: the treasure of Jerusalem, the head of Christ, the Stone of Destiny, parchments and clues to the bloodline of Christ, the treasure of the Knights Templar and much else besides.

Is there a hidden treasure at Rosslyn? One thing's for sure – people will never stop looking.

GETTING THERE

Rosslyn Chapel is six miles south of Edinburgh. Follow signs to the Edinburgh bypass and take the Straiton junction A701 Road to Penicuik and Peebles. After a short distance on the A701, the village of Roslin is signposted, take this road and, once in the village, Rosslyn Chapel is signed.

OPENING HOURS
Monday–Saturday 10.00 a.m. to 5 p.m.

Sunday 12 p.m. to 4.45 p.m.
Admission: Adults £6, Concessions £5, Children up to 18 years free

A LARGER BUILDING?

It would seem that Rosslyn Chapel was intended to be a much larger structure, with the present chapel only meant to be the choir of the bigger building. The baptistry on the western end of the chapel was added in the Victorian era.

SECRET CHAMBER?

These two solitary black slabs in the north isle of the chapel mark the entrance to the concealed crypt at Rosslyn. It is claimed that the crypt contains the remains of fully armoured knights lying as if asleep beneath the chapel. The poet and writer Sir Walter Scott is said to have gained entry to the crypt and may have used Rosslyn as inspiration for his *Lay of the Last Minstrel*.

WHO BUILT ROSSLYN CHAPEL?

It has often been suggested that the Knights Templar were involved in the construction of Rosslyn Chapel but in fact they were destroyed as a force over a hundred years before work began at Rosslyn.

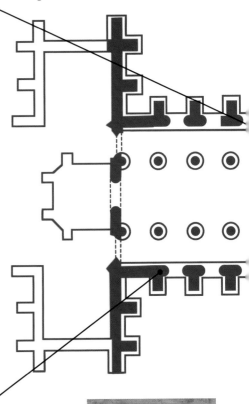

THE GREEN MEN OF ROSSLYN

Intriguingly, there are over 100 Green Men at Rosslyn Chapel. The Green Men of Rosslyn are unique in that they are found in various stages of life – some are young boys, some fully grown and we even find dead and skull-like Green Men in and around the chapel.

A STORY IN STONE

According to authors Ian Robertson and Mark Oxbrow, you can actually read Rosslyn Chapel as if it were a book in stone. The authors claim in their book, *Rosslyn and the Grail*, that if you start in the north-east corner of the chapel and work your way around, you can make out the cycle of the seasons and of life. The carving of the angel with the open book is said to be the start, with the nearby angel with the closed book the end.

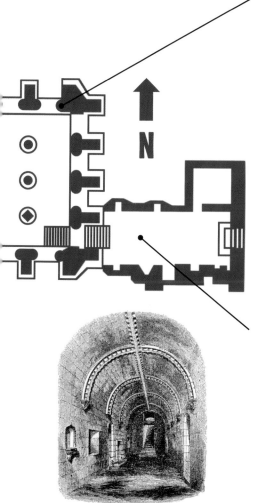

THE SACRISTY

The sacristy is often incorrectly referred to as the crypt. This is the oldest part of the present building, built even before the chapel itself. The sacristy contains some carvings that have retained their colour over the years, as well as the coats of arms of the Sinclair family. Of particular interest in the sacristy are pencil line drawings on the walls dating to the construction of the chapel and showing how some of the proportions of the original structure were laid out.

THE APPRENTICE PILLAR

Known as the Apprentice Pillar, the Prentice Pillar and even the Prince's Pillar, this monumental piece of stone carving is one of Rosslyn's best-known features. It is regarded as a masterpiece within the chapel but there is a grisly tale of murder and jealousy attached to it.

During construction of the chapel, the Master Mason wanted to create a wonderful pillar and travelled to Rome to learn more about his craft and visit the opulent churches at the centre of Christendom. He was absent for a long time and eventually his apprentice begged to be given the opportunity to undertake the work. The young apprentice produced the spiral design and intricate work we see today, far exceeding anything that the Master Mason could have achieved. When the Master Mason eventually returned, he was jealous of his pupil's great skill and murdered him, supposedly with a blow to the head from his mason's hammer. Two heads carved into the chapel near to the Apprentice Pillar are said to represent the slaughtered apprentice and the Master Mason, the latter hanged as a murderer.

Each generation that views the pillar has a fresh insight into the design and speculates on the inspiration behind the carving. In a twentieth-century interpretation of the work, it has been likened to the double-helix construction of DNA.

A carving of the head of the murdered apprentice
looks down from high in the chapel.

SINCLAIR

THE
ROSLIN
LEGEND

THE PRENTICE PILLAR
ROSLIN CHAPEL.

FOUNDED 1446
BY WILLIAM St Clair

Nº 101

RPP

TEMPLE CHURCH
London, England

S tanding in splendid courtly surroundings, between the Thames and Fleet Street, Temple Church has a fascinating story to tell.

In *The Da Vinci Code*, Temple Church is the scene of a false trail that Sophie and Langdon have followed. It also features as a location in the movie of the same name.

Originally built by the Knights Templar, the round church was consecrated on 10 February 1185 by Heraclius, patriarch of Jerusalem. It has also been speculated that Henry II of England was at this ceremony. Intended to be a replica of the round churches of the Holy Land and Middle East, specifically the Holy Sepulchre of Jerusalem, the church is an incredibly beautiful and tranquil place, with amazing acoustics.

There are marble effigies of nine knights on the floor of the round church, the most famous being William Marshal, Earl of Pembroke. It was William who acted as main mediator and liaison between King John and the barons in 1215.

Today, the church has the status of a royal peculiar rather than a private chapel. The Crown appoints the Master of the Temple and the upkeep of the edifice is the responsibility of both the Inner and Outer Temples (these are the ancient legal houses and companies on the site).

The round part of the church is the older portion, with the chancel section having been built in 1240. Henry III had at one point signalled his intention to be buried at Temple Church but was instead interred in Westminster Abbey, which he had built. One of his sons, who died in infancy, is, however, buried at the church.

GETTING THERE

Nearest Tube: Temple or Blackfriars

OPENING HOURS
Generally open Wednesday to Sunday
For specific opening times and details, contact the verger – 020 7353 3470, verger@templechurch.com

TEMPLARS IN LONDON

With the consecration of the building in 1185, Temple Church became the heart of the Templar activity in Britain. Receiving a good deal of royal patronage, the Templars enjoyed revered status under both Henry II and Henry III.

The Master of the Temple sat in Parliament as the first baron of the realm and was known as the *primus baro Angiae*. The Temple was often used as a bank by noblemen and as lodgings and a place of refuge by emissaries and kings. It was such associations that helped to make the Templars a powerful and influential force in the country.

The Temple and the surrounding area were home to many knights and novices from the order, along with warrior monks, chaplains and serving brethren. However, following the dissolution of the Knights Templar on Friday, 13 October 1307 (hence our modern superstition about the date Friday the 13th), the church and the London preceptory were taken over by Edward II and shortly afterwards the church passed into the hands of the Knights Hospitaller. It was the Knights Hospitaller who then rented the property and its surrounding buildings to two colleges of lawyers in the City of London. These two colleges then became known as the Inner and Middle Temples, surviving to this day.

A KNIGHT INTERRED

O n the floor of the round church at Temple are effigies of the bodies of nine medieval knights. The most famous of the nine is William Marshal, the Earl of Pembroke. Born in 1146, Marshal was a knight who served under King Henry II, Richard I, King John and for three years into the reign of Henry III. He married the second richest heiress in England at the time, Isabel de Clare, whose father had been the Earl of Pembroke. It was this title that William was granted upon his marriage.

William Marshal had been described by Stephen Langton, the Archbishop of Canterbury at the time, as the 'greatest knight that ever lived'.

Upon the death of King John, William was entrusted to ensure that King John's nine-year-old son, Henry, would accede to the throne and it was William who dealt with the barons at Runnymede at the signing of the Magna Carta. Indeed, William's charisma was such that two kings of France, Louis VII and Philip Augustus, trusted his word over that of the English royal house.

William wished to be buried as a Knight Templar, so just before his death he was invested into the order. He died on 14 May 1219 at Caversham in Oxfordshire.

GILBERT MARSHAL
fourth Earl of Pembroke (detail)

RENNES-LE-CHÂTEAU
Languedoc, France

The origins of the real story behind *The Da Vinci Code* can be traced directly back to a sleepy French village in the Languedoc region, close to the southern coast of France.

It is here that one of the most enduring and complex mysteries of the twentieth century has been played out, and there is a seemingly endless array of books and papers claiming to solve, once and for all, the true story about the priest, Abbé Bérenger Saunière, his possible treasure and what it all means.

The people of Rennes-le-Château today seem largely oblivious to the countless tourists and treasure hunters that visit the village. Notices have gone up around the area warning against unauthorised excavations but little can be done about the wild speculation that continues to rage. Where did Saunière get his seemingly endless supply of money from? Is there a treasure still to be unearthed at Rennes-le-Château? These and countless other questions remain unanswered.

It would seem that Saunière did find something at Rennes-le-Château, with the latest speculation being that a tomb and crypt were discovered beneath the church, possibly connected to the Habsburg family. However, as with all things to do with Rennes-le-Château, the truth about this is also wrapped inside a puzzle, locked in a conundrum. Rennes-le-Château has attracted rumour after countless rumour. In the end, it seems that Abbé Bérenger Saunière may have taken his secret to the grave.

GETTING THERE

Nearest Airport: Carcassonne

Rennes-le-Château is reached from the city of Carcassonne by taking the D118 south to Limoux. From Limoux continue on the D118 heading towards Quillan. At the village of Couiza, a sign will direct you left up the hill to Rennes-le-Château.

OPENING HOURS

1 May to 15 September 10.30 a.m. to 6 p.m.
16 September to 15 November 11.30 a.m. to 4.30 p.m.
16 November to 15 December 11.30 a.m. to 4 p.m. weekends
16 December to 10 January 11.30 a.m. to 4 p.m. every day
10 January to 29 February closed
1 March to 30 April 11.30 a.m. to 4 p.m. every day

TOUR MAGDALA

This imposing and remarkable structure was built by Bérenger Saunière to house his vast library. A stone staircase leads to the roof of the building, from which there is a magnificent view of the surrounding area.

BÉRENGER SAUNIÈRE

The parish priest of Rennes-le-Château and the central figure in the mystery surrounding this sleepy southern French village. Dan Brown uses the name Saunière for *The Da Vinci Code* character Jacques Saunière, the murdered curator of the Louvre museum and Sophie Neveu's grandfather.

RECENT EXCAVATIONS

In April 2001 and March 2002, a team led by the scholar Robert Eisenmann and author Michael Baigent made some preliminary archaeological investigations beneath the Tour Magdala and the church in Rennes-le-Château. Results seem to suggest that the team uncovered a possible crypt with tombs beneath the church.

WHERE IS IT?

Rennes-le-Château sits atop a rocky outcrop overlooking the Aude Valley in the Languedoc region of southern France. The nearest town is Couiza, at the foot of the hill upon which Rennes-le-Château is perched.

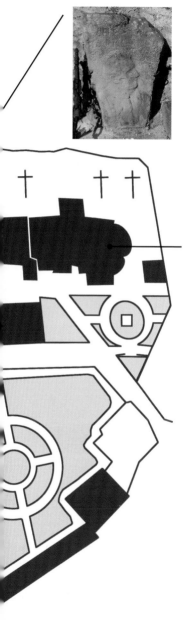

SAUNIÈRE'S GRAVE

The graves of both Bérenger Saunière and his maidservant Marie Denarnaud were until recently adjacent to one another in the church graveyard. However, at the order of the local mayor, Saunière's remains and tombstone have been removed to a new location inside the gardens of the Tour Magdala/Villa Bethanie complex. The moving of the body and tombstone was undertaken with military precision under the screen of night, with armed gendarmes sealing off the village to stop prying eyes and objectors.

THE CHURCH

Dedicated to St Mary Magdalene, the church possibly dates as far back as the eighth century, when Rennes-le-Château may have been known as Rhédae.

Over the porch lintel is a bizarre inscription, *Terribilis est locus iste* (This place is terrible). A statue of the demon Asmodeus supports a stoup near the door. The plaques depicting the Stations of the Cross contain bizarre inconsistencies. One shows a child swathed in Scottish plaid. Another has Pontius Pilate wearing a veil. Saints Joseph and Mary are each depicted holding a Christ child, as if to allude to the old legend that Christ had a twin.

GROTTE DU FOURNET — DITE DE LA MAGDELEINE

The journey to the alleged burial site of the Mary Magdalene is arduous but Saunière, a middle-aged priest, is said to have walked here most days to collect stones for his replica grotto. Why?

The grotto is magical. A coffin-shaped imprint is found in the centre, while a shallow grave is evident in the back recess of the cave. Could this be the burial site of Mary Magdalene and her daughter Sarah, the bloodline of Christ, the Holy Grail?

ANOMALOUS TILE OF MARY

After ascending one of two sets of 11 steps (22) that lead to the Tour Magdala, one is greeted with a tiled floor where one tile is just slightly different from the rest: it contains a red dot where the others are black. It points up the 22 stone steps, where a lone window points unambiguously at a grotto in the distance by the name of Grotte du Fournet — dite de la Magdeleine, which translates as the burial site of the Mary Magdalene.

THE NOBLE'S TOMBSTONE (MARIE DE NÈGRE D'ABLES)

Sadly, access to the cemetery is now restricted only to villagers but the remains of this provocative piece of the mystery are preserved in the museum in Rennes-le-Château. Before Saunière allegedly defaced the tombstone, it contained raised and offset letters and revealed the key to the parchments. Did the tombstone conceal the location of a treasure or secret?

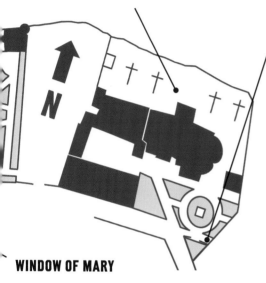

SAUNIÈRE'S GROTTO

This peculiar structure was built by Saunière with stones he personally collected near the Grotte du Fournet – dite de la Magdeleine. It once contained a statue of Mary Magdalene. It points at the Tour Magdala, which in turn points at the Grotto du Fournet. The bench in Saunière's grotto is inscribed with the letters XXSLX. Treasure hunters once destroyed the grotto. Though it has since been rebuilt, no one has deciphered the code.

WINDOW OF MARY

The window, which is found on the 22-step stone staircase of the Tour Magdala, is unambiguously fixated on the Grotte du Fournet – dite de la Magdeleine. A compass reading from the window reads 22 degrees; 22 July, of course, is the feast day of Mary Magdalene. Coincidence?

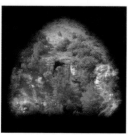

THE ASMODEUS STATUE

Immediately upon entering the church of St Mary Magdalene, and just after walking beneath the Latin inscription that states 'This place is terrible', one is greeted by a statue of the devil, or so it would first appear. Saunière commissioned the statue as part of his restorations. Years later, treasure hunters stole the head, which has since been replaced with another equally grimacing figure. The statue is believed to represent one of three things. Asmodeus, the ancient Hebrew guardian of King Solomon's treasure is the most popular interpretation. But just what is he guarding? Others believe that the statue represents Rex Mundi, the Cathar god of the underworld, or Satan. Did Saunière discover a Cathar secret? Still others believe that it portrays the Republic, the political demon that Saunière, a staunch monarchist, feared the most.

THE 'M' IN THE CHURCH

The restorations of Abbé Saunière are laden with clues, especially the configuration of statues he commissioned within the Church of St Mary Magdalene. Aligning the east–west corridor of the church and leading up to the pulpit are six primary statues of saints. Over the years, treasure hunters have observed that when the statues are connected in an unbroken line, they form the letter M. The saints in question are St Germaine, St Roch, St Antoine de Padoue, St Antoine and St Luc (on the pulpit), in this way spelling the French word GRAAL, the English equivalent of which is grail. The inverse of the M points at the statue of Mary Magdalene, whose feast day is 22 July. Opposite her is St Antoine the hermit, whose feast day is 17 January and who is associated with grottos. The numbers 22 and 17 occur with peculiar regularity in the mystery of Rennes-le-Château.

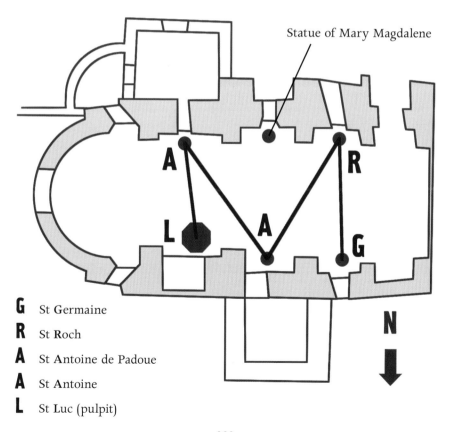

Statue of Mary Magdalene

G St Germaine

R St Roch

A St Antoine de Padoue

A St Antoine

L St Luc (pulpit)

CASTEL SANT'ANGELO
Rome, Italy

This building has been a tomb, a prison and a fortress but in Dan Brown's book *Angels and Demons* it assumes another role: that of the Illuminati lair. The Hassassin, who believes he is working for this secret organisation, has used Castel Sant'Angelo as a base from which to conduct his ritual murders of the four cardinals. Robert Langdon approaches the castle across the Ponte Sant'Angelo, which is lined by statues of angels carved by Bernini.

The Hassassin has used the Castel because of its proximity to the Vatican and the presence of a covered passageway linking the two buildings. In 1527, Pope Clement VII used the passageway, described charmingly in one guidebook as a pope-a-duct, to escape from German soldiers who were attacking the city of Rome. Clement took refuge in Castel Sant'Angelo for several months before returning to the Vatican with the remnants of his Swiss Guard.

Built as a mausoleum for the Emperor Hadrian, the tower was originally topped by a statue of Hadrian and had many other figures decorating it. It was then converted into a fortress and when the tower was besieged in AD 537, it is reported that the defenders hurled a torrent of marble deities down onto those attacking them, persuading them to give up the siege. In 590, Pope Gregory the Great led a procession through the streets of Rome to pray for relief from an attack of the plague. He saw a vision of the archangel Michael on top of the tower and this was taken as a sign of divine help. Since then it has been known as Castel Sant'Angelo.

GETTING THERE

Nearest Metro: Ottaviano or Lepanto

OPENING HOURS
Tuesday–Sunday
April to September 9 a.m. to 6 p.m.
October to March 9 a.m. to 2 p.m.
Admission: €5

THE VATICAN
Rome, Italy

Situated on the west bank of the River Tiber, the Vatican City covers an area of 109 acres in the heart of Rome and is an independent state, complete with its own postal service and passports. It was created in 1929, when Pope Pius XI signed the Lateran Treaty with the fascist dictator Mussolini, and has its own security force, the Swiss Guard, which is responsible for the personal security of the pope.

As well as being a historic attraction, the Vatican City is the religious and administrative centre of the Catholic Church – a faith with approximately one billion adherents. The head of the Church, the pope, is also head of state.

In 1984, the Vatican was declared by UNESCO to be a World Heritage Site, a status granted to places of outstanding cultural value.

In *Angels and Demons*, the Vatican is under threat from a hidden anti-matter device, a bomb powerful enough to destroy the buildings and the priceless art collection contained within them.

GETTING THERE

Nearest Metro: Cipro Musei Vaticani or Ottaviana San Pietro

OPENING HOURS
St Peter's Basilica: April–September 7 a.m. to 7 p.m.
October–March 7 a.m. to 6 p.m.
Admission: free

The Vatican Grottoes: April–September 7 a.m. to 6 p.m.
October–March 7 a.m. to 5.00 p.m.
Admission: free

The Vatican Museums: visiting times vary and can be checked on the Vatican website: www.vatican.va

Admission: €12, some concessions available

The Vatican Necropolis, where pagan and Christian tombs are located, can be visited by prior appointment.

Note: To enter St Peter's Basilica or the Vatican Museums you must pass through a security system common to most museums these days and queues can build up at busy times. There is also another checkpoint for visitors to pass through, at which anyone dressed inappropriately is turned away. To ensure a successful visit, do not wear shorts, women's skirts must cover the knee and the shoulders must be covered.

BALCONY

The balcony of St Peter's Basilica is the focal point for papal addresses to the crowds in St Peter's Square. It is also where newly elected popes are introduced to the world with the phrase *'habemus papem'* (we have a pope). In *Angels and Demons,* the balcony is the scene of the dramatic appearance by Camerlengo Ventresca just prior to his death.

VATICAN CITY

With a population of around 900 residents in 2004, the Vatican City is the smallest independent state in the world. This figure is augmented by the 3,000-plus people who work there for the Holy See, the official name given to the government of the Roman Catholic Church. The Vatican State also has territorial control over Castel Gandolfo, the official summer residence of the pope, situated in the Alban hills south of the city of Rome.

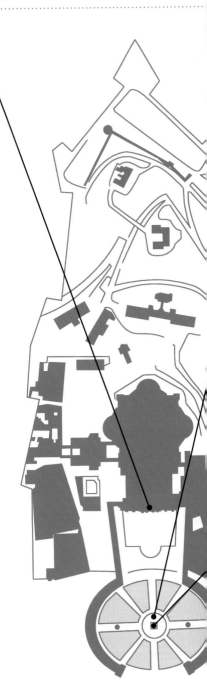

WEST PONENTE

This elliptical relief by Bernini represents the West Wind and is part of a series of markers set into the pavement of St Peter's Square. The blocks mark the compass bearings north, south, east and west, and the West Ponente is where the element of air is represented in *Angels and Demons*.

OBELISK

During the reign of Pope Sixtus V, the obelisk that dominates St Peter's Square was relocated from the Caligula Circus to its present position. Tradition tells that the mammoth job of moving the obelisk was completed in silence, at Sixtus's express command, so that the instructions of the foreman could be heard by the team of 900 men hauling on the ropes.

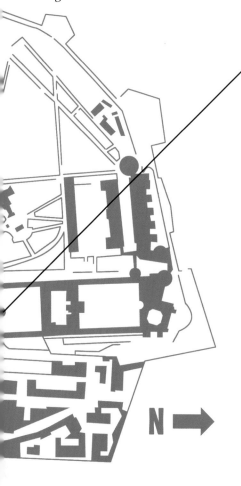

N →

ST PETER'S BASILICA

As you enter the basilica, Michelangelo's *Pietà* is on your right, protected by a glass screen. The statue depicts the Virgin Mary cradling the body of Jesus after the Crucifixion. Completed in 1499, it is considered the finest example of work on this theme and portrays a very young and serene Virgin. It is believed that Michelangelo was symbolising the purity of Mary in this sensitive representation.

The present basilica was begun in 1506 and finished in 1615, with several famous architects involved in its design and construction. Initially designed by Donato Bramante as a Greek cross, the plans were modified first by Raphael and then by Michelangelo, who conceived the dome. The façade was added by Carlo Maderno, then between 1655 and 1667 Bernini designed the elliptical piazza and the colonnades that lead to the basilica.

Bernini was also responsible for one of the most striking features of the interior of the basilica, the baldachin. This huge bronze canopy stands twenty-six metres high and is supported by four spiral columns. It stands over the supposed site of St Peter's tomb and excavations under the basilica conducted in the twentieth century uncovered tombs from the Roman era. In 1968, Pope Paul VI declared one of the bodies uncovered, that of an elderly man, to be the remains of St Peter the Apostle, although this is disputed by many and there is speculation that some of the bones found may be of animal origin.

SISTINE CHAPEL

During the papal conclave, as the cardinals gather to elect a new pope, they are shut inside the Sistine Chapel. When the conclave gets under way in *Angels and Demons*, the drama of the occasion is heightened by the fact that the cardinals are unaware of the threat posed to them by the stolen antimatter hidden somewhere in the Vatican.

The Sistine Chapel was constructed between 1473 and 1481 under the direction of Pope Sixtus IV. Many of the finest artists of the Renaissance were employed to decorate the chapel to a magnificent standard. On the side walls, for example, are frescos by Pinturicchio, Botticelli and Rosselli, depicting on the south wall the life of Moses and on the north wall scenes from the life of Christ.

It is the ceiling frescos by Michelangelo, however, that are the most remarkable feature of the chapel, painted between 1508 and 1512 for Pope Julius II. The characters of the Old Testament, including 40 generations of Christ's ancestors, cover the ceiling and it is remarkable to consider that the artist completed the work without using assistants. Michelangelo returned to the chapel again between 1535 and 1541 to add *The Last Judgement* on the west wall. In this fresco, with Christ taking the role of judge, two groups of figures are seen either ascending to heaven and redemption or descending to hell.

In addition to providing the location for the papal conclave, the Sistine Chapel serves as the private chapel of the pope.

SECRET ARCHIVES

The Vatican Apostolic Library, also known as the Vatican Secret Archives, contains one of the world's most important collections of manuscripts and early books. It is estimated to contain 1,600,000 printed books, 8,300 incunabula (of which 65 are printed on vellum), 150,000 manuscript volumes, 100,000 prints and engravings, 300,000 coins and medals, and 20,000 objects of art. It includes, for example, the remains of the imperial library of Constantinople purchased by Pope Nicholas V in the fifteenth century, and the oldest document in the archives is the *Liber diurnus Romanorum pontificum*, which dates back to the eighth century. To accommodate the vast collection takes over 50 miles of shelving, split into over 630 sections known as fonds.

Unlike Robert Langdon, who in *Angels and Demons* is left in the Secret Archives alone and causes great upheaval, scholars who visit the Secret Archives today benefit from an index room, photocopying facilities and a computer laboratory. Around 1,500 scholars each year are permitted to study the archives from 8.30 a.m. to 1.15 p.m., Monday to Saturday, except between 16 July and 15 September, when the archive closes.

There are several documents in the archive relevant to both *Angels and Demons* and *The Da Vinci Code*. The parchment of Chinon from 1308 confirms the absolution by Pope Clement V of leading members of the Knights Templars. Despite appearing to side with the French King Philip IV, the pope could not find evidence that the Templars were heretical. The documents relating to Galileo's trial can also be found in the archives and his signature can be seen on the final part of his testimony.

SWISS GUARD

Unlike the colourfully dressed members of the Swiss Guard posing for tourist photographs at the Vatican, the guards in *Angels and Demons* are frantically engaged in looking for the antimatter hidden within the Vatican.

Pope Julius II officially founded the regiment in 1506 when he engaged Swiss mercenaries to protect himself. The newly formed force was put to the extreme test during the Sack of Rome in 1527 when Pope Clement VII was besieged – only 42 out of his contingent of 189 guards survived.

Contrary to popular myth, the uniform worn by the guardsmen today was not designed by Michelangelo. It was created in 1914 and the red, yellow and blue are the colours of the Medici family, who provided two popes: Leo X and Clement VII.

To be eligible for entry into the Swiss Guard, men must be:

- a Swiss citizen;
- between 19 and 30 years old;
- over 5 ft. 8 in. tall;
- unmarried;
- Catholic and of 'irreproachable reputation'; and
- a previous member of the Swiss armed forces.

The new recruits swear allegiance to the pope thus:

> I swear I will faithfully, loyally and honourably serve the Supreme Pontiff [reigning pope named here] and his legitimate successors, and also dedicate myself to them with all my strength, sacrificing if necessary also my life to defend them. I assume this same commitment with regard to the Sacred College of Cardinals whenever the See is vacant.

THE PANTHEON
Rome, Italy

The Pantheon in Rome is the site of the tomb of the great artist Raphael. In *Angels and Demons*, the characters Vittoria Vetra and Robert Langdon are directed to the Pantheon by a line from a poem that reads: 'Santi's earthly tomb with demon's hole'. Raphael Santi (known to us today as simply Raphael) was buried in his present tomb in the Pantheon in 1833 and the building does possess an oculus or demon's hole in the roof. Sadly for the cardinals that Vetra and Langdon are trying to save, however, they have interpreted the clue incorrectly. The tomb they are looking for is not that of Raphael himself but one he designed, and the demon's hole refers to an ossuary annexe for burying multiple family members – the location they need to visit is the Chigi Chapel in the Church of Santa Maria del Popolo.

Situated on the Piazza della Rotunda, a busy square with plenty of vantage points from which to admire the portico of the Pantheon, the huge granite columns of the church are surmounted by an inscription to Marcus Agrippa. In front of the building stands an obelisk, originally built for the pharaoh Rameses II at the temple to the god Ra at Heliopolis in Egypt. Brought to Rome for the temple of Isis, the obelisk was moved to its present location in 1711. What Sophie and Langdon do not realise as they leave the Pantheon is how many more obelisks they will encounter on their path around Rome. In fact, any visitor to Rome can see more standing obelisks than are left in the whole of Egypt, thanks to the avid collection of the Roman Empire, when it controlled Egypt, of these impressive artefacts.

GETTING THERE

Nearest Bus Routes: 64, 70, 75, 119

OPENING HOURS
Monday–Saturday 8.30 a.m. to 7.30 p.m.
Sunday 9 a.m. to 6 p.m.
Holidays 9 a.m. to 1 p.m.
Admission: free

CHURCH OF SANTA MARIA AD MARTYRS

Converted into the Church of Santa Maria ad Martyrs in AD 609, the Pantheon is the best-preserved ancient Roman building. The structure visible today was built around AD 120 by the Emperor Hadrian as a temple to the many gods of Rome. The niches lining the inside of the circular building would originally have housed statues of the gods.

The building is constructed with perfect symmetry, with the height and diameter both being 43 metres. In the centre of the domed roof, there is a nine-metre skylight called the oculus. This illuminates the interior of the building, which has no other windows, and means that if you visit on a rainy day, you must be prepared to get wet. Originally, the roof was lined with bronze but this was taken and melted down for other purposes, including Bernini's baldachin in the Vatican.

In addition to Raphael's tomb, the Pantheon is also the resting place of two of Italy's kings, Vittorio Emanuele II and Umberto I.

OCULUS

The Pantheon was the first pagan temple to be converted into a church when it was consecrated as the Church of Santa Maria ad Martyrs in AD 609. It was dedicated to Christian martyrs and Pope Boniface IV arranged for the bodies of many Christians killed for their faith to be brought to the site and re-buried. A tradition holds that a horde of demons rose up through the hole in the roof as the church was being dedicated. This demon's hole is the cause of the mistake made by Vittoria Vetra and Robert Langdon over where they should be searching.

SANTA MARIA DEL POPOLO
Rome, Italy

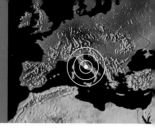

The Piazza del Popolo is a large elliptical space dominated by an Egyptian obelisk originally carved for the pharaoh Ramses II and erected in its current location in 1589. During the dominance of Rome by a later warrior leader, Napoleon Bonaparte, the carved Egyptian-style lions surrounding the base of the obelisk were added.

The Church of Santa Maria del Popolo occupies a space at the northern end (not the south-east corner as described in *Angels and Demons*) of the piazza that has had a number of different uses over the centuries. In the days of ancient Rome, the site was used for the tombs of the Domitia family and it was believed that the body or ashes of the Emperor Nero had been buried there. When Pope Paschal II had the ground consecrated in AD 1099, the unloved Nero's remains were supposedly thrown into the River Tiber.

The church was erected by public subscription by Paschal II, which led to its name, Santa Maria del Popolo (of the people). A later re-building on the orders of Pope Sixtus IV, with the façade by Andrea Bregno, was an early example of Renaissance architecture. Gianlorenzo Bernini, who amended the façade and remodelled the interior, made further alterations in the seventeenth century.

As you enter the church by the main door, there is a macabre monument to the architect Gisleni, who designed his own tomb. The skeleton of Gisleni is wrapped in a shroud and bears the inscription, 'Neither alive in this world nor dead in the next'.

GETTING THERE

Nearest Metro: Flaminio

OPENING HOURS
Monday–Saturday 7 a.m. to 12 p.m.; 4 p.m. to 7 p.m.
Sunday 8 a.m. to 1.30 p.m.; 4.30 p.m. to 7.00 p.m.
Admission: free

To the right of the entrance is the Rovere Chapel, which has a fresco of the nativity by Pinturicchio in addition to tombs of the Rovere family. In the Costa Chapel are the tombs of Giovanni Borgia (one of Pope Alexander VI's sons) and Vannozza Cattanei, his mother and the long-term mistress of the pope.

There are more Pinturicchio frescos in the vault, including *Sybils*, *Evangelists* and *Doctors of the Church*. Behind the altar are the tombs by Andrea Sansovino of cardinals Ascanio Sforza and Girolamo Basso della Rovere that were completed in 1509 and depict the cardinals in an unusual pose, leaning against the sarcophagus as though sleeping.

In the apse, the church also contains the oldest stained-glass windows in Rome, by the French artist Guillaume de Marcillat, which depict the life of Christ and the Virgin Mary. An icon of the Virgin is enshrined at the high altar and is known as the *Madonna del Popolo*.

In the Cerasi Chapel are two

masterpieces by Caravaggio: *The Crucifixion of St Peter* and *Paul on the Road to Damascus.* These pictures both have the main figures at the front of the composition and are examples of his technique of chiaroscuro – seeming to illuminate the figures against a darker background. The chapel also contains a painting by Annibale Carracci, *The Assumption of the Virgin.*

Despite all the fine Renaissance and Baroque details contained in the church, you are likely to find most visitors clustered at the Chigi Chapel, situated to the left of the entrance.

The Chigi Chapel is the scene of the discovery of the first murdered cardinal in *Angels and Demons* and represents the first altar of science, namely earth.

HABAKKUK AND THE ANGEL

The Old Testament prophet Habakkuk was visited by an angel who instructed him to visit Daniel in the lions' den. This story is told in Bel and the Dragon, a work that is not contained in the Book of Habakkuk in the Bible.

Habakkuk is supposed to have explained to the angel that he could not visit Daniel in Babylon and bring him food because he did not know the way to the city. The angel then lifted Habakkuk up by the hair and carried him there. In

the sculpture, which is opposite a statue of Daniel, Bernini depicts the moment when the angel is about to lift Habakkuk up.

Robert Langdon and Vittoria Vetra deduce that Bernini is the artist whose work will lead them to the altars of science that they need to visit to try and save the remaining cardinals. It is the direction in which the angel is pointing that gives the clue to the next location on their quest.

CHIGI CHAPEL

The authorities at the Church of Santa Maria del Popolo may be getting weary of the additional attention focused on this chapel because of its association with Dan Brown's *Angels and Demons*. Dan Brown has his protagonists visiting the church when it is under reconstruction and they struggle to locate the correct chapel. On the author's visit to the church, the Chigi Chapel was the only part of the building heavily obscured with scaffolding and plastic sheeting. Nevertheless, it is well worth spending time admiring the works of art within the chapel.

The Chigi Chapel was commissioned by Agostino Chigi, a banker, and designed by Raphael. Both Agostino and his brother Sigismondo are buried in the chapel beneath unusual pyramid-shaped tombs. Raphael designed the mosaics, showing God as the creator, and the statues of the prophets Jonah and Elias that were executed by Lorenzetto.

After Raphael's death in 1520, other artists carried out the execution of his designs. During the papacy of the Chigi pope Alexander VII, for example, Bernini was given the task of completing the chapel in addition to his other work on the church. There are two statue niches containing works by Bernini: *Daniel in the Lions' Den* and *Habakkuk and the Angel*.

Sebastiano del Piombo painted the *Birth of the Virgin* as the altarpiece. The original surname of Sebastiano was Luciani (a name he shares with Albino Luciani, the later Pope John Paul I), the 'del Piombo' was adopted after he was given the job of sealer of briefs by Pope Clement VII.

One feature that is prominent throughout the chapel is the coat of arms of the Chigi family: six hills or mountains arranged in a pyramid shape, surmounted by a star.

OSSUARY

In the floor of the Chigi Chapel is a marble slab that covers the entrance to the ossuary annexe where the remains of the Chigi family are buried.

This is the structure referred to in *Angels and Demons* as the 'oculus' or 'demon's hole' and is actually a feature of many chapels at the time. The figure of death, portrayed as a skeleton, could sometimes adopt the role of a *vitae testimonium*, a witness to life rather than the destroyer of the flesh. When the skeleton holds family crests and emblems, it is immortalising the name of the family and is enveloped in noble livery.

It is within the ossuary annexe that the body of the asphyxiated cardinal has been buried up to his waist in the earth beneath the tomb.

SANTA MARIA DELLA VITTORIA
Rome, Italy

Although one of the nearest metro stations to the church is Barberini, do not be confused by the description in *Angels and Demons* which locates it in the Piazza Barberini. You enter the church from Via Septembre XX and as soon as you cross the threshold the opulence of the interior becomes apparent. The whole church is decorated in a lavish style and the ceilings are covered with frescos depicting, among other themes, the ascent of St Paul into heaven.

For Robert Langdon and Vittoria Vetra, the ceiling details would presumably have been obscured by the smoke rising from the blaze that had been lit, representing the element of fire. The victim of the bonfire is a cardinal who is suspended high up in the church and who, despite their efforts, Robert and Vittoria are unable to save.

There was a real fire at the church in 1833 that destroyed the original high altar and the painting of Santa Maria della Vittoria, now replaced with a copy. The original had been brought to Rome after the battle of the White Mountain near Prague in the seventeenth century. A chaplain had hung an image of the Virgin Mary around his neck that was credited with granting success to the Catholic League forces and it was this painting that was installed in the newly constructed church, which in turn took its name from the famous victory.

The façade of the church was designed by Giovanni Battista Soria and the building was funded by Cardinal Borghese. Two of the chapels on the right-hand side of the church contain carved statue groups, one by Balzico re-creates

GETTING THERE

Nearest Metro: Republica or Barberini

OPENING HOURS
Monday–Saturday 7 a.m. to 12 p.m.;
3.30 p.m. to 7 p.m.
Sunday 8.15 a.m. to 10 a.m.; 3.30 p.m.
to 6 p.m.
Admission: free

the scene of the Virgin giving the scapular to St Simon Stock. Nearer to the high altar, the piece by Domenico Guidi is *The Dream of St Joseph*. Beautiful as these two sculptures are, the masterpiece in the church is the *Ecstasy of St Teresa* that is in the Cornaro Chapel to the left of the high altar.

Bernini captured the moment when St Teresa had a vision of a meeting with an angel. While viewing the *Ecstasy of St Teresa*, it is possible to switch on additional lights to illuminate the statue. During the author's visit, this required the insertion of a 50 euro cent coin – the effect is very well worth the trouble of acquiring the change.

On either side of the main sculpture, there are carved re-creations of opera boxes, from which prominent members of the Cornaro family appear to be observing events below.

THE ECSTASY OF ST TERESA

St Teresa of Avila was a nun who lived from 1515 to 1582 and was canonised in 1622. In 1970, she was granted the additional honour of being the first woman to be created a doctor of the church. Teresa joined a Carmelite convent and became renowned for her mental prayer. She is seen as a leading example of the contemplative life and her writings are still revered today.

Teresa suffered from poor health for much of her life and had mystical visions, which she described in her work. The particular moment captured so sensitively by Bernini in his sculpture is that when an angel pierced her with a dart or arrow of divine love. The spiritual or bodily pain that was caused by the dart is vividly captured in her account of the vision:

> He appeared to be one of the highest types of angel who seem to be all afire . . . In his hands I saw a long golden spear and at the end of the iron tip I seemed to see a point of fire. With this he seemed to pierce my heart several times so that it penetrated my entrails . . . The pain was so sharp that it made me utter several moans; and so excessive was the sweetness caused me by the intense pain that one can never wish to lose it.

An angel who is 'afire' seems to be a reference to a seraph, often painted red to denote the connection with fire.

The expression on the face of St Teresa that Bernini carved seems to suggest an experience more pleasurable than painful. It has been speculated by many people, including Robert Langdon, that it was a sexual experience.

The skill with which the gleaming white marble has been carved into the flowing folds of the clothing shows Bernini's talent to its fullest extent. There is a hidden source of natural light that is channelled onto the golden rays behind the two figures.

In the context of *Angels and Demons*, the statue is important literally as a pointer, using the tip of the angel's spear to indicate the next location or altar of science.

PIAZZA NAVONA
Rome, Italy

Originally the site of a stadium built by the Emperor Domitian, the piazza retains the dramatic proportions of the racetrack to which Romans flocked in the first century AD. The almost 300-metre-long piazza is broken up by three fountains and the *Fountain of the Four Rivers* is the central monument. This is where Robert Langdon grapples with the Hassassin in his attempt to save Cardinal Baggia from drowning.

One of the other two fountains in the Piazza Navona, the Fountain of the Moor at the southern end of the piazza, is partly the work of Bernini. The third fountain portrays Neptune grappling with an octopus, among an imaginative collection of sea creatures.

One of the other main features of the Piazza Navona is the Church of Sant'Agnese in Agone, designed by the architect Borromini, who was a great rival of Bernini. Tradition has it that the angels of the façade of the Church of Sant'Agnese are deliberately looking away from the fountain to snub Bernini, while one of the characters on the fountain has its head covered to shield it from the horror of viewing the church. In actual fact, the figure on the fountain with his head covered represents the River Nile, the source of which was unknown at the time the fountain was constructed, thus the head is concealed.

The piazza is a lively place and it is enjoyable to spend time at the many cafés and restaurants or admiring the work of artists who do portraits of tourists.

GETTING THERE

The piazza is not located near any of Rome's metro stations, although it is served by various bus routes: 64, 87, 116 and 116T. It is also not far from Castel Sant'Angelo or the Vatican and it is quite possible to stroll to the piazza from either of these locations.

PIAZZA NAVONA

The elongated space of the Piazza Navona is the location for the fourth altar of science in Robert Langdon's quest around the city of Rome. Bernini's *Fountain of the Four Rivers* in the centre of the piazza provides the element of water that completes the sequence: earth, air, fire and water.

FOUNTAIN OF THE FOUR RIVERS

Constructed between 1648 and 1651, the *Fountain of the Four Rivers* is mostly the work of students of Bernini, although designed by the great man himself. It is seen as one of the finest fountains in Rome and one of Bernini's major works of art.

The four rivers, each portrayed

by a human figure at the corners of the sculpture, represent the main rivers from each of the four continents known about at the time. These are the Danube, Nile, Ganges and River Plate. There is an additional allegorical connection to the four rivers that run from the Garden of Eden in the biblical story. Perched on top of the marble fountain is a massive granite obelisk, which was carved for the Emperor Domitian in around AD 81 and moved to its current location when the fountain was constructed.

By designing the fountain to support the obelisk on arches, Bernini has almost given the appearance that the obelisk is floating. The patron of the construction, Pope Innocent X, has his family crest and the family symbol of the dove on top of the obelisk. In *Angels and Demons,* it is the direction in which this dove is facing that leads Robert Langdon to the location of the Illuminati lair.

A story recounted by tour guides, arising from the rivalry between Bernini and Borromini, is that the latter spread rumours that the obelisk was unsafe. To demonstrate that this was nonsense, Bernini climbed the obelisk, attached a piece of string to it and tied the other end to one of the buildings in the piazza. Could this be the story that inspired Dan Brown to credit Robert Langdon with scaling the fountain?

CONSTANTINE I (THE GREAT)

One of the most controversial issues within *The Da Vinci Code* is the portrayal of the Roman Emperor Constantine I as the author of lies and deceits perpetrated by the Church and the destroyer of the sacred feminine. Robert Langdon is given the task of explaining to Sophie that, 'The Priory [of Sion] believes that Constantine and his male successors successfully converted the world from matriarchal paganism to patriarchal Christianity . . .'

The role of Constantine in choosing Christianity as the religion of the Roman Empire and his own deathbed conversion is portrayed in the novel in a negative way. Many of Dan Brown's detractors have highlighted the interpretation of Constantine's impact on Christianity as one of the main weaknesses of *The Da Vinci Code*. Brown credits Constantine with concealing the relationship between Jesus and Mary Magdalene, which is the most incendiary part of the novel for those who hold traditional beliefs. To understand why this Roman emperor is still causing debate so long after his death we need to look at what is known about him.

At the beginning of his biography of Constantine, Michael Grant sagely points out that, 'Impartiality, in the later Roman empire, was not generally required of a "historian".' Our knowledge of Constantine is mainly limited to artefacts such as coins and to written evidence from contemporary and later writers. These were usually Christian admirers whose gratitude to him for sanctioning their religion blinds them to many of his faults. We have to be careful in consequence not to believe that we completely understand the emperor or can be entirely sure of all aspects of his story. In addition, it should be understood that Constantine was an extremely complex character.

Flavius Valerius Constantinus was the illegitimate son of Constantius Chlorus. He was born around AD 273. At the age of about 20, he must have been delighted when his father was appointed caesar, or assistant emperor, to Emperor Maximian, who controlled the western empire, while the emperor who had particular care for the eastern empire, Diocletian, took Galerius to be his junior co-ruler. This rule by two emperors, or augusti, with the assistance of two caesars, was known as the Tetrarchy.

One of Constantius's tasks was to return Britain to the empire, since at that time it was being ruled as an independent state by a rebel administration. Launching a successful invasion in 297, Constantius ended the ten-year separation and went on to have success against German troublemakers. Elsewhere, his fellow caesar, Galerius, and Emperor Diocletian were fighting enemies in the east.

Diocletian, enthusiastically supported by Galerius, wished to bring unity to the empire by ensuring that the traditional gods were worshipped and around 297 ordered that all administrators and soldiers should make sacrifice to these gods on pain of dismissal.

The by now large Christian minority found such sacrifice repugnant. Six years later, an edict ordered the destruction of churches and the scriptures. The clergy were arrested and released only after a pagan sacrifice was made. In April 304, all Christians were ordered to sacrifice or die. While strictly speaking the edict was empire-wide, it had virtually no impact in the west, since it was not generally enforced. In the east, however, Galerius especially became an enthusiastic anti-Christian zealot and many were undoubtedly killed as a result of the policy.

A year later, Diocletian, by now in poor health, persuaded Maximian to abdicate simultaneously with him and leave the empire to their caesars. Galerius and Constantius became the emperors and both then appointed caesars to assist them. Significantly, they both had ambitious adult sons, neither of whom was chosen for elevation to this rank.

This could only lead to trouble.

The disappointed Constantine joined his father, who was planning a campaign against the Picts in what is now Scotland. It was successful but Constantius died at York in 306. Constantine immediately claimed that his father had appointed him

senior emperor in the west and the army supported him enthusiastically. This did not please the other rulers. As a consequence, until the year 313, civil wars were fought as rivals battled for supremacy. Constantine was an unscrupulous negotiator and politician, as well as a good general, and one by one the others died or were killed.

In the year 312, Constantine entered Italy to confront his rival, Emperor Maxentius, and was successful in the north. Advancing on Rome, he expected to lay siege to the city but Maxentius preferred to risk a pitched battle and the armies met just across the Milvian Bridge. Constantine ordered his troops to carry banners bearing what some argue is a Christian symbol and he won the day. When Maxentius's army tried to scramble back into the city, the bridge collapsed and the emperor was drowned. The victor is said to have entered the city carrying his enemy's head on a spear.

Lactantius, who had converted to Christianity and was favoured by Constantine, states that before the Battle of Milvian Bridge the emperor had a vision that told him to have the monogram symbol called the Chi-rho, for Christ, placed on his soldiers' shields. Another Christian, Eusebius of Caesarea, had a version that his emperor had seen a cross of light in the sky, above the sun, bearing the inscription CONQUER BY THIS, and the whole army having seen it were inspired by the divine intervention. It should be pointed out that Eusebius, particularly, is a questionable source of information. Jacob Burckhardt, the celebrated Swiss historian, said that Eusebius was the 'first thoroughly dishonest historian of antiquity'.

Constantine's last rival was Licinius and he invaded his territory in 316, after deliberately provoking a quarrel and weakening his co-emperor. Licinius believed, perhaps with some justification, that the Christians within his part of the empire were undermining him on behalf of Constantine, who was advertising himself as their great supporter. The fact that Constantine's mother Helen was known to be a Christian also swayed support his way. The worried Licinius tried to protect himself by expelling Christians from the civil service and the military but he did not persecute them as Galerius and Diocletian had done until he had cause to believe that some bishops were traitors to him. They were executed and their churches razed to the ground.

Constantine, the avenger, invaded his territory again and Licinius was deposed, although his life was spared as a sign of Constantine's mercy. Yet only the next year Licinius was put to death and at the same time his nine-year-old son was also killed. Not even his apologists could reasonably argue that Constantine was not unscrupulous when he felt the need to safeguard his own interests. Rather like a cuckoo in a nest, he had eventually eliminated his weaker rivals and now he had the whole empire to himself.

Remembering that such a vast territory had always been at risk from rebellion or invasion in the past – which is why the shrewd Diocletian had instituted the Tetrarchy – Constantine appointed his son Crispus, from his first marriage, as caesar. But Crispus's reign was to end violently several years later when he was executed on his own father's orders. It is said that Constantine's second wife, Fausta, had fallen in love with her young stepson but was rejected by him and had her revenge by accusing him of gross impropriety, after which Constantine had him killed. Fausta had sons of her own and no doubt harboured ambitions for their future. Shortly afterwards, perhaps suspecting that he had been duped, the emperor ordered that his wife should be suffocated in a steam bath. Constantine may have been the first 'Christian' emperor but he also had the distinction of being one who had both a son and a wife killed.

Constantine realised that while religion could be a divisive force it could also be used to unify the disparate parts of his large empire. He was personally attracted to the cult of the sun, Sol, and issued coins with this deity on the reverse. As a soldier, he must also have been aware of the cult of Mithras, born on 25 December, who was highly popular with the military. But, always the pragmatist, Constantine also recognised that the Christians had a well-established communication system and a hierarchy that, despite sectarian squabbling, knitted them together in a way that paganism, with all its forms of worship and multitude of gods, could not. Constantine, therefore, threw his weight behind the Christians.

In his *History of Rome*, Max Cary explains that by this time 'Christianity was still a long way from being the universal religion of the Roman Empire'. He continues: 'Yet they had planted their propaganda cells in every province; their clergy had constituted itself into a powerful aristocracy; above all, they had captured a high proportion of the more thoughtful inhabitants of the empire.' The opportunist emperor seized the chance of using this hierarchy to control a state religion just as he used the military to control the lives of his subjects.

Constantine acted as chairman at important meetings of the Christian leaders and convened the Council of Nicaea, where it was decided which doctrines were to be orthodoxy and which were to be condemned as heresy. He was confident enough to lecture on church affairs, although he delayed his own baptism until he realised that he was at death's door. Receiving baptism, of course, washed away all the sins he had committed during his life and he could enter heaven's portal as innocent as a tiny child. It also took him some years to decide to relinquish the traditional pagan title assumed by his predecessors in office, Supreme Pontiff (*Pontifex Maximus*), which was then assumed by successive popes and is still used today.

Constantine confiscated the riches of pagan temples and filled his coffers with the profits. Some of this wealth was spent on strengthening and reorganising elements of the army. He also raised levels of taxes, which even his Christian apologists remarked upon. His mother, who has become known as St Helena, a woman of very obscure birth but many legends, helped to spend much of her son's wealth by founding religious establishments and is reputed to have journeyed to Jerusalem, where she claimed to have discovered the True Cross with divine help.

Constantine himself founded a new capital city on an old Greek site called Byzantium, renaming it Constantinople (Constantine's city) in 330. This is now Istanbul, Turkey. By now, though still calling itself the Roman Republic, the empire no longer had many features distinguishing it from a complete autocracy.

On his death in 337, Constantine had intended that the empire should be divided among his surviving sons – Constans, Constantius II and Constantine II – and nephews Hannibalianus and Delmatius – to rule cooperatively. Soon only the sons survived, all other adult male members of the family were murdered. Then his sons began disputes and civil wars. Attempted usurpations arose which resulted in Constantius II becoming sole emperor in 350. Though the western half of the empire was subject to complex irresistible pressures, including barbarian incursions and internal disunity to which it finally succumbed, the eastern (Byzantine) empire continued with varying success for over a thousand years more.

While Constantine himself led a life far from our ideas of a benevolent Christian ruler, it is certainly true that his actions shaped the progress of the early Church. In the introduction to *The Da Vinci Code,* Dan Brown asserts that: 'All descriptions of artwork, architecture, documents and secret rituals in this novel are accurate'; however, he does not claim that every historical detail is correct. In questioning his interpretation of events such as the Council of Nicaea, many opponents of Brown's have sought to cast doubt on other aspects of the book's contents. Not so much 'conquer by this' as 'contest by this'.

Mosaic of Constantine the Great in Hagia Sophia, Istanbul.

243

LEONARDO DA VINCI

ANALYSING THE EVIDENCE

The first of two main background themes contained within Dan Brown's *The Da Vinci Code* is that a secret bloodline of the house of David exists and was supposedly perpetuated through the union of Jesus Christ with Mary Magdalene. The second theme, and the one that gives the book its title, is that Leonardo da Vinci somehow left codified messages pertaining to the bloodline within his incredible works of art.

Leonardo da Vinci was a remarkable man. His works still generate amazement and admiration among all who gaze upon them. But did he really hide cryptic clues to the so-called holy bloodline within his paintings?

In their book *The Templar Revelation*, Clive Prince and Lynn Picknett look at two of Leonardo's most famous works and argue that both hold distinct and definite motifs. This in turn leads the authors to conclude that Leonardo did indeed codify these particular works. The two works in question are *The Last Supper* and *The Madonna of the Rocks* (the first version in the Louvre, which is sometimes referred to as *The Virgin of the Rocks*).

It would take an entire book, or two, to properly analyse the paintings in question. Here, we will take a look at the two paintings mentioned and consider the main body of evidence used to support this theory.

THE LAST SUPPER

The *Last Supper* is a truly breathtaking piece of work. Executed between 1494 and 1498, this painting is actually a mural upon a wall in the refectory of the Convent of Santa Maria delle Grazie in Milan, Italy. It's a most remarkable piece, with a striking three-dimensional quality. It captures a split second in time: the moment that Jesus, at the last supper of the title, tells his followers that one amongst them will betray him. The representation of expressions, movement and anatomy within the work is close to perfection.

In *The Templar Revelation* by Prince and Picknett, the authors claim that certain features of *The Last Supper* are clues to a secret known by Leonardo.

The Convent of Santa Maria delle Grazie where *The Last Supper* is housed.

The mural on the refectory wall of the Convent of Santa Maria delle Grazie.

THE CHALICE

The first anomaly that should be noted is actually something that is missing from the picture: there is no central cup or chalice upon the table of *The Last Supper*. Most other depictions of this scene show a central receptacle, one that has gone on to play the main role in Holy Grail lore as the cup that held the blood of Christ at the Crucifixion. In Leonardo's depiction, we see several small glasses but no central grail.

THE CENTRAL THEME

If we look to the middle of the piece, it's interesting to note that the two central characters of Jesus and St John (sometimes known as the Younger or the Beloved) are leaning away from each other at very similar angles – not only that

but their clothes are almost mirror images of each other's apparel. One is wearing a blue cloak and a red robe, the other a red cloak and a blue robe. It is this character leaning away from Jesus that has attracted most speculation. In *The Templar Revelation*, Prince and Picknett claim that far from being St John, the person we are seeing is in fact a woman. Their interpretation is that this character is Mary Magdalene and that Leonardo has included her here to represent both the sacred feminine and to attest to the supposed fact, as postulated in *The Holy Blood and the Holy Grail* by Baigent, Lincoln and Leigh, that Jesus and Mary were actually married. Furthermore, Prince and Picknett believe that the V shape formed by the two central characters leaning away from each other also represents the sacred feminine, a feature picked up by Dan Brown in *The Da Vinci Code*.

THE DISEMBODIED HAND

To the left of the strange feminine-looking character, as we look, is the figure of St Peter with his left hand seemingly resting on the shoulder and across the neck of the John/ Mary figure. Prince and Picknett claim that this is a threatening gesture and provides more evidence that it is Mary Magdalene who is represented in the mural. From the Gnostic gospel of Mary Magdalene we learn that Mary and Peter were at odds with each other over the teachings of Christ and over the affections he seems to have bestowed upon Mary above the other disciples.

Also of note is the so-called 'disembodied hand'. If you look slightly to the left and below the figure of Peter, you will notice at table height a hand clutching what seems to be a dagger or knife of some sort. This is the so-called disembodied hand, which doesn't seem to belong

to any of those visible in the picture. However, in the restored version of the mural (started in 1979 and finished in 1999 by Pinin Brambilla Barcilon, amid much controversy), it appears as though the hand could belong to Peter, although this is not completely clear.

LEONARDO'S SELF-PORTRAIT

To the right of the central theme, there are three characters who seem to be arguing with one another and gesticulating towards Jesus. The second to last person here is generally accepted to be a self-portrait of Leonardo as St Thaddeus (also known as St Jude). There is a precedent for this. In his earlier work *The Adoration of the Magi*, Leonardo painted himself into the work on the far right of the piece, also looking away from the central holy scene. Is this act of looking away another clue to the real feelings of Leonardo towards the holy family and the Church?

THE MADONNA OF THE ROCKS

C onfusingly, there are two versions of this painting, which is also known as *The Virgin of the Rocks*. The first version now hangs in the Grand Gallery of the Louvre in Paris (see opposite), while the second is displayed in London's National Gallery (see below). In *The Da Vinci Code*, it is the first version that Sophie Neveu single-handedly lifts off the wall and threatens to damage while attempting to make good her escape from the Louvre.

The original commission for this work was made by the Confraternity of the Immaculate Conception in 1483, who wished it to be the centrepiece of a trio of paintings for their altar in the chapel of the Church of San Francesco Grande in Milan.

However, it seems that all did not go to plan. The confraternity had originally specified the necessary dimensions of the work to Leonardo, as they already had the frame in which they intended to hang the finished piece. The theme that the painting was commissioned to depict was an event found in Christian legend but not in the published gospels. This event was a supposed meeting between the holy family and an infant John the Baptist in a cave during the flight into Egypt. The archangel Uriel protects John the Baptist and the whole story seems to have been intended as a justification for the later baptism of Jesus by John, an event not at all necessary for a sinless Jesus. In this meeting, Jesus confers upon John the authority to baptise him in later life. The confraternity were horrified at the finished work, refusing to pay Leonardo for the painting, and the whole sorry event ended in a very acrimonious lawsuit that dragged on for some 20 years.

So why would the confraternity have been so aghast at the depictions within the painting? According to Prince and Picknett, there are some striking elements within the piece that bear closer scrutiny. The most obvious problem you encounter when looking at this masterpiece is who is John and who is Jesus? The two children sit across from each other, with the infant next to the Virgin Mary being blessed by the child under Uriel's protection. There is no obvious way of telling who is who and many have speculated that it is John and not Jesus who is bestowing the blessing, making John the pre-eminent infant figure. There also seems to be some deliberate placement of the hands of both the Virgin

mother and of Uriel. The Virgin's left hand hovers, some say menacingly, above the head of the infant on the right of the scene, while the archangel Uriel makes a pointing gesture below the Virgin's hand in the direction of the other child. The authors of *The Templar Revelation* postulate that this placement of the hands does indeed signal the fact that the child on the right, the one doing the blessing, is John. The theory goes that the hand of Mary hovers, grasping an invisible head, whilst the outstretched finger of Uriel appears exactly where an invisible throat would be, cutting across it. This, they argue, is a codified depiction of the future beheading of John the Baptist and so ties the infant on the right to the character of John. It is an interesting and intriguing theory that demands more research from art historians.

LEONARDO: SAINT OR SINNER?

Leonardo da Vinci was without question a genius: a man whose imagination and creative skill were leagues ahead of his contemporaries and whose processes of thought were centuries ahead of his time.

There is no doubt that a mind such as Leonardo's *could* have conjured up the supposed clues that he is claimed to have hidden within his work but dispute still rages over whether or not this was something he *would* have actually done. For example, as described, the figure to the left of Jesus (as we look) in *The Last Supper* that some believe to be Mary Magdalene would appear to have definite feminine features and characteristics. But Leonardo painted many individuals in an asexual manner. That is, many of his figures can be quite feminine even though they are undoubtedly meant to depict male characters. A classic example of this is the wonderful painting of John the Baptist that Leonardo executed towards the end of his life (see page opposite). This figure has soft feminine lines and, facially at least, is strikingly asexual in its features. Another example is the *Mona Lisa*. With no eyebrows and that enigmatic smile, if one were to remove the long feminine hair from the *Mona Lisa*, one would be left with a distinctly asexual-looking face.

What we can be certain of is that Leonardo's main commissions were religious in nature and the Church was one of his main employers. For him to be seen as openly heretical would, therefore, have been a very dangerous game to play.

The only way to decide on these matters is to actually stand in front of the works in question and make your mind up for yourself. Whether or not he was a heretic, a member of a clandestine secret order, or just a man out of time, one thing is for certain – his work will continue to bring joy and be a marvel to behold.

SIR ISAAC NEWTON

The monument to Sir Isaac Newton in London's Westminster Abbey proves to be a vital location in *The Da Vinci Code* as Robert Langdon and Sophie Neveu attempt to solve the riddles left for them by her grandfather.

Newton is also named as one of the Grand Masters of the Priory of Sion, supposedly holding the position from 1691 to 1727. This would make Newton a predecessor of Sophie's grandfather Jacques Saunière, the museum curator whose death has sparked the chain of events in the novel. The Priory of Sion is the secret organisation, thought to have been protecting a great secret through centuries, that Dan Brown uses to provide a backdrop to the quest for the Holy Grail.

Using a clue that has caused them some confusion, Robert and Sophie are searching for a tomb that matches the description: 'In London lies a knight a Pope interred'. Rather than a Roman Catholic pope, it turns out to be Alexander Pope, friend and admirer of Sir Isaac Newton, Newton himself being the knight to whom the riddle refers.

The monument to Sir Isaac Newton is made of marble and was carved by Michael Rysbrack to celebrate some of Newton's great achievements. A relief panel shows boys using some instruments critical to Newton's optical discoveries: a prism and a telescope. Newton himself has been carved in a reclining position, leaning on a pile of his most famous books, including the *Philosophia naturalis principia mathematica* (The Mathematical Principles of Natural Philosophy) commonly known as the *Principia*. In the background of the design is a pyramid to which is attached a globe bearing the signs of the zodiac.

In popular culture, Sir Isaac

Newton is portrayed as discovering the concept of gravity after an apple fell on his lap while he sat in his garden. In *The Da Vinci Code*, Dan Brown uses the word 'apple' as the answer to the cryptex riddle associated with Newton. The scope of the discoveries made by Newton and his impact on the scientific advances made in the seventeenth century are much broader than this superficial analysis suggests.

The young Isaac Newton had a troubled childhood; his father died before he was born and after his mother remarried she moved away, leaving him in the care of his grandmother. His education was interrupted as a result of his family circumstances but eventually his abilities were recognised and he went to Trinity College, Cambridge.

At this time, the discoveries of scientists such as Copernicus and Galileo were still not fully accepted and the geocentric, i.e. earth-centred, model of the universe was still on the curriculum. At some stage in his studies, Newton began to question the classical version of astronomy, dominated by the work of Aristotle and Plato, and to gain an interest in the new theories. Some notes that he wrote in 1664 contained the line: 'Plato is my friend, Aristotle is my friend, but my best friend is truth.'

His early work in mathematics formed the basis of the fundamental theorem of calculus and was described in *De methodis serierum et fluxionum* (On the Methods of Series and Fluxions). As a Fellow of Trinity College, he lectured on the optical discoveries he had made and was invited to give a paper to the Royal Society on light and colours.

As he continued to study planetary motions, he met the astronomer Edmond Halley, who encouraged him to publish his work on dynamics. Shortly afterwards *De motu corporum in gyrum* (On the Motion of Bodies in an Orbit) was produced and this work was then expanded and updated into the *Principia*. The *Principia* contained Newton's three laws of motion, still familiar to schoolchildren today, and the law of universal gravitation.

Newton was a Protestant, albeit an unusual one, and he spent time interpreting the prophesies of the prophet Daniel. These studies were published after his death as *Observations upon the Prophesies of Daniel and the Apocalypse of St John*. He was also interested in the science of alchemy, the notion that one compound could be changed into another by the alteration of its constituent elements. Newton devoted considerable time to his alchemical studies and he collected and copied documents in the Hermetic tradition.

In 1696, he was appointed to the lucrative position of Warden of the Mint and moved to London, where he took his duties seriously and was actively involved in preventing counterfeit coins being circulated.

His international reputation as a scientist and his position as president of the Royal Society gave him a unique place in the British social hierarchy. His great work *Opticks* was published in 1704 and in 1705 he was knighted by Queen Anne, the first scientist to receive this honour.

When Newton died in 1727, his importance was acknowledged by his state funeral and burial in Westminster Abbey. The monument described above to mark his achievements was completed in 1731.

William Blake's homage to Newton.

FRANÇOIS-BÉRENGER SAUNIÈRE

F rançois-Bérenger Saunière was born on 11 April 1852 in the small village of Montazels in the Languedoc. His parents were Marguerite and Joseph Saunière and his father had at one time been mayor of the town.

The eldest of seven children, Saunière was a strong athletic character with a large frame. He entered the seminary at Carcassonne in 1874 and was ordained as priest in June of 1879. One of his first posts was as the priest of the small village of Alet-les-Bains from 1879 to 1882. He then moved on to the equally tiny village of Clat, where he stayed until 1885.

Up until this point, Saunière was just a humble priest serving the small communities in which he lived but things would change dramatically when he was appointed as priest of the hamlet of Rennes-le-Château in 1885. Saunière's anti-republican tendencies came to the fore and he became very outspoken in his support for the French monarchy. He voiced his views from the pulpit and as a result was asked by the Church authorities to leave the diocese in December 1885. In July 1886, however, he was reinstated due to popular demand from the villagers of Rennes-le-Château.

It is in Rennes-le-Château that Bérenger Saunière became embroiled in a mystery that has echoed down to the present day

257

Saunière's birthplace in the village of Montazels, close to Rennes-le-Château.

through books such as *The Holy Blood and the Holy Grail* and, more recently, *The Da Vinci Code*. Although not directly mentioned in *The Da Vinci Code*, it would appear that Dan Brown is making reference to Bérenger Saunière with the character of Jacques Saunière, the Grand Master of the Priory of Sion who is murdered in the Louvre early in the novel.

During his stay in Rennes-le-Château, Saunière embarked on an ambitious programme of renovations to his church and presbytery, and he spent much more money than he received in his small income from the Church. Speculation has since raged about the secret source of his wealth, and tales of treasure, holy bloodlines and much else have grown up around this mysterious priest and his activities at this small French village. Like any mystery that is so far removed in time, most of this is pure speculation. Recent research has shown that Saunière was involved in the dubious act of trafficking masses, where he would charge for the saying of mass on behalf of an individual. It seems that Saunière had taken adverts out in local and national papers to advertise this service and that much of his mysterious wealth may well have come from this source.

Saunière had an ambiguous relationship with his housekeeper, Marie

Denarnaud, living with her family when he first arrived and then supposedly imparting his secrets to Marie alone before his death. How much of Saunière's wealth was down to the much-written-about 'secret' and how much can be accredited to the trafficking in masses, one can only guess at.

Saunière died on 22 January 1917 after suffering a heart attack on 17 January. He was buried in the ancient churchyard at Rennes-le-Château, with his faithful housekeeper, Marie, being buried beside him when she died in 1953. The residents of Rennes-le-Château called her the 'priest's Madonna'.

Recently, amidst much controversy, the mayor of Rennes-le-Château had the body of Bérenger Saunière moved to a new plot within the walls of the domain. People must now pay an entrance fee in order to pay their respects to one of the great mystery figures of the twentieth century.

Saunière's room at Villa Bethanie, where he died on 22 January 1917.

BERNINI

Gianlorenzo Bernini (1598–1680) was an outstanding artist who was fortunate enough to learn his craft at an early age from his sculptor father, Pietro, originally a Florentine. They moved to Rome from Naples in 1606 when Gianlorenzo was about eight years of age, and after his talent was recognised, he was employed by some of the most powerful figures in Italy, including the Barberini and Borghese families. Father and son worked together in the Church of Santa Maria Maggiore and on the Villa Borghese. Cardinal Maffeo Barberini, who became Pope Urban VIII, employed Gianlorenzo and was his greatest patron.

Having access to the Vatican meant that the young Bernini was able to study the classical statues there and with the much-admired Greek and Roman techniques at the forefront of his mind, he was able to achieve great acclaim for his sculpture. One of his works is so remarkably similar to the art of the ancient world that until quite recently it was believed to date from around 300 BC, the Hellenistic era.

The seventeenth century was a period of history when Europeans of culture, power and wealth were recognising and rediscovering the art of the ancient world. Many of the beautiful sculptured figures of the classical period had been damaged by the passage of so many centuries and, if they were to be appreciated in their former glory, restoration was thought desirable. Bernini had the eye, the artistic 'feel' and the talent to replace missing and damaged parts and knit them almost seamlessly into the ancient stonework. The more he did, the more familiar he became with the methods by which the old masters had caused rock to be transformed into the imitation of flesh.

He was also able to study the High Renaissance masterpieces and it is recognised that his acquaintance with Michelangelo's work influenced him in the *St Sebastian* that he produced around the year 1617. His portrait bust of Cardinal Robert Bellarmine about seven years later received great acclaim. This was the same Bellarmine who warned Paolo Foscarini against defending the Copernican view of the solar system.

Bernini admired the technique and innovatory work of the fiery Caravaggio, who lived from about 1572 to 1610. Caravaggio painted dramatic and sometimes shockingly realistic pictures such as the *Supper at Emmaus*, where a plump-faced Christ is blessing the food on the table in front of him while his companions, whom he had met on the road after his death and resurrection, are caught in the moment of astonishment as they recognise their master. Bernini took Caravaggio as an exemplar and, like him and earlier artists, used living people, not only the rich and powerful but also the poor, ugly and undistinguished, to be the models for his works.

Bernini's marble sculpture, *The Ecstasy of St Teresa*, in the Church of

Self-portrait of Bernini as a young man.

Santa Maria della Vittoria in Rome, which he completed around 1646, is regarded as a masterpiece, catching as it does a fleeting moment of time frozen in stone. This work shows an angel bearing a fire-tipped spear, which Robert Langdon in *Angels and Demons* recognises as being a clue to the location of the next murder. Earlier in his life, Bernini had depicted the Greek god Apollo amorously pursuing Daphne, the daughter of a river-god, who escaped by turning into a laurel tree. Her body is caught at the very moment of metamorphosis.

Bernini, however, was not only an outstanding sculptor. He was also a distinguished architect and painter. In 1629, Urban VIII appointed him the principal architect at St Peter's,

Rome, and his tomb is Bernini's work. The 26-metre-high bronze and gold baldachin, or canopy, over the high altar is also Bernini's, as are other well-known features around the Eternal City, including churches and wildly imaginative fountains. It is in this baroque urban setting that Robert Langdon and Vittoria Vetra search for the missing cardinals in *Angels and Demons. The Fountain of the Four Rivers* in the Piazza Navona, for example, provides the element of water at the end of Langdon's quest. This particular feature was commissioned by Pope Innocent X.

Until Bernini's work was completed, the way from the papal apartments to St Peter's was a gloomy narrow staircase. It was transformed by the creation of the magnificent

Bernini's sculptures are scattered all over Rome, like his angels on the Ponte Sant'Angelo.

Scala Regia, which was considered a much more fitting route for the pope. Bernini's later works included the angels on the Ponte Sant'Angelo.

There was a blow to his reputation when the bell towers which he had designed and began to place over the façade of St Peter's proved too heavy and started to cause the building to crack. They had to be removed in 1646, which must have been a humiliating experience for Bernini.

So eager was Pope Alexander VII to leave his mark on Rome by employing Bernini that on the very day he became pope, when he might be thought to have had so many other things on his mind, he sent for the architect to discuss

completion of St Peter's Basilica. The same pope was concerned to enhance his family chapel, the Chigi Chapel in Santa Maria del Popolo, with Bernini's sculptures. This is the chapel containing the demon's hole, the locus of the first element, earth, where the first cardinal is murdered in *Angels and Demons*.

The colonnade in St Peter's Square is Bernini's work, comprising 284 columns decorated with 140 statues of saints. He thought big and with the riches of the Roman Catholic Church being harnessed to provide the huge sums of money being lavished on these works, for the greater glory of God, he could afford to do so. But the glory days came to an abrupt end in the early 1670s when Clement X was forced to cut expenditure and Bernini's architectural commissions ceased. He was by then an old man.

Many artists are not recognised as geniuses until after they have passed away but Bernini was not one of them. He was created a papal knight by Gregory XV in recognition of his talent and services to the Church. His pride in his achievements was palpable and his own mother, no doubt infected by the same pride, is quoted as saying that he behaved 'almost as if he were master of the world'.

His greatest patron, Urban VIII, said that Bernini 'was made for Rome and Rome for him'. It is a fitting epitaph.

CELESTINE V

A humble Neapolitan born around 1215, Pietro di Morrone became a Benedictine monk at the age of 17 and some time later was ordained as a priest. He was attracted to the character of John the Baptist, who, as we learn in the Bible, lived in the wilderness. So did Pietro, at first near Mount Morrone, from whence comes part of his name. He wore the roughest clothing with a heavy iron chain around his waist and ate very sparingly and plainly, often fasting. Spending his time in prayer and work, he wished for little more than to live a blameless and virtually solitary life but he was destined to be disappointed.

Word spread about this holy man and others flocked to imitate his lifestyle. Towards the end of his life there are said to have been 36 monasteries where others tried to follow his example. These monks became known, after he was elevated to pope, as Celestines.

Following the death of Pope Nicholas IV in April 1292, the papal throne remained empty for well over two years. In those times, instead of a very large conclave of cardinals assembling to elect a new pope, the electoral college was very small. In fact, they numbered only twelve in total: six Romans, four Italians and two Frenchmen. There were many jealousies and differences between them, with each having his own loyalties and ambitions. One of the factors in Italy and Germany, for example, was the bitter and often bloody rivalry between the Guelphs, supporters of the papacy, and the Ghibellines, who backed the Roman emperor and his allies. Each cardinal and his backers had no intention of elevating a rival to power.

Pietro was not the only faithful follower of Jesus who despaired at this failure to elect a holy father but he was reported to the conclave as having predicted that there would be terrible consequences for the Church if a new pope were not chosen within four months. Prophecies from holy ascetics such as Pietro were given a great deal of respect in the medieval period, as their lifestyle was thought to make them more receptive to the will of God.

His words concentrated the minds of the conclave, who decided that the best way out of their predicament was to elect Pietro himself. His reaction when his peace was disturbed by the arrival of high-level representatives can only be imagined. He had no personal ambition; all he wanted was to be left alone to lead his simple life of prayer and contemplation. Yet he was being told that he had been elected by the will of God. He was probably tempted to refuse the honour but with typical humility he accepted what was being forced upon him. The 79-year-old recluse became not only a spiritual leader but an earthly ruler virtually overnight. He was, unsurprisingly perhaps, not up to the job.

Some believed that he was the first legitimate pope to inherit the keys of St Peter since Emperor Constantine the Great had regularised the Christian Church and in so doing granted corrupting earthly power and wealth to its leader. Pietro, who now took the title Celestine V, was clearly not tainted with ambition and desire for luxuries.

King Charles of Naples, recognising the value of being the pope's guardian, persuaded the new incumbent to journey towards his kingdom to be formally crowned. Only three cardinals had arrived at Aquila when Charles, anxious to have the deed completed, ordered that the coronation take place there and then. It was more formally repeated a short while later, believed to be the only time a pope has received two coronations. The inappropriateness of this, given the unworldliness of Celestine, is obvious. He had travelled to the kingdom of Naples on the back of a donkey, imitating Jesus on Palm Sunday.

One of Celestine's many mistakes was to create twelve new cardinals: seven French and the rest Neapolitans. This was a factor in the slightly later relocation of the seat of the papacy to Avignon in France. He alienated many by making arbitrary decisions, granting favours and approving unwise appointments, but it must be remembered that nothing in his long life had prepared him for this situation. Worldly and cunning self-seekers saw many opportunities to take advantage of Celestine's simplicity, though it is difficult to understand much of what went on at this time since most of his actions were annulled by his successor and few records were kept.

Charles urged Celestine on to Naples and on arrival the new pope insisted on taking up residence in a humble cell modelled on the hut he had occupied as a hermit. He became worried that the work he was forced to do in connection with the administration of the Church was interfering with his spiritual devotions and that he was putting his soul in danger. His embittered and largely unconsulted cardinals quickly realised what an error they had made.

Cardinal Caetani, an expert in canon law, was asked to advise his brethren on the question of whether a pope could voluntarily relinquish his office. It was by then clear that Celestine himself was not opposed to the idea. But as the pope was considered to have no earthly superior, it was hard to know to whom he might offer his abdication. Caetani found solutions to this difficulty.

When the possibility of Celestine stepping down became known, the news must have caused a stir throughout Christendom but nowhere more so than in Naples. Charles of Naples naturally opposed the idea and protest rallies were organised. Celestine, who had apparently not reached a final decision, was begged not to stand down. The holy father, despite any imperfections that they may have perceived, was loved by the Neapolitan masses.

A week later, however, Celestine announced that he had relinquished his throne and that the cardinals were free to elect a successor. No doubt he was

The coronation of Celestine V.

looking forward to going back to his mountain wilderness, his fasting and his prayers without the cares of office. He was to be sorely disappointed.

Shortly afterwards, none other than Benedict Caetani, the man who had advised upon the abdication and declared it legal, was elected pope. He took the name Boniface VIII. His character was in very sharp contrast to that of simple Celestine.

Boniface processed towards Rome, taking Celestine, now dressed again in his rough garb, with him. When the opportunity arose, Celestine escaped and, despite the search by agents of the new pope, evaded capture for some time. He was greeted enthusiastically by monks who had known him for many years but Boniface, who knew that his predecessor was much admired, had no intention of having a potential rival left at large for long.

Eventually, Celestine was recaptured, apparently while trying to escape to Greece, and incarcerated in a castle tower near Anagni. Nine months later he was dead. It has been claimed that the poor old man was badly treated and that he died as a result of this, perhaps actually being murdered, but others argue that it must be remembered that out of personal choice he is likely to have been on a virtual starvation diet and he was a very old man. His spirituality was recognised by Pope Clement V in 1313, who declared him to be a saint.

Celestine's remains were taken to the church of his order at Aquila, where they are still venerated today. It only remains to add that his skull has a mysterious hole in it. This evidence was used by Dan Brown to establish a precedent for a papal murder when his character Robert Langdon makes reference to it in *Angels and Demons*.

BONIFACE VIII

B oniface VIII became Supreme Pontiff in 1294 after his predecessor, Celestine V, controversially resigned. His election was of questionable validity, largely because it could well be argued that if a pope is elected by the will of God, then it is not possible for him to resign from office. Therefore, if Celestine V could not legally relinquish his office, Boniface's papacy was illegitimate.

Boniface had advised Celestine V on the legality of his abdication and was aware of the precarious nature of his own appointment. Once in office, he attempted to secure his position first by having his unworldly predecessor imprisoned. Celestine still had powerful admirers and Boniface was concerned that he might be restored to office, even against his own will. Celestine subsequently died under mysterious circumstances and in *Angels and Demons* Dan Brown makes reference to the fact that Boniface has been implicated in his death.

Boniface's other tactic for ensuring his stronghold on office was to assert his supremacy over secular rulers. This policy was to have serious consequences both for him and his contemporaries.

According to the *Catholic Encyclopedia* of 1913, on 18 November 1302 Boniface issued a papal bull known as *Unam Sanctam*, which:

> lays down dogmatic propositions on the unity of the Church, the necessity of belonging to it for the attainment of eternal salvation, the position of the Pope as supreme head of the Church, and the duty thence arising of submission to the Pope in order to belong to the Church and thus to attain salvation . . .

Boniface believed such a declaration was necessary at this time because his authority was being challenged by the powerful and unscrupulous King Philip IV (the Fair) of France. But his assertion that popes were superior to earthly rulers set him on a collision course with Philip and others including Albert of Habsburg (German king and duke of Austria) and the powerful Italian Colonna family. Acceptance of papal supremacy would mean that their actions were always open to scrutiny by the pope and subject to his approval or disapproval. Decisive government could then be compromised by papal interference in matters of state.

The pope's quarrel with Philip IV of France became so bitter that the king was excommunicated in 1303. France was facing an interdict that would mean no church services could take place, with potentially severe consequences for the nation. Guillaume de Nogaret, councillor and keeper of the seal, therefore persuaded Philip to let him take an expedition to forcibly persuade Boniface of the need to cooperate with the French. Making common cause with the Colonnas, ancient enemies of Boniface's family, Nogaret captured the pope with a force of over 1,500 men, some of whom were willing to kill him. Boniface suffered at their hands but his life was spared. Local supporters of his family then rose against the invaders and it became prudent to release the pope, who had clearly received a terrible shock.

Nogaret's plan had been to take Boniface to France and enforce cooperation but now he had to return home empty-handed. However, within a month the pope was dead, the result, it has been alleged, of the ill treatment he had received.

Dante Alighieri, politician and poet, non-practising doctor and pharmacist, was another opponent of Boniface and in his *Divine Comedy* he envisaged that, after his death, Boniface would be consigned to the eighth circle of hell for the sin of simony – corruptly trading money for church appointments. In the *Inferno*, Dante describes an encounter with a previous pope, Nicholas III, who has been accused of the same offence and condemned to eternal damnation with his head down a hole and flames burning the soles of his quivering feet.

Less than a year and the short reign of Pope Benedict XI later, a French pope, Clement V, was elected. He was the first of a series of popes under the 'protection' of the French king and therefore much inclined to cooperate with the monarch. It was under the papacy of Clement V that Philip IV carried out his infamous campaign against the Knights Templar, an action discussed in *The Da Vinci Code*.

COPERNICUS

The astronomer better known today by the Latinised name he adopted later in life was born Mikolaj Nicolas Copernik at Torun in a Polish province of Royal Prussia in the year 1473. The youngest of four children, son of a father in the copper trade who was a civic dignitary, a local politician and magistrate, his early life was spent at the house in Torun and a country summer residence boasting a vineyard.

When Nicolas was ten, his father died and while he continued living mainly in the family home, his guardianship passed into the hands of his maternal uncle, Lucas, a canon of Frauenburg Cathedral.

Lucas ensured that Nicolas received a good education. In 1488, he attended the cathedral school at Wroclawek and then went on to the cathedral school in the capital city at the time, Krakow. Lucas was by now a bishop and it was his wish that both Nicolas and his elder brother should have successful careers in the Church. With his connections, this would not have been difficult.

We are told that Nicolas studied mathematics, astronomy, geography, philosophy and, of course, Latin, without which no Christian child of the time could possibly have been considered properly educated. This course of study should not be thought of in terms of the modern university curriculum, however. Basically, the teachings of Aristotle and Ptolemy's perception of the universe were covered and mathematical computation was an essential element. Apt students equipped with this knowledge could understand the calendar with particular reference to the holy days of the church, astrology and the casting of horoscopes.

Having learned all he felt he needed to know after four years at university, Nicolas returned home without the formality of graduating, which was common at the time. He was fortunate in that there was enough family money to enable him to purchase his own copies of some of the books he wanted to own in order to develop his own ideas. He was also fortunate in that the newly developed printing presses were enabling scholars like himself to buy books at reasonable prices, whereas, only a generation before, manuscripts, which had to be laboriously, painstakingly and often inaccurately copied by scribes, were prohibitively expensive. Some of the books that Copernicus bought are still in existence and bear his signature.

No doubt under the guidance of Bishop Lucas, who wished to ensure his nephew's future prospects, Copernicus then entered Bologna University in Italy to study canon law, a three-year course. At the same time, the bishop secured for him a salaried position as canon of Frauenburg Cathedral, in return for which there were, perhaps surprisingly, no duties. The comfortably provided-for student was able to supplement his official studies with Greek, more mathematics and astronomy.

Lodging with a professor who was undertaking astronomical research, Copernicus was able to observe astral phenomena which fascinated him and set his fertile brain thinking. He began developing his own theories and by 1500 Copernicus was in Rome, celebrating the jubilee and lecturing in astronomy and mathematics.

After returning to Poland to be officially inducted as a canon at Frauenburg, not having completed his degree course at Bologna, he then persuaded the cathedral authorities and his uncle that he should return to Italy, this time to study medicine and law. It might seem that Copernicus was by way of being the eternal student, with a range of interests much wider than that of the common man. This is true, but what he really wanted to do was to continue his astronomical studies, this time at Padua, while during a period in Ferrara he became a doctor of canon law. By 1512, he had returned to Frauenburg, taken up duties as a canon and set up his own observatory in a tower. This was about a century before the invention of the telescope and it can only be imagined what use Copernicus could have made of that device.

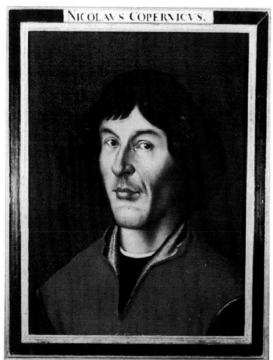

NICOLAVS COPERNICVS.

He had already had a book of translations of obscure poetry published and in 1514 he chose to circulate handwritten copies of *Commentariolus* (Little Commentary) to some of his close acquaintances. This set out some of his theories such as: a) the universe does not have one centre; b) the centre of the earth, therefore, is not the centre of the universe; c) the rotation of the earth gives the impression that the stars are rotating; but d) the earth revolves round the sun. Shortly afterwards, he began his great work *De revolutionibus orbium*

coelestium libri VI (Six Books Concerning the Revolution of the Heavenly Orbs).

By this time, the pope had set up the Fifth Lateran Council, which intended to improve the calendar, and he sought the advice of Copernicus, among others. Copernicus chose not to go to Rome but replied by letter, stating his belief that the revolutions of the heavenly bodies were not well enough understood yet.

Wars disturbed the peace of Poland to the extent that Copernicus became, variously, an administrator, an ambassador during peace talks and the successful organiser of the defences of Allenstein Castle during a siege but he still found time to pursue his astronomical investigations. During the 1520s, his bishop threatened that if he did not accept ordination as a priest, his income would be stopped but Copernicus refused.

The Roman Catholic Church was by now very concerned with the rise and spread of Protestantism in northern Europe and revolutionary ideas about religion now being hotly debated were to a certain degree linked to Copernicus's theories regarding the universe.

The official stance at the time was that the earth was the centre of all things and everything in the sky revolved around it. To believe otherwise could be very dangerous, as, after all, if the pope's pronouncements must be accepted by all orthodox Catholics, then ideas running counter to church teaching must be considered unorthodox, even heretical.

Ptolemy, an Egyptian, had proposed the earth-centred model in AD 150 after studying earlier works, including those theories held by the Greek philosopher Aristotle. The earth, a fixed mass located at the centre of all things, was surrounded by a closed space, the universe, which contained the sun and fixed stars all within a spherical envelope outside which nothing existed. The Church was happy with this ancient wisdom, which made much sense to the casual observer, and it had been accepted for well over a thousand years.

Copernicus died in 1543 unable to guess what an effect he would have on this orthodoxy after his death. He had turned philosophical and religious beliefs upside down but it was not until the Italian scientists Bruno and Galileo took up his theories that the storm broke in earnest.

Giordano Bruno, a Dominican priest, was condemned by the Inquisition for suggesting that space was endless and that there may be other worlds inhabited by people perhaps superior to ourselves. He was burned at the stake for this heresy in 1600, refusing to abjure his beliefs even to save his life. In 1633, Galileo, under threat of torture and a miserable death, was forced to recant all belief in Copernicus's theories, for which he was merely sentenced to life imprisonment. The powerful Catholic hierarchy was often brutal and it ruthlessly destroyed all dissent from its approved doctrines.

Copernicus is referenced in *Angels and Demons* in the context of a group of scientists whose work the Church had banned and whose beliefs were considered dangerous and contrary to scripture. It is even suggested by one of the characters, Maximilian Kohler, that Copernicus was murdered, although there is no historical evidence to back up such a claim. As Langdon and Vetra search the Vatican's Secret Archives they discover documents written by Copernicus, Galileo and Newton amongst the stacks. What sort of radical thinking would mean that over 400 years after a scientific discovery Copernicus might still have a place in a hidden vault?

GALILEO

In *Angels and Demons*, the scientist Galileo is presented as a member of the Illuminati and an opponent of the Catholic Church. He is credited with writing a pamphlet called *Diagramma della Verità* that was confiscated by the Vatican. Once they find the document in the Vatican's Secret Archives, Langdon and Vittoria Vetra use it to follow the path of Illumination around Rome. The relevance of Galileo's work to the debate on the conflict between the Church and science has already been discussed in the earlier narrative section. Here, we look at the life of the man whose impact on our understanding of astronomy has been decisive.

Of the many humiliations which can be heaped upon a person, being forbidden to speak what one believes to be the truth must rank as one of the most galling. Truly free speech is a rare commodity even in modern times and well worth preserving where it exists. In earlier periods, it was severely curtailed, with draconian penalties for those who dared to offend the men of might and power. The astronomer and physicist Galileo Galilei was one who did so offend and had cause to remark, 'I do not feel obliged to believe that the same God who has endowed us with sense, reason and intellect has intended us to forgo their use.' Imagine, then, his feelings when he was forced publicly to lie and deny his own beliefs to save his life.

Born in 1564 in Pisa, Italy, he was the son of Vincenzo, a celebrated composer, player of the lute and music theorist who experimented with acoustics in relation to the vibrating of instrumental strings. Galileo was taught at home and went to the university in his home town until lack of finance forced him to leave. However, he was still able to become professor of mathematics at that university for a short while before he moved to Padua and taught geometry, mechanics and astronomy until 1610.

He was required to teach a syllabus that included the assertion that the earth was at the centre of the universe and the sun and planets charted their course around it. This was the truth as the Roman Catholic Church saw it but it had been challenged by Copernicus. Galileo had the advantage over Copernicus of owning a refracting telescope, which he had constructed after receiving information from Holland about this new invention. The Dutch version was very much inferior to his own. To his delight, he could now see objects such as the moons orbiting Jupiter and by observation and calculation he realised that Copernicus's theory of heliocentricity (the sun as the centre of what we now call the solar system) was correct.

Galileo observed that the planet Venus had phases like our Moon, suggesting that it orbited the sun as the earth does. He studied sunspots and was the first to note that the moon had mountains and craters despite the fact that the ancient Greek Aristotle, whose theories were supported by the Church as incontrovertible fact, had stated that it was a perfect sphere.

Galileo solved the astronomical problems he encountered by observation, consideration of the facts learned and the application of logic. Scientists of the present day will not be surprised by his methods but the approach was not common in the sixteenth and early seventeenth centuries. His English contemporary, Francis Bacon, author of *Novum Organum,* wrote describing similar procedures that became known as the Baconian method.

An illustration of the way Galileo demonstrated that accepted ideas could be refuted by experiment was his legendary use of the Leaning Tower in his native town. It was held that objects fell at a rate proportional to their weight. So a cannonball was thought to fall faster than a pebble, for instance. He ascended the tower and dropped objects of different weights which all, to the astonishment of observers, hit the ground at exactly the same moment. Galileo was not afraid to question orthodox wisdom whenever observation showed it to be false but he made enemies of many contemporaries by the vehemence of his arguments and by ridiculing their claims to superior knowledge.

Galileo knew there was concern that some of his beliefs were held to be against the teachings of scripture, so he travelled to Rome in 1616 to argue the validity of his controversial theories. He was interrogated by the Inquisition, which declared that some of his beliefs were heretical and scientifically false. He must renounce them, he was told. He obeyed

and promised not to carry on teaching those points which offended the established doctrines. The following year, a decree was issued prohibiting the dissemination of works which were declared heretical and those advocating the truth of the Copernican claims were given special mention.

The Church today argues with some justification that it did not object to scientific experiment as such and points to the fact that Copernicus, some of whose theories much of Galileo's astronomical work confirmed, was himself a churchman and had not been persecuted for his theories. But the Church also now admits that the ecclesiastical authorities in Galileo's time were wrong to adhere to a false principle, namely the proper use of scriptural belief. It is said that Galileo urged that the Bible should teach men to go to heaven, not how the heavens go.

Cardinal Bellarmine, who had great influence in the Sacred College, wrote to Paolo Foscarini, a much-respected contemplative Carmelite friar, theologian and mathematician who supported some of Galileo's theories, saying:

> If real proof be found that the sun is fixed and does not revolve around the earth, but the earth round the sun, then it will be necessary, very carefully, to proceed to the explanation of the passages of scripture which appear to be contrary, and we should rather say that we have misunderstood these than pronounce that to be false which is demonstrated.

The trial of Galileo.

This sentence suggests that the cardinal had difficulty in finding the exact words to avoid impaling himself on a spike that he might require to wriggle off at some time in the future. The whole letter, while couched in the friendliest terms, is a reminder that Foscarini is on thin ice. The book which Foscarini had published supporting Copernican theories was placed on the *Index librorum prohibitorum* (Index of Forbidden Books) in 1616.

Galileo, despite his earlier warning and promise to keep his own counsel, and having received an assurance from Pope Urban VIII in 1624 that, provided he treated Copernican theory purely as a mathematical proposition, he would be tolerated, published a book with the convoluted title, *Dialogo sopra i due Massimi Sistemi del Mondo, Tolemaico e Coperncano* (Dialogue Concerning the Two Chief World Systems). As a consequence, he was summoned to Rome in 1633 to face the Inquisition a second time and was found guilty of heresy.

He chose to accept the verdict, accept that he had been wrong and to promise not to offend again. Having a passionate belief, indeed a certainty, that his controversial beliefs were correct, it can be imagined that this must have caused him considerable turmoil. Nevertheless, his acquiescence was sufficient to allow the Inquisition to spare his life, though he was condemned to permanent imprisonment.

By 1638, possibly due to his earlier observations of sunspots, he was totally blind and was therefore allowed to move to his own home in Florence to be kept under close house arrest until he died in 1642. Voltaire (1694–1778) said, 'Those who can make you believe absurdities can make you commit atrocities.' Perhaps those who condemned Galileo to his sad end have their excuse here.

MICHELANGELO

The Italian Renaissance artist Michelangelo di Lodovico Buonarroti Simoni was born in the provincial town of Caprese, Tuscany, on 6 March 1475, but the family soon returned to Florence, where, in 1488, Michelangelo announced his intention to become an artist.

His father, in common with most well-to-do men of his time regarded artists as being among the lower strata of society and was not at all pleased by this development. But despite his opposition, the boy eventually began a three-year apprenticeship with Domenico Ghirlandaio, who ran a prosperous art workshop.

Ghirlandaio was a trained goldsmith but like so many craftsmen and artists of his time he could turn his hand to various creative tasks. He was particularly noted as a panel painter and was a master of fresco. His painting of an old man and his grandson, a naturalistic depiction of a scarred, warty, bulbous-nosed fellow with a smooth-skinned little lad of about three or four, is a masterpiece. Michelangelo must have learned much during his apprenticeship but was later at pains to play down his debt to his old master.

Michelangelo had what one might call today an artistic temperament. He felt beholden to no man and Vasari (1511–74) quotes him, in his *Lives of the Artists*, as saying, 'I cannot live under pressures from patrons, let alone paint.' In fairness, it must be admitted that for the ability to portray every aspect of people, from the highest to the lowest, he was unparalleled. It was his misfortune that, since an artist could only exist by pleasing rich patrons, he was caught between the jealousies and rivalries of the Roman papacy and the ruling family in Florence, the Medici. For such a conceited man, this must have been galling.

His early career saw him leave Florence for Rome, during the period when the Medici were driven out. He returned after the reformist zealot priest Girolamo Savonarola, who had become dictator and ordered the destruction of works of art in the Bonfire of the Vanities, had been overthrown and executed.

Pope Julius II initially wanted Michelangelo to work on a suitably imposing papal tomb but on being summoned back to Rome in 1508 he was instead directed to paint 12 apostles on the ceiling of the Sistine Chapel. This was going to mean working in fresco, though the artist thought of himself as a sculptor. It has been suggested that other artists who were jealous rivals

of Michelangelo had engineered this commission in a medium he was not used to, though it was one with which he would have been familiar from his apprenticeship. The idea was to cut him down to size.

Michelangelo and the pope discussed improving on the original fairly simple commission and it finally metamorphosed into an ambitious plan for well over 300 figures. The artist had prepared preliminary sketches and it was agreed that he should depict what he saw fit. Assistants were drafted in. The project grew increasingly complex and Michelangelo was unhappy with the early work. He dismissed all his assistants, removed what had been done thus far and started again on his own. He refused to let anyone but Julius see the work in progress.

The pope was impatient to see it completed and put great pressure on Michelangelo, who laboured meticulously on. Under this pressure, although not totally finished, it was unveiled in August 1511. It was tremendously influential and the great Raphael was so moved by what he saw that he changed his own technique, adopting a more sculptural and flowing style. Michelangelo is quoted as saying, 'After four tortured years, more than four hundred over-life-sized figures, I felt as old and as weary as Jeremiah. I was only 37, yet friends did not recognise the old man I had become.' His relief at

The Sistine Chapel and a detail from one of Michelangelo's frescos: a close-up of the face of God

applying the last brush stroke one day in 1512 must have been immense.

In the mid-1530s, he was given another monumental commission. The Last Judgement was to be the subject, a project probably conceived by Pope Paul III's predecessor, Clement VII, before his death. It was inspired by the desire to depict humanity needing salvation and cast an eye back to the 1527 Sack of Rome in the time of Pope Clement VII by unruly and unpaid forces of the Holy Roman Emperor Charles, and the ongoing pressures of the Reformation.

In 1535–6 the work began. The result was in complete contrast to the confidence of the Sistine Chapel ceiling. *The Last Judgement* is a sad and pessimistic vision of the mouth of hell above an altar bearing the crucifix, with the symbol of Christ standing between humanity and damnation. Naked souls ferried over the Styx by Charon are about to enter their eternal punishment while fortunate figures rise to heaven. The work received much criticism and the more controversial elements of some of the figures later received strategic overpainting.

Michelangelo acquired much of his knowledge of human anatomy through having dissected human corpses, though it was strictly banned by the Church. It may be also be noted that he included himself in *The Last Judgement* in the flayed skin of St Bartholomew.

Despite the outrage some felt at *The Last Judgement*, Pope Paul III commissioned frescos for his own chapel, which were completed in 1550. By now in his 75th year, Michelangelo could look back at a successful career with satisfaction but was so driven that he continued working, towards the end making drawings of the Crucifixion and writing poetry. He also carved the *Pietà* that is now in Florence Cathedral Museum, intending for it to grace his own tomb.

Since 1546, he had increasingly turned his attention to architecture and was appointed chief architect of St Peter's. It has been said that he did his later work solely for the glory of God but it would be hard to deny that he also had in mind the glory of Michelangelo. Several of the scenarios depicted in *Angels and Demons* took place in the shadow of his works around the Eternal City.

He had reached the very great age of 88 early in 1564 when he died and was interred in Santa Croce, Florence. His most famous sculpture is generally accepted to be his *David*, fashioned between 1501 and 1504, a symbol of strength and anger. When it was seen by the people of Florence, still traumatised by the Savonarola period and the expulsion of the Medici, it was adopted as a symbol of their fighting spirit and willingness to overcome their enemies.

RAPHAEL

R affaello Santi, or Raphael as he is called in the English-speaking world, was the son of the artist and poet Giovanni Santi di Pietro. Born in 1483 in Urbino, he was taught by his father, who was a painter of 'no great merit', according to Raphael's first biographer Vasari, until his father's death in 1494. By 1499, he was assisting Perugino and becoming familiar with the techniques of Pinturicchio, from whom he perhaps learned his mastery of perspective. His first major work, *The Marriage of the Virgin*, clearly reflects the influence of Perugino. Throughout his tragically short career he was constantly updating his expertise as he analysed the works of others.

He knew the reputations of Florentine artists and sought them out in order to learn more. In Florence, during a period of about four years up to 1508, he learned more of his trade from Fra Bartolommeo, the genius Leonardo da Vinci and the temperamental Michelangelo. His speciality was portraits and he painted several Madonnas. Leonardo's *Madonna and Child with St Anne* clearly inspired him, and Raphael picked up the lighting and shading techniques of the older man. In his *Deposition of Christ*, which is now in the Borghese Gallery in Rome, he obviously drew from Michelangelo's extensive anatomical knowledge but the darker elements are not there – this is a calmer, more appealing approach. From Fra Bartolommeo, a Dominican friar, he perhaps absorbed some of the sentiment that art should not be commercial but should serve as a substitute for the words in the Bible: the scriptures in pictures, a visual aid to devotion.

In 1508, Pope Julius II, who was at this time negotiating with Michelangelo over the Sistine Chapel project, summoned Raphael to Rome to decorate apartments at the Vatican, at the suggestion of the architect Bramante. Among his other works in Rome following this commission, Raphael painted a fresco in the Villa Farnesina, produced cartoons for tapestries to be hung in the Sistine Chapel and, in 1515, painted St Cecilia in the Church of San Giovanni in Bologna.

He was given architectural commissions in St Peter's and was awarded overall responsibility on the death of Bramante in 1514. Many of the pieces of ancient classical sculpture, which were being newly appreciated in Rome, were in need of conservation and all those bearing Latin inscriptions became Raphael's responsibility. In the year 1517, he was appointed commissioner of antiquities for Rome. This work, however, did not prevent him taking on private clients. In the Church of Santa Maria del Popolo, for example, he was asked to design a chapel for the Chigi family, which was completed by Bernini. It is here that Dan Brown sets the scene of the first cardinal's murder in *Angels and Demons*. A striking sketch of a Sibyl, the basis of an intended painting for the same chapel, shows the ease with which Raphael captured not only human form but also flowing drapery.

Some of Raphael's paintings have an almost photographic quality. His ability to use light and shade and his mastery of perspective are exemplified in his work *The Canigiani Holy Family*, which he completed around 1506 while still in his early twenties. While it is possible to see the influence of the more experienced painters from whom he had been learning, he developed and honed his own methods of showing perfection and gentleness in the human face which few others could hope to capture.

Raphael was a dark, handsome man with plenty of charm. He seems to have made himself popular amongst those with whom he came into contact, to the extent that he was named 'the prince of painters'.

He died in 1520 and in 1521 the great humanist and neo-Platonist Pandolfo Pico della Mirandola wrote the following to the Duchess Isabella Gonzaga of Mantua:

Bust of Raphael by Giuseppe Fabris.

When he died, the heavens wanted to give one of the signs they gave when Jesus Christ expired . . . Here people are talking about nothing but the death of this exceptional man, who has completed his first life at the young age of 37. His second life – that of fame, which is subject neither to time nor death, will endure for all eternity . . .

Tomb of Raphael in the Pantheon.

The fact that people were still publicly mourning his passing a year later is a tribute to his popularity as one of the finest, if not the greatest, artists of all time. Had he been spared for as long as Michelangelo, it is intriguing to speculate what he might have achieved.

At the time of his death, Raphael was working on *The Transfiguration*, which was ultimately completed by his pupil Giulio Romano. This altarpiece was placed at the head of his coffin at the funeral mass held in the Vatican, although Vasari claimed that Raphael was an atheist. If there is any truth in that claim, then the prominent display of the picture at the funeral in the heart of the Catholic Church for one who had no faith is supremely ironic. Christ is ascending to a heaven in which the deceased possibly has no belief.

It is at Raphael's tomb in the Pantheon, Rome, that Robert Langdon first stops when rushing from church to church in his attempt to rescue the hostage cardinals in *Angels and Demons*. In 1833, the remains of Raphael are believed to have been discovered under the statue of the Madonna del Sasso, which is where Vasari, in his biography of the painter, claimed they had been laid to rest. Lorenzo Lotti, usually called Lorenzetto, a sculptor who had been a colleague of Raphael, had been commissioned to fashion this statue of the Madonna. The bones were reburied in the Pantheon with a bust depicting the artist in a niche above the tomb. The epitaph inscribed on Raphael's tomb translates as: 'Here lies Raphael by whom the mother of all things [meaning Nature] feared to be overcome whilst he was living, and whilst he was dying, herself to die.'